AF531583

Auditing and Cost Accounting

Dr. Anoop Pant

RANDOM PUBLICATIONS
NEW DELHI (INDIA)

Auditing and Cost Accounting

ISBN 978-93-5111-394-2

Published in 2014 in India by

RANDOM PUBLICATIONS

4376-A/4B, Gali Murari Lal, Ansari Road
New Delhi-110 002
Phone : +91-11-43580356, +91-11-23289044
e-mail: randomexports@gmail.com, sales@randompublications.com, info@randompublications.com

Type Setting by : Keystoneprintads, Delhi-110051
Printed at : Mehra Printers, Delhi-110 092

Preface

Auditing is a systematic and scientific examination of the books of accounts and records of business to enable the auditor to satisfy himself that the profit and loss account and the balance sheet are properly drawn up so as to exhibit a true and fair view of the financial state of affairs of the business and profit or loss for the financial period. The term auditing has been distinguished from accounting and investigation The main point of distinction is that accountancy is concerned with the preparation of financial statements whereas auditing is concerned with checking of these financial statements and reporting on the financial position and result of operation of the organisation. Investigation is undertaken for some special purpose i.e. to determine the extent of fraud or to determine the purchase price of the organisation and the like.

Cost Accounting is the process of accounting for costs from the point at which expenditure is incurred or committed to the establishment of its ultimate relationship with cost centre and cost units. Cost accounting profession got recognition in 1939 in India. It has been made compulsory for specified manufacturing companies. Cost Accounting has the objectives of determining Product costs, facilitate planning and control of regular business activities and supply information for taking short term and long-term decisions. Cost Accounting is useful in different areas such as materials, labour, overheads, stock valuation etc.

Financial Accounting is concerned with providing information to external users. It does not provide detailed cost information for different jobs, processes or departments. It also does not possess an adequate system of standards to evaluate the Performance of departments and employees. There are two major methods of costing- job costing and process costing. Job costing includes Contract, Batch and Multiple costing. Costing system should be developed in an organisation to fit in the general organisation of the business. Cost and Financial Accounting are different from each other.

Besides being a Chartered Accountant an auditor should possess certain other qualities, such as knowledge of relevant laws, intelligence, tactfulness, vigilance, honesty and integrity courage, impartiality, broadmindedness, patience, perseverance, maintaining secrecy of his client, commonsense etc.

I thank all members of my team who have helped in the preparation of the book. My special thanks go to "Random Publications" who have published the book.

– Dr. Anoop Pant

Contents

1

Fundamentals of Auditing

UNDERSTANDING AUDITS

The common group of audits covers a broad range of assessment types, most of which relate to financial issues (e.g., real estate, financial portfolio, tax-related assessments, or accounting practice business assessments). Audits are confusing processes that are defined by the relationship of the auditor to the authority requesting the assessment and the entity being audited. Today we see the discipline of auditing under fire because some major auditing and consulting firms have shown themselves lacking in compliance with industry established ethics codes of conduct. The media is ripe with news describing the conflict generated by the consultants/auditors when they ignored the principles of their profession and advised clients to misrepresent themselves to the public. They created an inter-dependence between their customers and their firms that enriched both entities at the expense of the employees and stockholders.

Auditors are required, by the nature of their profession, to render opinions (attestations) based upon valid evidence relating to the condition of their customers' accounting practices. The auditor is liable for the accuracy of the opinion rendered. This liability is a constant reminder of the extensive responsibilities entrusted to a person identified as an auditor. Responsibilities are not to be taken lightly by people who conduct audits or desire to become auditors. A plaintiff may bring suit against an auditor under common statutory, or both common and statutory law. Auditing is a serious discipline. Auditors must be the most experienced, knowledgeable, professionally qualified individuals in a discipline. National Property Management Association represents the greatest potential for finding individuals uniquely qualified to be auditors in the discipline of Personal Property (Asset) Management.

IDEA

Economic decisions in every society must be based upon the information available at the time the decision is made. For example, the decision of a bank to make a loan to a business is based upon previous financial relationships with that business, the financial condition of the company as reflected by its financial statements and other factors. If decisions are to be consistent with the intention of the decision makers, the information used in the decision process must be reliable. Unreliable information can cause inefficient use of resources to the detriment of the society and to the decision makers themselves. In the lending decision example, assume that the barfly makes the loan on the basis of misleading financial statements and the borrower Company is ultimately unable to repay. As a result the bank has lost both the principal and the interest. In addition, another company that could have used the funds effectively was deprived of the money.

As society become more confusing, there is an increased likelihood that unreliable information will be provided to decision makers. There are several reasons for this: remoteness of information, voluminous data and the existence of confusing exchange transactions. As a means of overcoming the problem of unreliable information, the decision-maker must develop a method of assuring him that the information is sufficiently reliable for these decisions. In doing this he must weigh the cost of obtaining more reliable information against the expected benefits. A common way to obtain such reliable information is to have some type of verification (assessment) performed by independent persons. The audited information is then used in the decision making process on the assumption that it is reasonably complete, accurate and unbiased.

ORIGIN

The term audit is derived from the Latin term 'audire,' which means to hear. In early days an auditor used to listen to the accounts read over by an accountant in order to check them Auditing is as old as accounting. It was in use in all ancient countries such as Mesopotamia, Greece, Egypt. Rome, U.K. and India. The Vedas contain reference to accounts and auditing. Arthasashthra by Kautilya detailed rules for accounting and auditing of public finances. The original objective of auditing was to detect and prevent errors and frauds.

Auditing evolved and grew rapidly after the industrial revolution in the 18th century With the growth of the joint stock companies the ownership and management became separate. The shareholders who were the owners needed a report from an independent expert on the accounts of the company managed by the board of directors who were the employees. The objective of assessment shifted and assessment was expected to ascertain whether the accounts were true and fair rather than detection of errors and frauds. In India the companies Act 1913 made assessment of company accounts compulsory

With the increase in the size of the companies and the volume of transactions the main objective of assessment shifted to ascertaining whether the accounts were true and fair rather than true and correct. Hence the emphasis was not on arithmetical accuracy but on a fair representation of the financial efforts The companies Act.1913 also prescribed for the first time the qualification of auditors The International Accounting Standards Committee and the Accounting Standard board of the Institute of Chartered Accountants of India have developed standard accounting and auditing practices to guide the accountants and auditors in the day to day work The later developments in auditing pertain to the use of computers in accounting and auditing. In conclusion it can be said that auditing has come a long way from hearing of accounts to taking the help of computers to examine computerised accounts

ROLE OF AUDITING

THE DEMAND FOR AUDITING IS A RESULT OF FOUR UNDERLYING FACTORS

The complexity of the system refers to the activity in an institution or business, along with the interaction of the exchanges of information, which often make the proper recording of transactions and allocations of costs difficult to track. The physical remoteness of the system increases the likelihood both of intentional or unintentional error and of demand for an independent party to examine the records. Bias and motives of the provider create a demand for an independent party to lend credibility to the company's financial or property system statements. For example, management may be more optimistic about the status of the property system than the Government. The optimism may be based on accurate or inaccurate statements of the property department. The property department may have a vested interest in presenting an optimistic picture of the system. Consequences associated with the reliability of information are cause for verification when the information is used for costly business decisions, such as buy-outs, new contracts, stock evaluation, market pricing, etc. To understand the auditing process, you should become familiar with the definitions that are important to auditing.

DEFINITION OF AUDITING

A systematic process of objectively obtaining and evaluating evidence regarding assertions about economic actions and events to ascertain the degree of correspondence between those assertions and established criteria and communicating the results to interested users.

SYSTEMATIC PROCESS

As a systematic process, auditing is a logical, purposeful, structured approach to decision-making; it is not an unplanned, haphazard process.

OBJECTIVELY OBTAINING AND EVALUATING EVIDENCE

Auditing involves the collection of evidence. Evidence represents the information collected by the auditor that will affect the auditor's decision process. Although evidence itself may be more or less conclusive in nature, the process of collecting and evaluating evidence should be objective.

ASSERTIONS ABOUT ECONOMIC ACTIONS AND EVENTS

Assertions are related to the financial statements of the organization being audited. The auditor is given information and statements from the auditee. These statements represent the auditee's assertions about actions and events and include not only the statements themselves but also the accounting system and process. (This statement looks, at first glance, to relate only to economic issues and financial statements. However, if you understand that property is in fact a function of economic values and that financial statements include statements of assets and inventories, you can see where property issues fit.)

DEGREE OF CORRESPONDENCE BETWEEN ASSERTIONS AND ESTABLISHED CRITERIA

Correspondence here means the comparison of the assertions of the auditee to the established criteria.

The established criteria may include, but are not limited to, the sorces such as:

- Generally Accepted Accounting Practices(GAAP)
- Federal Acquisition Regulations (FAR)
- State or Municipal Regulations
- Corporate Policies and Procedures

COMMUNICATING RESULTS TO INTERESTED USERS

The communication of the auditor's assurance or information is referred to as attestation, or the attest function. Attestation is a communicated statement of opinion (judgment) based upon convincing evidence by an independent, competent, authoritative person concerning the degree of correspondence in all material respects of accounting information communicated by an entity with established criteria.

FEATURES

- Assessment is a systematic and scientific examination of the books of accounts of a business;
- Audit is undertaken by an independent person or body of persons who are duly qualified for the job.
- Audit is a verification of the results shown by the profit and loss account and the state of affairs as shown by the balance sheet.
- Audit is a critical review of the system of accounting and internal control.
- Audit is done with the help of vouchers, documents, information and explanations received from the authorities.

- The auditor has to satisfy himself with the authenticity of the financial statements and report that they exhibit a true and fair view of the state of affairs of the concern.
- The auditor has to inspect, compare, check, review, scrutinize the vouchers supporting the transactions and examine correspondence, minute books of share holders, directors, Memorandum of Association and Articles of association etc., in order to establish correctness of the books of accounts.

STANDARDS

PROFESSIONAL STANDARDS

Auditing standards represent a measure of the quality of audit work performed. They are broad conceptual guidelines that serve as a model for all auditors and should remain relatively stable over time. Generally Accepted Auditing Standards (GAAS) are standards published by the American Institute of Certified Public Accountants (AICPA). The Auditing Standards Board issues pronouncements entitled Statements of Auditing Standards (SASs).

Auditing procedures, on the other hand, represent specific audit tasks to be performed. For example, to comply with an auditing standard that requires audits to be properly planned, the auditor may perform the specific audit procedure of holding a preliminary planning meeting with client personnel.

COMMON STANDARDS

The examination is to be performed by a person or person having adequate technical training and proficiency as an auditor. In all matters relating to the assignment, the auditor must maintain an independent mental attitude. Due professional care is to be exercised in the performance of the examination and the preparation of the report.

STANDARDS OF FIELDWORK

Audits must be adequately planned and properly supervised. Proper planning must be undertaken to insure effective results. Planning must include the requirements for personnel and the logistics to support the personnel undertaking audits. Existing internal controls must be studied and evaluated to define the tests to be applied to the subject audit. Sufficient competent evidential matter is to be obtained through inspection, observation, inquiries, and confirmation to afford a reasonable basis for an opinion regarding the statement under consideration.

Internal Control

Internal controls consist of the plan of an organization and all of the coordinate methods and measures adopted within a business to safeguard its assets, check the accuracy and reliability of its accounting data, promote operational efficiency, and encourage adherence to the prescribed managerial policies. Internal controls represent the means by which a company processes its accounting transactions so that reliable financial information can be generated and safeguards its assets.

Sufficient Competent Evidential Matter

Competent matter demands that the evidence is valid and relevant. An auditor must exercise professional judgement in determining the relevance of specific pieces of evidence and the objectivity, timeliness, and relationship to conclusions as to the overall fairness of the statements drawn from the audit.

STANDARDS OF REPORTING

The report shall either contain an expression of opinion regarding the financial statements, taken as a whole, or an assertion to the effect that an opinion cannot be expressed. When an opinion cannot be expressed, the reasons should be stated. In all cases the report should contain a clear-cut indication of the character of the auditor's examination and the degree of responsibility he/she is taking.

SUGGESTED CODE OF PROFESSIONAL ETHICS

- *Independence – Integrity – Objectivity*: An auditor should maintain integrity and objectivity and, when engaged in the practice of property management, be independent of those served.
- *Common and technical standards*: An auditor should observe the profession's common and technical standards and strive continually to improve competence and quality of services.
- *Responsibilities to clients*: An auditor should be fair and candid with clients and serve them to the best of the auditor's ability, with professional concern for their best interests, consistent with the auditor's responsibilities to the public.
- *Responsibilities to colleagues*: An auditor should conduct himself/herself in a manner that will promote cooperation and good relations among the members of the profession.
- *Other responsibilities and practices*: An auditor should conduct himself/herself in a manner that will enhance the stature of the profession and its ability to serve the public.
- *Auditor's Legal Liability*: We live in a litigious society. The auditor today can reasonably expect his or her every action regardless of how right or wrong it may be to be questioned in a court of law and possibly to result in substantial damages being awarded. Privity of Contract is a relationship between two or more parties that creates a contractual duty. In an auditing context, the auditor and client

have a privity or contractual relationship that is usually established by a contract called an engagement letter. Usually, however, third parties such as investors or creditors are not parties to the contract and are said to have a nonprofit relationship. Due professional care is the performance of, and reporting on, a professional engagement with the degree of care, competence, learning, and experience commonly possessed by other embers of the auditing profession and required by professional standards.

NEGLIGENCE

It is the failure of the auditor to perform or report on an engagement with the due professional care and competence of a prudent auditor. The auditor is negligent if he or she fails to do what the ordinary, reasonable, prudent auditor would do, or does what the prudent auditor would not do. Sometimes negligence may be referred to as simple or ordinary. Simple negligence, ordinary negligence, and negligence are synonymous.

Gross Negligence

It is a serious occurrence of negligence tantamount to a flagrant or a reckless departure from the standard of due care. These terms are frequently used interchangeably and are equivalent to sloppy auditing or lack of a reasonable basis for a belief.

A plaintiff in establishing gross negligence must prove each of the following assertions:

- The auditor made a representation about a material fact with lack of reasonable support.
- The purpose of the representation was to induce reliance by another (for example, a client or a third-party user of the financial statements).
- The representation was relied upon by the client or a third party.
- The reliance caused damages to the client or third party.

Fraud occurs when an auditor issues an opinion on the financial statements knowing that the financial statements or the audit report thereon are false. Fraud differs from gross negligence in that the auditor does not merely lack reasonable support for belief, but has both knowledge of the falsity and intent to deceive a client or third party.

EXPRESSION OF OPINION

When we speak of the objective, we rationalize the thinking process to formulate a set of attainable goals, with reference to the circumstances, feasibility and constraints. In money matters, frauds and errors are common place of occurrence. Apart from this, the statements of account have their own purpose and use of portraying the financial state of affairs. The objective of audit, naturally, should be to see that what the statements of account convey is true and not misleading and that such errors and frauds do not exists as to distort what the accounts should really convey. Till recently, the principal emphasis was on arithmetical accuracy; adequate attention was not paid to appropriate application of accounting principles and disclosure, for ensuring preparation of accounting statement in such a way as to enable the reader of the accounting statement to form a correct view of the slate of affairs.

Quite a few managements took advantage of the situation and manipulated profit or loss and assets and liabilities to highlight or conceal affairs according to their own design. This state of affairs came up for consideration in the Royal Mail Steam Packet Company's Case as a result of which the Companies Acts of England and India were amended in 1948 and 1956 respectively to require the auditor to state inter alia whether the statements of account are true and fair. This is what we can take as the present day audit objective. The implication of the substitution of "true and fair" need to be understood. There has been a shift of emphasis from arithmetical accuracy to the question of reliability to the financial statements. A statement may be reliable even though there are some errors or even frauds, provided they are not so big as to vitiate the picture.

The word "correct" was somewhat misplaced as the accounting largely consists of estimates. However, you should not infer that the detection of errors and frauds is no longer an audit objective; it is indeed an audit objective because statements of account drawn up from books containing serious mistakes and fraudulent entries cannot be considered as a true and fair statement. To establish whether the financial statement show a true and fair state of affairs, the auditors must carry out a process of examination and verification and, if errors and frauds exist they would come to his notice in the ordinary course of checking. But detection of errors of frauds is not the primary aim of audit; the primary aim is the establishment of a degree of reliability of the annual statements of account. If there remains a deep laid fraud in the accounts, which in the normal course of examination of accounts may not come to light, it will not be construed as failure of audit, provided the auditor was not negligent in the carrying out his normal work.

TYPES OF AUDITS

- Audits of Financial Statements
- Compliance Audits
- Contract
- Federal and State law
- Policies and Procedures
- Operational Audits
- Effectiveness
- Efficiency

DETECTION OF FRAUD & ERRORS

The term fraud means the willful misrepresentation made with an intention of deceiving others. It is a deliberate mistake committed in the accounts with a view to get personal gain.

In accounting, fraud means two things:

- Defalcation involving misappropriation of either cash or goods
- Fraudulent manipulation of accounts not involving defalcation.

FRAUD COVERS THE FOLLOWING

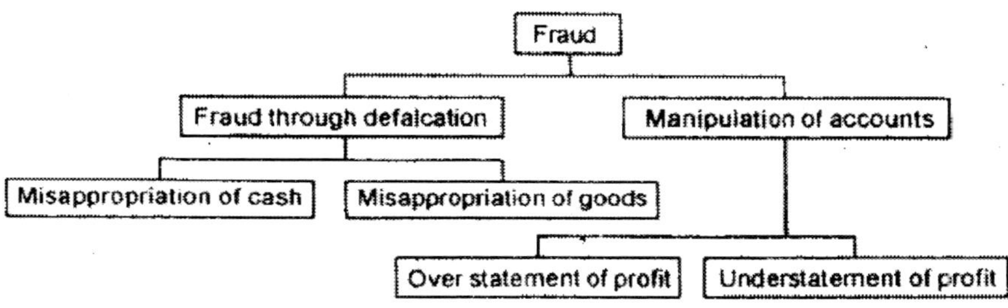

FRAUD THROUGH DEFALCATION

Following are the methods of defalcation involving misappropriation of cash or goods:

- By misappropriating the receipt by not recording the same in the cashbook
- By destroying the carbon copy or counter foil of the receipt and misappropriating the cash received
- By entering lesser amount on the counterfoil and misappropriating the difference between money actually-received and the amount entered on the counterfoil of the receipt book.
- By not recording the receipt of sale of a casual nature for example sale of scrap, sale of old newspapers etc.
- By omitting to record cash donations received by non-profit making charitable institutions
- By misappropriating the cash received on discounting the bills receivable and showing them as bills outstanding on hand.
- By misappropriating cash received from debtors and concealing the same by giving artificial credit to the debtors in the form of bad debts, discount or sales return etc.
- By adopting the method of "teeming and lading" or "lapping process". Under this method cash received from one debtor is misappropriated and deficiency in that debtors account is made good when another payment is received from second debtor by crediting the second debtors account less by that amount. This process is carried out round the year.

- By suppressing the cash sales by not recording them or by treating the cash sales as credit sales.
- By misappropriating the sale proceeds of VPP sales or sales of goods on approval basis by treating the transaction as goods received or not approved.
- By under casting receipt side total of the cashbook
- By recording fictitious or bogus payments
- By recording more payments than actual amounts paid by altering the figures on the vouchers.
- By showing the same payment twice.
- By showing credit purchases as cash purchases and misappropriating the amount
- Recording personal expenses as business expenses
- By not recording discounts and allowances given by the creditors and misappropriating the amounts
- By overcasting the payment side total of the cashbook
- Recording fictitious and inflated purchases and misappropriating that amount.
- By suppressing the credit notes for returns and showing the full payment to creditors.
- By including the names of dummy workers or the workers who have? The job in the wage sheets and misappropriating the amount.
- By over casting the total of wages sheets and drawing that amount for misappropriation.
- By misappropriating the undisbursed wages.

FRAUD THROUGH MANIPULATION OF ACCOUNTS

It implies presentation of accounts more favorably than what they actually are. Window dressing means showing a wrong picture. The fraud through manipulation of accounts is also known as window dressing because accounts are manipulated to show a wrong picture of the profit or loss of the business and its financial state of affairs. Commonly this type of fraud is committed by the people at the top management level. This does not involve any misappropriation of cash or goods but it is either over statement of profit or understatement of the same. Such fraud is committed with certain objective and is relatively difficult to detect.

LIMITATIONS OF AUDITING

At this stage, it must be clear that the objective of an audit of financial statements is to enable an auditor to express an opinion on such financial statements. In fact, it is the auditor's opinion which helps determination of the true and fair view of the financial position and operating results of an enterprise. It is very significant to note that the AAS-2 makes it a subtle point that such an opinion expresses by the auditor is neither an assurance as to the future viability of the enterprise nor the efficiency or effectiveness with which management has conducted affairs of the enterprise.

Further, the process of auditing is such that it suffers from certain inherent limitations, i.e., the limitation which cannot be overcome irrespective of the nature and extent of an audit procedure. It is very important to understand these inherent limitations of an audit since understanding of the same would only provide clarity as to the overall objectives of an audit.

The inherent limitations are:

- First of all, auditor's work involve exercise of judgment, for example, in deciding the extent of audit procedures and in assessing the reasonableness of the judgment and estimates made by the management in preparing the financial statements. Further much of the evidence available to the auditor can enable him to draw only reasonable conclusions there from.
- The audit evidence obtained by an auditor is commonly persuasive in nature rather than conclusive in nature. Because of these factors, the auditor can only express an opinion. Therefore, absolute certainty in auditing is rarely attainable. There is also likelihood that some material misstatements of the financial information resulting from fraud or error, if either exists, may not be detected.
- The entire audit process is commonly dependent upon the existence of an effective system of internal control. Further, it is clearly evident that there always be some risk of an internal control system failing to operate as designed. No doubt, internal control system also suffers from certain inherent limitations. Any system of internal control may be ineffective against fraud involving collusion among employees or fraud committed by management.
- Certain levels of management may be in a position to override controls; for example, by directing subordinates to records transactions incorrectly or to conceal them, or by suppressing information relating to transactions. Such inherent limitations of internal controls system also contribute to inherent limitations of an audit.

IMPORTANCE

- *Errors are Located*: Auditing is helpful for business. The error can be located through it. The location and correction of error is possible through auditing. The true and fair information about business is available.
- *Frauds are Discovered*: Auditing is helpful for business. The discovery of fraud is possible through it. The guilty persons can be held responsible. The auditing accounts show fair about business.

- *Loans Become Easy*: Auditing is useful for business. Lenders for granting loans accept the auditor's accounts. The reputation of borrowers increases due to auditing. Thus auditing accounts help the businessman to expand his activities.
- *Advise about Weakness*: Auditing is useful for business. The people can seek advise from auditors. The auditors are professional and they know their work very well. They can spotlight the grey area. It is the duty of the business man to act upon the advise of the auditors.
- *High Moral Values*: Auditing is essential for business. There is moral check on the management and other staff. Auditing puts the pressure on the staff of work honestly. There is no pending work so there is less chance of errors and frauds.
- *Tax Payments*: Auditing is useful for business, tax authority accept audited accounts for assessment of taxes. There is no further inquiry or investigation from department. The audited accounts lessen the worries of business people.
- *Tax Owners*: Auditing is useful for business. The tax authorities accept audited accounts for assessment of taxes. There is no further inquiry or investigation from tax department. The audited accounts lessen the worries of business people.
- *Efficiency Improves*: Auditing is beneficial for business. The auditing determines the efficiency of employees. The training and qualifies management is an asset for any business. Such management can play dynamic role in framing and implementing the policies.
- *Dispute is settled*: Auditing is essential for business. The audited accounts are helpful to settle the disputes. The audited accounts become the basis of making decisions. The dispute may relate to infringement of patents or trademarks.
- *Planning Becomes Possible*: Auditing is helpful for business. The audits accounts present true and fair view of business activities. The facts and figures can be used to prepare budge and estimates for the next years. The projected cash receipts and payments, income statement and balance sheet can be prepared.
- *Improvement of Internal Control*: Auditing is helpful for business. The auditor can point out the weakness of internal control system. The business management can take steps to remove these weaknesses. The effective control systems are essential for large-scale business enterprises.
- *Fluctuation in Profits*: Auditing is helpful for business. The auditor can make the detailed study to find of fluctuation in profits. There are various reasons for changes in profits. The auditor can determine the true cause of such changes.
- *High Credit Rating*: The auditing is beneficial for business. The auditing accounts increase the credit standing of any business house.

The lenders can rely on audited accounts for granting credit facility. In fact auditing is a screening test of business entity.

- *Listing at Stock Exchange*: The auditing is beneficial for business. The listing of securities at stock exchange is optional. The public limited companies can get registration at stock exchange. Stock exchange management for registration purpose accepts the audited accounts.
- *Shareholders Protection*: Auditing is beneficial for owners. The shareholders feel that their rights are protected through auditing. They can know the performance of management. Audited accounts help to determine the value of shares.
- *Partner Satisfaction*: Auditing is helpful for partners. The sleeping partner feels satisfaction when there are audited. The managing partners can use business property for their personal benefit. There is moral check on managing partners.
- *Proprietors*: Auditing is useful for proprietors. The audited accounts help the sole traders that their business is going on properly. The error and fraud are pointed out auditors. The owners can determine the efficiency of their employees or assistants.
- *Beneficiary*: Auditing is valuable for beneficiaries. The auditor of a trust can nominate any person as trustee to look after the property of a trust. Auditing can safeguard the right of beneficiaries. There is a moral check on the trustee to follow the by – laws of trust.
- *Deceased Estate*: The auditing is helpful for dependents of decreased person. The audited accounts presents true and fair view of financial statements. The family can rely on audited accounts for distributing the estate of deceased person.
- *Insolvency*: The auditing is beneficial for creditors. The audited accounts show true and fair view of state of affairs of sole proprietorship or partnership. The creditor can get their money first and then owners can get refund of capital. The audited accounts help to settle the cases at an early date.
- *Better Performance of Tax Department*: Auditing is beneficial for government. Tax officers accept the audited accounts. The assessment order can be issued without further clarification. There is saving of money and time due to audited accounts. The performance of tax officers is improved.
- *Exact Revenue Amount*: Auditing is beneficial for government. The collection of revenue is possible at an early date. The people are allowed to deposit various kinds of taxes. The recovery of income is made at the start of the year. The government can start welfare project on the basis of total revenue collected.
- *Progress of Economy*: Auditing is essential for government policies. The true fair view is stated in audited accounts. The stage of

economic progress can be determined. The government can take measures to raise the rate of economic growth.

- *Purchase of Private Business*: Auditing is helpful for government. The private business houses may not work in favour of common public. The government can take over such business units. The purchase price is decided on the basis of auditing of accounts.
- *Sale of Government Business*: Auditing is useful for government. The policy can be framed on the basis of audition accounts. The management comes to know the value of business. The government can sell state – owned unit to private sector. The bid price is settled on audited accounts.
- *Inspectors*: The auditing is helpful for government. The auditing accounts show the fair value of all assets. The value of assets is the basis of tax. This issue can be settling through audited accounts. The auditors are experts in their field. They know all methods of property valuation. They can issue certified the government agencies for valuation of property.
- *Insurers can Settle Claims*: Auditing is essential for insurers. The settlement of fire or marine insurance claims is easy through audited accounts. The policy holders and insurance company can settle actual loss of property.
- *No Loss to Lenders*: Auditing is essential for lenders. The banks and other lenders ask the borrowers to submit audited accounts before granting loans. The audited accounts are helpful to check the trust worthiness of customers.
- *Creditor are Protected*: Auditing is essential for creditors. They can know the true performance of their debtors. The creditor can accept this promise only when he feels that debtor is reliable businessman. Auditor accounts provide basic information about reliability.
- *Bidders Can Offer High Rate*: Auditing is helpful for bidders. Audited accounts provide information about net worth of any business. The people interested in purchasing the business can rely on such information. They know the fair value of business. They can offer reasonable price through open bidding.
- *Better Pay to Employees*: Auditing is helpful for employees. They are interests in profits. Auditing accounting proves true and fair view of profit. The employees can demand higher pay, fringe benefits and participating in profits. Audit of accounts with the independent person help the employees to make settlement with the employers.
- Investors Can Take Decisions: Auditing is helpful for inventors. The audited accounts can be used to calculate value of shares and other securities. The bargains power is given to the people who have money and they want earn income. They can protect their rights through reliable information.

2

Audit Planning

Meaning

As per Auditing and Assurance Standard, "Basic Principles Governing an Audit", Audit Planning is one of the basic principles. Accordingly, it states "The auditor should plan his work to enable him to conduct an effective audit in an efficient and timely manner. Plans should be based on knowledge of the client's business.

Plans should be made to cover, among other things:

- Acquiring knowledge of the client's accounting systems, policies and internal control procedures;
- Establishing the expected degree of reliance to be placed on internal control;
- Determining and programming the nature, timing, and extent of the audit procedures to be performed;
- Coordinating the work to be performed. Plans should be further developed and revised as necessary during the course of the audit." AAS-8 further expounds this principle. According to it, planning should be continuous throughout the engagement and involves
  - Developing an overall plan for the expected scope and conduct of the audit; and
  - Developing an audit programme showing the nature, timing and extent of audit procedures.

Changes in conditions or unexpected results of audit procedures may cause revisions of the overall plan of and the audit programme. The reasons for significant changes may be documented.

Objectives of Planning

Adequate audit planning helps to:

- Ensure that appropriate attention is devoted to important areas of the audit.
- Ensure that potential problems are promptly identified;
- Ensure that the work is completed expeditiously;

- Utilize the assistants properly; and
- Co-ordinate the work done by other auditors and experts.

In planning his audit, the auditor will consider factors such as complexity of the audit, the environment in which the entity operates his previous experience with the client and knowledge of the client's business. The auditor may wish to discuss elements of his overall plan and certain audit procedures with the client to improve the efficiency of the audit and to coordinate audit procedures with work of the client's personnel. The overall audit plan and the audit programme, however, remain the auditor's responsibility.

Factors

Planning his audit, the Auditor will consider the following factors:

- *Complexity of the Audit*: The scope of work and reporting responsibilities is analyses in order to determine the complexity of audit.
- *Environment in which the entity operates*: This enables the Auditor to understand various operational aspects of audit, e.g. extent of computerization, nature of internal controls, general attitude of personnel, etc.
- *Previous experience with the client*: By analysing the previous year's audit working papers and other relevant files, the Auditor should pay particular attention to matters that required special consideration and decide whether they might affect the work to be done in the current year.
- *Knowledge of the client's business*: This is required to establish the overall audit plan. The Auditor will be able to
  - Identify areas of special audit consideration
  - Evaluate the reasonableness both of accounting estimates and management representations
  - Make judgments regarding the appropriateness of accounting policies and disclosures.
- *Discussion with Client*: The Auditor can discuss his overall plan and certain audit procedures with the client to improve the efficiency of the audit and to coordinate audit procedures with work of the client's personnel. The overall audit plan and the audit Programme, however, remain the Auditor's responsibility.
- *Sources of Informayion*: The Auditor should obtain a level of knowledge of the client's ness that will enable him to identify the events, transactions and practices that, in his judgment, may have iificant effect on the financial information. The Auditor can gain knowledge of client's "business from:
  - Client's Annual Reports to Shareholders.
  - Minutes of Meetings of Shareholders, Board of Directors and

important Committees.
- Intemal Financial Management Reports for current and previous periods, including Budgets, if any.
- Previous year's Audit Working Papers, and other relevant files.
- Personnel responsible for non-audit services to the client who may be able to provide information on natters that may affect the audit.
- Discussions with Client.
- Client's Policy and Procedures Manual.
- Relevant publications of the ICAI and other professional bodies, Industry Publications, Trade Journals,
- Magazines, Newspapers or Textbooks.
- Consideration of the state of the economy and its effect on the client's business.

Development of Plan

The auditor should consider the following matters in developing his overall plan for the expected scope and conduct of the audit:

- The terms of his engagement and any statutory responsibilities.
- The nature and timing of reports or other communication.
- The applicable legal or statutory requirements.
- The accounting policies adopted by the client and changes in those policies.
- The effect of new accounting or auditing pronouncements on the audit.
- The identification of significant audit areas.
- The setting of materiality levels for audit purposes.

Conditions requiring special attention, such as the possibility of material error or fraud or the involvement of parties in whom directors or persons who are substantial owners of the entity are the act of examining vouchers is referred to as vouching. It is the practice followed in an audit, with the objective of establishing the authenticity of the transactions recorded in the primary books of account. It essentially consists of verifying a transaction recorded in the books of account with the relevant documentary evidence and the authority on the basis of which the entry has been made; also confirming that the amount mentioned in the voucher has been posted to an appropriate account which would disclose the nature of the transaction on its inclusion in the final statements of account.

On these considerations, the essential points to be borne in mind while examining a voucher are:

- That the date of the voucher falls within the accounting period;
- That the voucher is made out in the client's name;
- That the voucher is duly authorized;

- That the voucher comprised all the relevant documents which could be expected to have been received or brought into existence on the transactions having been entered into, i.e., the voucher is complete in all respects; and
- That the account in which the amount of the voucher is adjusted is the one that would clearly disclose the character of the receipts or payments posted thereto on its inclusion in the final accounts.

After the examination is over, each voucher should be either impressed with a rubber stamp or initialed so that it may not be presented again in support of another entry.

Audit Programme

It is desirable that in respect of each audit and more particularly for bigger audits an audit programme should be drawn up. Audit programme is nothing but a list of examination and verification steps to be applied set out in such a way that the inter-relationship of one step to another is clearly shown and designed, keeping in view the assertions discernible in the statement of account produced for audit or on the basis of an appraisal of the accounting records of the client. In other words, an audit programme is a detailed of the accounting records of applying the audit procedures in the given circumstances with instructions for the appropriate techniques to be adopted for accomplishing the audit objectives.

Businesses vary in nature, size and composition; work which is suitable to one business may not be suitable to be rendered by the auditor are the other factors that vary from assignment to assignment. Because of such variations, evolving one audit programme applicable to all business under all circumstances is not practicable. However it becomes a necessity to specify in details in the audit programme the nature of work to be done so that no time will be wasted on matters not pertinent to the engagement and any special matter or any specific situation can be taken care of.

An audit programme consists of a series of verification procedures to be applied to the financial statements and accounts of a given company for the purpose of obtaining sufficient evidence to enable the auditor to express an informed opinion on such statements.

For the purpose of programme construction, the following points should be kept in view:

- Stay within the scope and limitation of the assignment.
- Determining the evidence reasonable available and identify the best evidence for deriving the necessary satisfaction.
- Apply only these steps and procedures which are useful in accomplishing the verification purpose In the specific situation.
- Consider all possibilities of error.
- Co-ordinate the procedures to be applied to related items.

Amplification is not necessary of the above points except the one under evidence: that is the very basis for formulation of opinion and an audit programme is designed to provide for that by prescribing procedures and techniques. What is best evidence for testing the accuracy of any assertion is a matter of expert's knowledge and evidence. This is the primary taks before the auditor when he draws up the audit programme. Transactions are varied in nature and impact; procedures to be prescribed depend on prior knowledge of what evidence is reasonable available in respect of each transaction

Factors, Advantages and Disadvantages of Audit Programme

Factors

While construction an audit programme, the Auditor should keep the following points in his mind:

- To operate within the scope and limitations of the assignment.
- To determine the evidence reasonably available and identify the best avidence for deriving the necessary satisfaction.
- To apply only those steps and procedures, which are useful in accomplishing the verification purpose in the specific situation.
- To consider all possibilities of error.
- To co-ordinate the procedures to be applied to related items.

Advantages

- It provides the assistant carrying out the audit with total and clear set of instructions of the work generally to be done.
- It is essential, particularly for major audits, to provide a total perspective of the work to be performed.
- Selection of assistants for the jobs on the basis of compatibility becomes easier when the work is rationally planned, defined and segregated.
- Without a written and pre-determined programme, work is necessarily to be carried out on the basis of some 'mental' plan. In such a situation there is always a danger of ignoring or overlooking certain books and records. Under a properly framed programme, the danger is significantly less and the audit can proceed systematically.
- The assistance, by putting their signature on programme, accepts the responsibility for the work carried out by them individually and, if necessary, the work done may be traced back to the assistant.
- The principal can control the progress of the various audits in hand by examination of audit programmes initiated by the assistants deputed to the jobs for completed work.
- It serves as a guide for audits to be carried out in the succeeding year.

- A properly drawn up audit programme serves as evidence in the event of any charge of negligence being brought against the auditor. It may be of considerable value in establishing that he exercised reasonable skill and care that was expected of professional auditor.

Disadvantages

- The work may become mechanical and particular parts of the programme may be carried out without any understanding of the object of such parts in the whole audit scheme.
- The programme often tends to becomes rigid and inflexible following set grooves; the business may change in its operation of conduct, but the old programme may still be carried on. Changes in staff or internal control may render precaution necessary at points different from those originally decided upon.
- Inefficient assistants may take shelter behind the programme i.e., defend deficiencies in their work on the ground that no instructions in the matter is contained therein.
- A hard and fast audit programme may kill the initiative of efficient and enterprising assistants.
- All these disadvantages may be eliminated by imaginative supervision of the work carried on by the assistants; the auditor must have a receptive attitude as regards the assistants; the assistants should be encouraged to observed matters objectively and bring significant matters to the notice of supervisor/principal.

Audit Working Papers

Meaning

The audit working papers constitute the link between the auditor's report and the client's records.

Documentation is one of the basic principles listed in AAS 1. according to AAS 3, documentation refers to working papers prepared or obtained by the auditor and retained by him in connections with performance of his audit.

The objects of an auditor's working papers are to record and demonstrate the audit work from one year to another.

Therefore, working papers should provide for:

- Means of controlling current audit work;
- Evidence of audit work performed;
- Schedules supporting or additional item in the accounts; and
- Information about the business being audited, including the recent history.

Working papers are varied in nature but the foundation of all working paper can be traced to:

- The basic constitutional document like memorandum and Articles of association, partnership Deed, trust deed, etc.;
- The contents of the minute books;
- The contents of the balance sheet and the profit and loss account; and
- The letter of engagement.

Importance of Audit Working Papers

- IT provides guidance to the audit staff regard to the manner of checking the schedules.
- The auditor is able to fix responsibility on the staff member who signs each schedule checked by him.
- It acts as an evidence in the court in the court of law when a charge of negligence is brought against the auditor.
- It acts as the process of planning for the auditor so that he can estimate the time that may be required for checking the schedules.

The auditor should adopt reasonable procedures for custody and confidentiality of his working papers and should retained them for a period of time sufficient to meet the needs of his practice and satisfy any pertinent legal or professional requirements of record retention.

Factors Determining Form and Content of Audit

Working Papers

Working papers should record the audit plan, nature, timing and extent of auditing procedures performed, and the conclusions drawn from the evidence obtained.

The form and content of working papers are affected by matters such as:

- Nature of the engagement.
- Form of the auditor's report.
- Nature and complexity of the client's business.
- Nature and condition of the client's records and degree of reliance on internal controls.
- Need in particular circumstances for direction, supervision and review of work performed by assistants.

Working papers should be designed and properly organized to meet the circumstances of each audit and the auditor's needs in respect thereof. The standardization of working papers (for example, checklists, specimen letters, standard organisation of working papers) improves the efficiency with which they are prepared and reviewed. It also facilitates the delegation of work while providing a means to control its quality. Working papers should be sufficiently complete and detailed for an auditor to obtain an overall understanding of the audit. The extent of the documentation is a matter of professional judgement since it is neither necessary nor practical that every observation, consideration, consideration or conclusion is documented by the auditor in his working papers.

Audit File

A permanent audit file normally includes:

- Information concerning the legal and organizational structure of the entity. In case of a company, this includes the memorandum and Article of association. In the case of a statutory corporation, this includes the act and regulations under which the corporation functions.
- Extracts or copies of important legal documents, agreements and minute relevant to the audit.
- A record of the study and the evaluation of the internal controls related to the accounting system. This might be in the form of narrative descriptions, questionnaires or flow charts, or some combination thereof.
- Copies of audited financial statements for previous years.
- Analysis of significant ratios and trends.
- Copies of management letters issued by the auditor, if any.
- Record of communication with the retiring auditor, if any, before acceptance of the appointment as auditor.
- Notes regarding significant accounting policies.
- Significant audit observations of earlier years.

The Current File

The current file normally includes:

- Correspondence relating to acceptance of annual reappointment.
- Extracts of important matters in the minutes of board meetings and general meetings as relevant to audit.
- Evidence of the planning of the audit and audit programme.
- Analysis of transactions and balances.
- A record of the nature, timing and extent of auditing procedures performed, and the results of such procedures.
- Evidence that the work performed by assistants was supervised and reviewed.
- Copies of communication with other auditors, experts and other third parties.
- Letters of representation or confirmation received from the client.
- Conclusions reached by the auditor concerning significant aspects of the audit, including the manner in which exceptions and unusual matters, if any, disclosed by the auditor's procedures were resolved or treated.

- Copies of the financial information being reported on the related audit reports.

Functions/Importance

- It provides guidance to the audit staff with regards to the manner of checking the schedules.
- The auditor is able to fix responsibility on the staff member who sign each schedule checked by him.
- It acts as an evidence in the court of law when a charge of negligence is brought against the auditor.
- It acts as the process of planning for the auditor so that he can estimate the time that may be required for checking the schedules.

The auditor should adopt reasonable procedures for custody and confidentiality of his working papers and should retain them for a period of time sufficient to meet the needs of his practice and satisfy any pertinent legal or professional requirement of record retention. Clarification On The Auditor's Rights Where Clients And Other Auditors

Seek Access To Their Audit Working Papers:

- Auditing and Assurance standard, "Basic principles governing an audit", states in para6: "The auditor should respect the confidentiality of information acquired in the course of his work and should not disclosed any such information to a third party without specific authority or unless there is a legal or professional duty to disclosed". Auditing and Assurance standard (AAS), "Documentation", states: 'working papers are the property of the auditor. The auditor may at his discretion, make portions of or extracts from his working papers available to his client. "AAS further requires", inter alia, that the "auditor should adopt reasonable procedures for custody and confidentiality of his working papers."
- part l of the second schedule to the chartered Accountants Act, 1949, provides that "A Chartered Accountant in practice shall be deemed to be guilty of professional misconduct, if he disclosed information acquired in the course of his professional engagement to any person other than his client, without the consent of his client or otherwise than as required by any law for the time being in force."
- Request are sometime received by the members of the institute, who have/had been performing the duties as the auditor of an enterprises, to provide access to their audit working papers. The request may be made by the clients or other auditors of the enterprise or its related enterprise such as a parent enterprise.
- It is hereby clarified that except to the extent, an auditor is not required to provide the client or the other auditors of the same enterprise or its related enterprise such as a parent or a subsidiary,

access to his audit working papers. The main auditors of an enterprise do not have right of access to the audit working papers of the branch auditors. In the case of a company, the statutory auditor has to consider the report of the branch auditor and has a right to seek clarifications and/or to visit the branch if he deems it necessary to do so for the performance of the duties as auditor. An auditor can rely on the work of another auditor, without having any right of access to the audit working papers of the other auditor. For this purpose, the term 'auditor' includes 'internal auditor'.

Features

As audit working papers are quite useful they should be prepared properly.

They should have the following essentials:

- *Standard form*: They should be prepared in a standard form. The subject matter should be arranged under various heading and subheadings.
- *Proper layout*: There should be proper design and layout of the working papers. This will bring uniformity into the maintenance of working papers.
- *Space for margins*: There should be enough space for margin after each note for noting down the auditor's remarks and decisions.
- *Proper organisation and arrangement*: The working papers should be properly organized and arranged. In other words the working papers should be so organized and arranged that the auditor will be able to locate any particular matter easily.
- *Completeness*: The audit working papers should be complete in all respects. They should contain detailed information on all essential facts or points.
- *Clarity and Accuracy*: The working papers should be quite clear and self explanatory. The information contained in the working papers should be accurate.
- *Good quality paper*: Paper of good quality should be used for working papers as they are subject to frequent handling further the paper used should be of uniform and convenient size so that they can be easily filed.

3

Cost

DEFINITION OF COST

In business, retail, and accounting, a cost is the value of money that has been used up to produce something, and hence is not available for use anymore. In economics, a cost is an alternative that is given up as a result of a decision. In business, the cost may be one of acquisition, in which case the amount of money expended to acquire it is counted as cost.

In this case, money is the input that is gone in order to acquire the thing. This acquisition cost may be the sum of the cost of production as incurred by the original producer, and further costs of transaction as incurred by the acquirer over and above the price paid to the producer. Usually, the price also includes a mark-up for profit over the cost of production. Costs are often further described based on their timing or their applicability.

ACCOUNTING VS OPPORTUNITY COSTS

In accounting, costs are the monetary value of expenditures for supplies, services, labour, products, equipment and other items purchased for use by a business or other accounting entity. It is the amount denoted on invoices as the price and recorded in bookkeeping records as an expense or asset cost basis.

Opportunity cost, also referred to as economic cost is the value of the best alternative that was not chosen in order to pursue the current endeavour—*i.e,* what could have been accomplished with the resources expended in the undertaking. It represents opportunities forgone. In theoretical economics, cost used without qualification often means opportunity cost.

COMPARING PRIVATE, EXTERNAL, SOCIAL, AND PSYCHIC COSTS

When a transaction takes place, it typically involves both private costs and external costs. Private costs are the costs that the buyer of a good or service pays the seller. This can also be described as the costs internal to the firm's production function. External costs, in contrast, are the costs that people other than the buyer are forced to pay as a result of the transaction. The bearers of such costs can be either particular individuals or society at large. Note that external costs are often both non-monetary and problematic to quantify for comparison with monetary values.

They include things like pollution, things that society will likely have to pay for in some way or at some time in the future, but that are not included in transaction prices. Social costs are the sum of private costs and external costs. For example, the manufacturing cost of a car reflects the private cost for the manufacturer. The polluted waters or polluted air also created as part of the process of producing the car is an external cost borne by those who are affected by the pollution or who value unpolluted air or water.

Because the manufacturer does not pay for this external cost and does not include this cost in the price of the car, they are said to be external to the market pricing mechanism. The air pollution from driving the car is also an externality produced by the car user in the process of using his good. The driver does not compensate for the environmental damage caused by using the car. A psychic cost is a subset of social costs that specifically represent the costs of added stress or losses to quality of life.

COST ESTIMATES AND COST OVERRUN

When developing a business plan for a new company, product, or project, planners typically make cost estimates in order to assess whether revenues/ benefits will cover costs. This is done in both business and government. Costs are often underestimated resulting in cost overrun during implementation. Main causes of cost underestimation and overrun are optimism bias and strategic misrepresentation.

Reference class forecasting was developed to curb optimism bias and strategic misrepresentation and arrive at more accurate cost estimates. Cost Plus, is where the Price = Cost plus or minus X per cent, where x is the percentage of built in overhead or profit margin.

COST MANAGEMENT

Cost management is the process by which companies control and plan the costs of doing business. Individual projects should have customised cost management plans, and companies as a whole also integrate cost management into their overall business model. There is no single accepted definition for this term, because it has such broad applications and possible strategies.

When properly implemented, cost management will translate into reduced costs of production for products and services, as well as increased value being delivered to the customer. For a company's management to be effective overall, cost management must be an integral feature of it. It is easiest to understand this concept if it is explained in the context of a single project.

For instance, before a project is started, the anticipated costs should be identified and measured. These expenses should then be approved before any purchasing occurs.

During the process of completing a project, all incurred costs should be noted and kept in a record of some kind, to help ensure that the costs are controlled and kept in line with initial expectations, to the extent that this is possible. Taking this approach to cost management will help a company determine whether they accurately estimated expenses at first, and will help them more closely predict expenses in the future. Any overspending can also be monitored in this way, and either eliminated in future projects or specifically approved if the expense was necessary.

Cost management cannot be used in isolation; projects must be organized and tailored with this strategy in mind. Starting a project with cost management in mind will help to avoid certain pitfalls that may be present otherwise. If the objectives of the project are not clearly defined at first, or are changed during the course of the project, cost over-runs will be more likely.

If costs are not fully researched before the project, they may be underestimated, thereby inflating the expectation of the project's success unrealistically. Construction projects are subject to their own particular challenges; these can include constraints in the form of laws and regulations that must be planned around.

If the project is completely and clearly defined, this will facilitate effective management of the costs it will incur. Effective cost management strategies will help a team deliver a finished project within the allocated budget, while also making it as valuable as possible to the company. There is always the possibility of unexpected costs, but preparation in the form of cost management will likely make them much easier to deal with when they occur.

COST BEHAVIOUR

The most important building block of both microeconomic analysis and cost accounting is the characterization of how costs change as output volume changes. Output volume can refer to production, sales, or any other principle activity that is appropriate for the organization under consideration. The following discussion examines the volume of production in a factory, but the same principles apply regardless of the type of organization and the appropriate measure of activity. Costs can be variable, fixed, or mixed.

VARIABLE COSTS

Variable costs vary in a linear fashion with the production level. However, when stated on a per unit basis, variable costs remain constant across all production levels within the relevant range. The following two charts depict this relationship between variable costs and output volume.

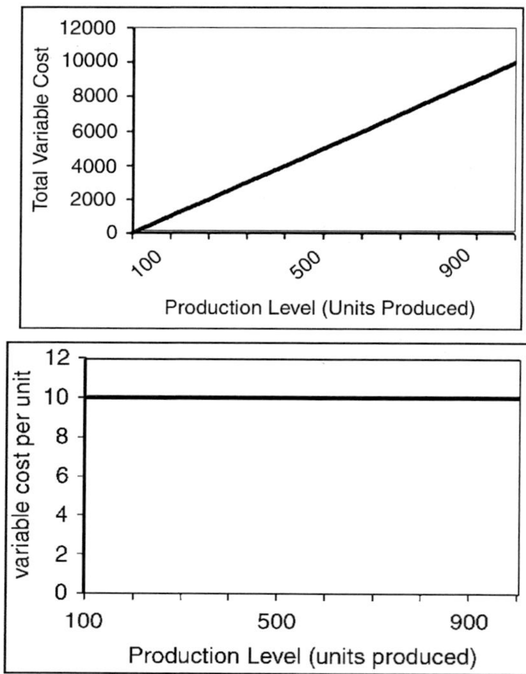

A good example of a variable cost is materials. If one pair of pants requires $10 of fabric, then every pair of pants requires $10 of fabric, no matter how many pairs are made. The fabric cost is $10 per unit at every level of production. If one pair is made, the total fabric cost is $10; if two pairs are made, the total fabric cost is $20; and if 1,000 pairs are made, the total fabric cost is $10,000. Hence, the total cost is increasing and linear in the production level.

FIXED COSTS

Fixed costs do not vary with the production level. Total fixed costs remain the same, within the relevant range. However, the fixed cost per unit decreases as production increases, because the same fixed costs are spread over more units. The following two charts depict this relationship between fixed costs and output volume.

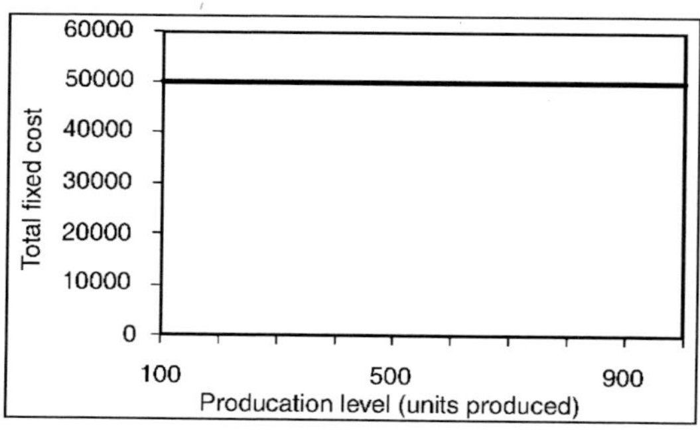

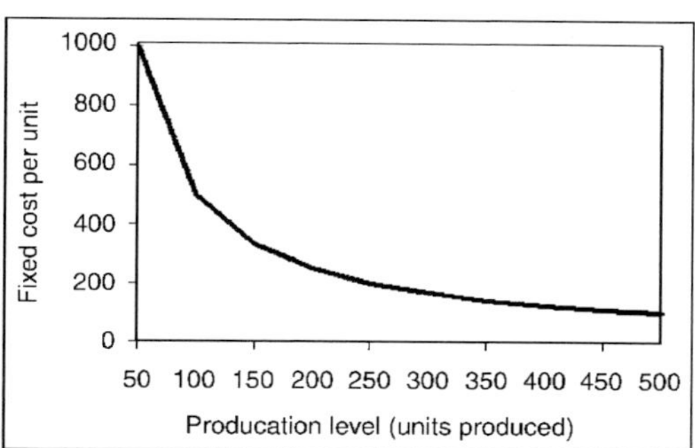

In this example, fixed costs are $50,000. The first chart shows that fixed costs remain $50,000 at all production levels from 100 units to 1,000 units. The second chart shows that the fixed cost per unit decreases as production increases. Hence, when 100 units are manufactured, the fixed cost per unit is $500 ($50,000 ÷ 100). When 500 units are manufactured, the fixed cost per unit is $100 ($50,000 ÷ 500).

RELEVANT RANGE

The relevant range is the range of activity over which these relationships are valid. For example, if the factory is operating at capacity, increasing production requires additional investment in fixed costs to expand the facility or to lease or build another factory. Alternatively, production might be reduced below a threshold at which point one of the company's factories is no longer needed, and the fixed costs associated with that factory can be avoided. With respect to variable costs, the company might qualify for a volume discount on fabric purchases above some production level. The relevant range for characterizing fabric as a variable cost ends at that production level, because the fabric cost per unit of output is different when the factory produces above that threshold than when the factory produces below that threshold.

MIXED COSTS

If, within a relevant range, a cost is neither fixed nor variable, it is called semi-variable or mixed. Following are two common examples of mixed costs.

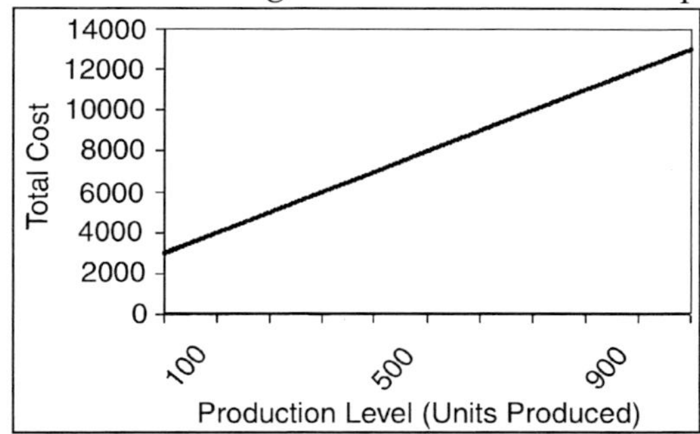

In this example, although the total cost line increases in production, it does not pass through the origin because there is a fixed cost component. An example of a cost that fits this description is electricity. A fixed amount of electricity is required to run the factory air conditioning, computers and lights.

There is also a variable cost component related to running the machines on the factory floor. The fixed component in this example is $3,000 per month. The variable cost component is $10 per unit of output. Hence, at a production level of 500 units, the total electric cost is $8,000 [$3,000 + ($10 x 500)].

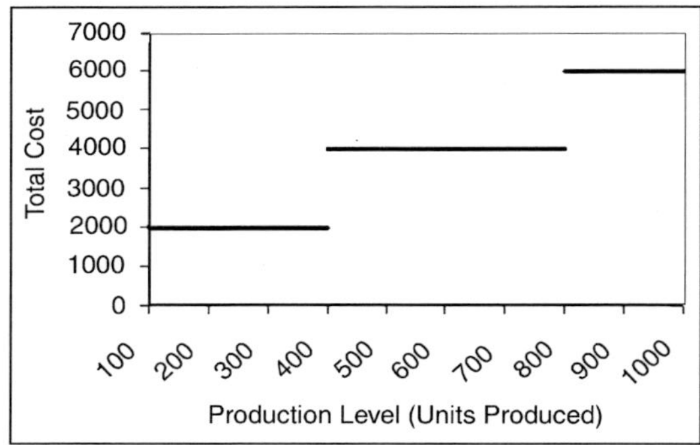

The mixed cost illustrated in the above chart is called a step function. An example of such cost behaviour would be the total salary expense for shift supervisors. If the factory runs one shift, only one shift supervisor is required. In order for the factory to produce above the maximum capacity of a single shift, the factory must add a second shift and hire a second shift supervisor, so that total shift supervisor salary expense doubles. If the factory runs three shifts, three shift supervisors are required.

COST BEHAVIOUR ASSUMPTIONS IN MANAGEMENT ACCOUNTING VERSUS MICROECONOMICS

Microeconomic analysis usually assumes decreasing marginal costs of production, sometimes followed by increasing marginal costs of production beyond a certain production level. Hence, economists' graphs of the total cost of production and the average per-unit cost of production show smooth, curved functions.

Management accountants usually assume the linear relationships depicted in the previous graphs. Linearity is a more accurate description of many situations encountered by management accountants than the economists' curves, and even when linearity constitutes a simplifying assumption it is almost always sufficiently descriptive for the task at hand.

BASIC COST MANAGEMENT CONCEPTS

Multi-product firms have to account for costs that can be tied to a product, direct costs. They also have to account for indirect costs not directly measurable. A 'cost object' can be a product, service, process or any items which management requires cost information. The way that costs are assigned depends on their nature. A direct costs is easily traceable with a high degree of accuracy and indirect, or overhead, cost cannot be easily identifiable with a particular object. Product costs are costs allocated to a product; this is not just physical products. All other costs are period costs. Such costs are expenses to the income statement in the period they are incurred. Product costs are recognised as an expense in the income statement only when the product is sold. Prior to sale the cost of products is shown as an asset due to the accrual principle.

The stages in the allocation of overheads to products are as follows;

- Identify overhead costs collected from production and service cost centres and apportion as appropriate and possible.
- Once identified allocate to production departments.
- Allocate overheads to a single product by dividing the number of products into the total overhead. The resulting sum can then be applied as cost to the product.
- Total Overheads of a Production Costs Centre ($s)/Level of Activity (units)

Predetermined overhead absorption rates are estimates of future expenditures. Estimates are used becuase some overhead costs are not known for some time until afterthey have incurred. Normal costing is where the cost object is determined using the actual costs for the direct the direct costs and a predetermined rate for the allocation of indirect costs. Functional-based cost accounting classifies all costs as either fixed or variable in relation to changes in the volume of units produced.

Activity-based costing tries to capture changes in technology by apportioning oveheads to product costs taking into account activity and transactions that drive the cost. An activity cost pool is where the costs of an activity under the ABC system are accumulated. Drives are factors that cause changes in the use of resources. The focus in ABC is managing activities instead of costs. Absorption costing is where the cost of inventories is determined in order to include an appropriate share of variable and fixed costs.

Fixed costs are allocated on the basis of normal operating capacity. In variable costing, only the production costs are used. Using absorption costsing, production overhead costs are included as a product cost whereas in variable costing they are treated as a period cost. This leads to different values of inventory and therefore different net profit figures. *The difference in profits derived from the application of the two methods can be reconciled by the following:*

- Fixed Overhead Absorption Rate * Movement of Inventories in a period = Difference in Profits

ACTIVITY BASED COSTING

Activity Based Costing is an accounting technique that allows an organization to determine the actual cost associated with each product and service produced by the organization without regard to the organizational structure. It is developed to provide more-accurate ways of assigning the costs of indirect and support resources to activities, bushiness processes, products, services, and customers.

ABC systems recognize that many organizational resources are required not for physical production of units of product but to provide a broad array of support activities that enable a variety of products and services to be produced for a diverse group of customers. The goal of ABC is not to allocate common costs to products. The goal is to measure and then price out all the resources used for activities that support the production and delivery of products and services to customers.

CONCEPT OF ACTIVITY-BASED-COSTING

Activity Based Costing is an accounting technique that allows an organization to determine the actual cost associated with each product and service produced by the organization without regard to the organizational structure. It is developed to provide more-accurate ways of assigning the costs of indirect and support resources to activities, bushiness processes, products, services, and customers. ABC systems recognize that many organizational resources are required not for physical production of units of product but to provide a broad array of support activities that enable a variety of products and services to be produced for a diverse group of customers.

The goal of ABC is not to allocate common costs to products. The goal is to measure and then price out all the resources used for activities that support the production and delivery of products and services to customers. An organization performs activities to do its business. These activities define the kind of business you are in: a ship owner has an activity to unpack boats; an accounting firm prepares tax returns; a manufacturer produces products; a council delivers services; a university teaches students. All activities consume resources.

It is the consumption of these resources that adds to overhead costs. The basis of Activity Based Costing is: look at the activities required to produce the cost of the product or service. The activities consume resources and the cost of these can be calculated.

The amount of activity required for each product and service is determined, hence the real cost can be determined:

- The activity is the work that is done.
- The resource is what the activity uses to do the work *e.g.* people, equipment, and services. Resources cost money.
- The cost of the activity depends on the quantity of resources used to accomplish the activity.
- The cost driver for an activity is the factor that influences the amount of the resources that will be consumed by this activity.

- The activity driver measures how much of the activity is used by the cost object. Example: Product A is delivered once a month, whereas product B is delivered once a week. Products A and B require a different number of deliveries, hence the cost of the delivery activity should be assigned to each product on the basis of the number of deliveries each uses.
- The cost object is whatever it is you wish to cost. It could be a product, service, process, job or customer.

While traditional costing arbitrarily allocates overhead costs, ABC traces overhead costs by looking at the activities that each product and service calls upon. With ABC the products consume the activities. It is the activities that cost money. If there were no activities, no resources would be consumed. It is the activities that you do that define your business.

USE OF ACTIVITY-BASED-COSTING

Activity-Based-Costing is necessary for the following reasons:

- Identify opportunities to reduce costs and/or increase efficiency
- Obtain actionable information to negotiate price increases for unprofitable clients
- Quantify the cost of non-value added activities such as errors and reworks
- Stratify overhead costs so they can be managed more effectively
- Understand TRUE profitability of your customers, products, or services
- Understand why profitability may be mediocre despite good strategic fundamentals

HOW DOES ABC WORK?

The first stage in an initial ABC study is to develop a fundamental understanding of the Resources and Activities of an organization. The Resources are then mapped to the Activities, thereby quantifying the cost of performing each of these Activities. These costs are traced to Cost Objects providing tremendous insight into where an organization is making and losing money.

ABC MODEL

The objective of an ABC implementation is to relate all of the costs of doing business to products, services, or customers.

Developing the initial model consists of the following five steps:

- Define Cost Objects
- Determine Activities that are supported by Resources
- Develop Cost Drivers to link Activities to Cost Objects
- Develop Resource Drivers to link Resources to Activities
- Identify the Resources of an organization

Identify Resources

Resources represent the expenditures of an organization. Examples include production labour, sales and marketing labour, occupancy and utilities, equipment, and supplies. These are the same costs that are represented in a traditional accounting view; unlike traditional accounting, ABC links these costs to products, customers, or services.

Identify Activities

Activities represent the work performed in an organization.

ABC Activities for the sales department in a typical organization might include:

- Attending trade shows and other events
- Distributing samples
- Evaluating products and improving product knowledge
- Making customer service calls
- Making sales calls to existing customers
- Making sales calls to potential customers
- Training product representatives

Traditional accounting will often break the cost of the sales department into salaries, benefits, allocated rent, supplies, and so on. Unlike traditional accounting, which reports what the costs are, ABC accounts for these costs based on what activities caused them to occur.

By determining the actual activities that occur in various departments, such as accounting, customer service, and sales, it is then possible to more accurately relate these costs to customers, products, and services.

Identify Cost Objects

ABC provides profitability by one or more cost object, usually represented by products, customers, and/or services. Cost Object profitability is utilized to identify money losing customers, to validate separate divisions or business units, or to measure the performance of individual projects, jobs, or contracts.

Defining the outputs to be viewed is an important step in a successful ABC implementation.

Determine Resource Drivers

Resource Drivers provide the link between the expenditures of an organization and the Activities performed within the organization. For example, the total salary of a customer service representative would likely be allocated to the Activities performed based on the amount of time spent performing the Activity. If 50 per cent of her time is spent performing the activity, taking orders for existing customers, 50 per cent of her salary would be allocated to this Activity.

Determine Cost Drivers

Determination of Cost Drivers completes the last stage of the model. Cost Drivers trace, or link, the cost of performing certain Activities to Cost Objects. For example, taking orders for existing customers may be linked to specific customers based on the number of orders taken, if each order takes approximately the same amount of time. If order taking time varies based on the customer, this cost may be linked based on another driver or multiple drivers.

OPERATING COST

Operating costs are the recurring expenses which are related to the operation of a business, or to the operation of a device, component, piece of equipment or facility.

BUSINESS OPERATING COSTS

For a commercial enterprise, operating costs fall into two broad categories:

1. Fixed costs, which are the same whether the operation is closed or running at 100 per cent capacity
2. Variable costs, which may increase depending on whether more production is done, and how it is done (producing 100 items of product might require 10 days of normal time or take 7 days if overtime is used. It may be more or less expensive to use overtime production depending on whether faster production means the product can be more profitable).

Business Overhead Costs

Overhead costs for a business are the cost of resources used by an organization just to maintain its existence. Overhead costs are usually measured in monetary terms, but non-monetary overhead is possible in the form of time required to accomplish tasks.

Examples of overhead costs include:

- Cost of electricity for the office lights
- Payment of rent on the office space a business occupies
- Some office personnel wages

Non-overhead costs are incremental costs, such as the cost of raw materials used in the goods a business sells. Operating Cost is calculated by Cost of goods sold + Operating Expenses. Operating Expenses consist of:. Administrative and office expenses like rent, salaries, to staff, insurance, directors fees etc.. Selling and distribution expenses like advertisement, salaries of salesmen.

EQUIPMENT OPERATING COSTS

In the case of a device, component, piece of equipment or facility, it is the regular, usual and customary recurring coststing or purchasing the equipment. Operating costs are incurred by all equipment—unless the equipment has no cost to operate, requires no personnel or space and never wears out. In some cases, equipment may appear to have low or no operating cost because either the cost is not recognized or is being absorbed in whole or part by the cost of something else.

Equipment operating costs may include:

- Salaries or Wages of personnel
- Advertising
- Raw materials
- License or equivalent fees imposed by a government
- Real estate expenses, including
  - Rent or Lease payments
  - Office space
  - Furniture and equipment
  - Investment value of the funds used to purchase The land, if it is owned instead of rented or leased
  - Property taxes and equivalent assessments
  - Operations taxes, such as fees assessed on transportation carriers for use of highways
- Fuel costs such as power for operations, fuel for production
- Public Utilities such as telephone service, Internet connectivity, etc.
- Maintenance of equipment
- Office supplies and consumables
- Insurance
- Depreciation of equipment and eventual replacement costs
- Damage due to uninsured losses, accident, sabotage, negligence, terrorism and routine wear and tear.
- Taxes on production or operation
- Income taxes

Some of these are not applicable in all instances.

For example:

- A solar panel placed on one's home for use in generating electric power generally has only capital costs; once it's running there are no personnel costs, utility costs or depreciation and it uses no extra land so it has no real operating costs; however there may need to be taken into account costs of replacement if damaged.
- An automobile or any other item purchased for personal use has no salary cost because the owner does not charge themselves for operating the device.
- An item which is leased may have some or all of these costs included as part of the purchase price.

It might be questionable to assert that the cost of ten extra people on the sales force are an incremental cost or an overhead cost, since the wages for these people are both overhead and incremental. The staff needed to keep the shop operational are mostly considered as overhead.

OVERHEAD COST

In business, overhead, overhead cost or overhead expense refers to an ongoing expense of operating a business. The term overhead is usually used to group expenses that are necessary to the continued functioning of the business, but cannot be immediately associated with the products/services being offered. Overhead expenses are all costs on the income statement except for direct labour,direct materials and direct expenses. Overhead expenses include accounting fees, advertising, depreciation, insurance, interest, legal fees, rent, repairs, supplies, taxes, telephone bills, travel and utilities costs.

Overhead can be classified under four headings:

1. Classification on behaviour of expenditure
2. Classification on the nature of expenditure
3. Element-wise classification
4. Functional classification

TARGET COSTING

As a totally new product and its industry develops, it starts to compete based on its new technology, concept, and/or service. Competitors emerge and the basis for competition evolves to other areas such as cycle time, quality, or reliability. As an industry becomes mature, the basis of competition typically moves to price. Profit margins shrink. Companies begin focusing on cost reduction. However, the cost structure for existing products is largely locked in and cost reduction activities have limited impact. As companies begin to realise that the majority of a product's costs are committed based on decisions made during the development of a product, the focus shifts to actions that can be taken during the product development phase. Until recently, engineers have focused on satisfying a customer's requirements.

Most development personnel have viewed a product's cost as a dependent variable that is the result of the decisions made about a products functions, features and performance capabilities. Because a product's costs are often not assessed until later in the development cycle, it is common for product costs to be higher than desired. This process is represented in Figure.

TRADITIONAL COST MANAGEMENT APPROACH

Target costing represents a fundamentally different approach.

It is based on three premises:

1. Orienting products to customer affordability or market-driven pricing,
2. Treating product cost as an independent variable during the definition of a product's requirements, and

3. Proactively working to achieve target cost during product and process development.

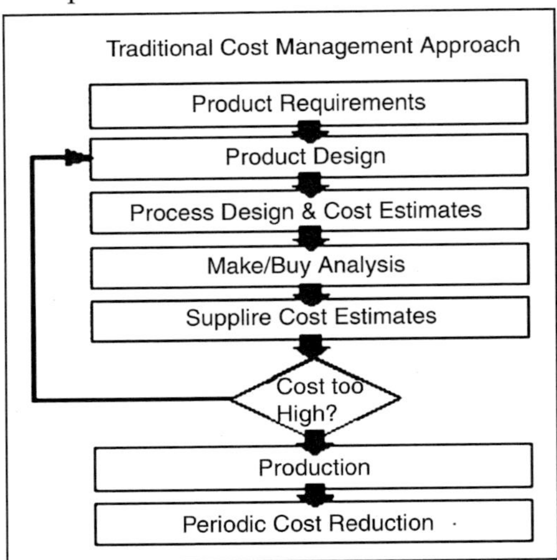

This target costing approach is represented in Figure.

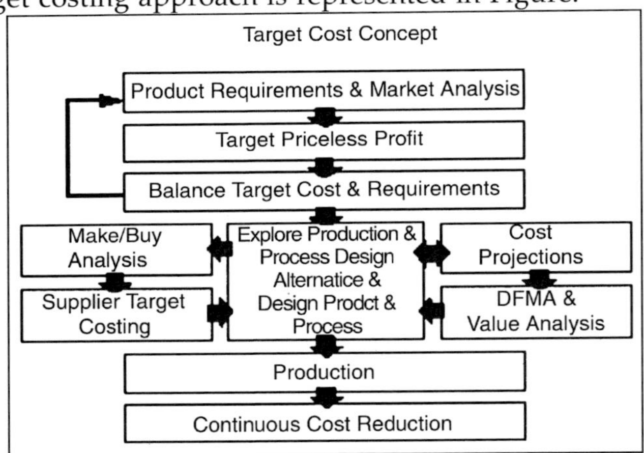

Target costing builds upon a design-to-cost (DTC) approach with the focus on market-driven target prices as a basis for establishing target costs. The target costing concept is similar to the cost as an independent variable (CAIV) approach used by the U.S. Department of Defence and to the price-to-win philosophy used by a number of companies pursuing contracts involving development under contract. The following ten steps are required to install a comprehensive target costing approach within an organization.

1. *Re-orient culture and attitudes*: The first and most challenging step is re-orient thinking towards market driven pricing and prioritized customer needs rather than just technical requirements as a basis for product development. This is a fundamental change from the

attitude in most organizations where cost is the result of the design rather than the influencer of the design and that pricing is derived from building up a estimate of the cost of manufacturing a product.

2. *Establish a market-driven target price*: A target price needs to be established based upon market factors such as the company position in the market place (market share), business and market penetration strategy, competition and competitive price response, targeted market niche or price point, and elasticity of demand. If the company is responding to a request for proposal/quotation, the target price is based on analysis of the price to win considering customer affordability and competitive analysis.
3. *Determine the target cost*: Once the target price is established, a worksheet is used to calculate the target cost by subtracting the standard profit margin, warranty reserves, and any uncontrollable corporate allocations. If a bid includes non-recurring development costs, these are also subtracted. The target cost is allocated down to lower level assemblies of subsystems in a manner consistent with the structure of teams or individual designer responsibilities.

Table. Target Cost Calculation Worksheet

Sign	Price/Cost Element	Estimate	% Factor	Per Unit Factor	Amount
	Manufacture's suggested Retail Price			$495.00	
–	Standard Dealer Margin		30%	$ –	$(148.50)
=	Cost to Retailer			$ 346.50	
–	Shipping/Distribution Cost to Retailer		0%	$15.00	$ (15.00)
=	Selling Price to Retailer			$331.50	
–	Distribution Cost/Mark-up		15%	$ –	$(49.37)
–	Shipping/Logistic Cost to Distribution Center		0%	$ 17.00	$ (17.00)
=	Manufactur's Selling Price			$264.78	
–	Profit Margin		8%	$ –	$ (21.18)
–	Warranty Cost		2%	$ –	$ (5.30)
–	Corporate Allocations		10%	$–	$ (26.48)
–	Business Unit Selling, General and Administrative		12%	$ –	(31.77)
	Non Recurring Development Cost	1200000			
	Estimated Production Volume	200000			
–	Allocated Non Recurring				

	Development Cost		$ 6.00	$ (6.00)
=	Business Unit Target Cost			$ 174.05
–	Overhead	45%	$ –	$ (78.32)
=	Direct Target Cost (Labour and Material			$ 9573

4. *Balance target cost with requirements*: Before the target cost is finalized, it must be considered in conjunction with product requirements. The greatest opportunity to control a product's costs is through proper setting of requirements or specifications. This requires a careful understanding of the voice of the customer, use of conjoint analysis to understand the value that customers place on particular product capabilities, and use of techniques such as quality function deployment to help make these tradeoff's among various product requirements including target cost.
5. *Establish a target costing process and a team-based organization*: A well-defined process is required that integrates activities and tasks to support to support target costing. This process needs to be based on early and proactive consideration of target costs and incorporate tools and methodologies described subsequently. Further, a team-based organization is required that integrates essential disciplines such as marketing, engineering, manufacturing, purchasing, and finance. Responsibilities to support target costing need to be clearly defined.
6. *Brainstorm and analyse alternatives*: The second most significant opportunity to achieve cost reduction is through consideration of multiple concept and design alternatives for both the product and its manufacturing and support processes at each stage of the development cycle. These opportunities can be achieved when there is out-of-the-box or creative consideration of alternatives coupled with structured analysis and decision-making methods.
7. Establish product cost models to support decision-making. Product cost models and cost tables provide the tools to evaluate the implications of concept and design alternatives. In the early stages of development, these models are based on parametric estimating or analogy techniques. Further on in the development cycle as the product and process become more defined, these models are based on industrial engineering or bottom-up estimating techniques. The models need to be comprehensive to address all of the proposed materials, fabrication processes, and assembly process and need to be validated to insure reasonable accuracy. A target cost worksheet can be used to capture the various elements of product cost, compare alternatives, as well as track changing estimates against target cost over the development cycle.

8. Use tools to reduce costs. Use of tools and methodologies related to design for manufacturability and assembly, design for inspection and test, modularity and part standardization, and value analysis or function analysis. These methodologies will consist of guidelines, databases, training, procedures, and supporting analytic tools.
9. Reduce indirect cost application. Since a significant portion of a product's costs are indirect, these costs must also be addressed. The enterprise must examine these costs, re-engineer indirect business processes, and minimize non-value-added costs. But in addition to these steps, development personnel generally lack an understanding of the relationship of these costs to the product and process design decisions that they make. Use of activity-based costing and an understanding of the organization's cost drivers can provide a basis for understanding how design decisions impact indirect costs and, as a result, allow their avoidance.
10. Measure results and maintain management focus. Current estimated costs need to be tracked against target cost throughout development and the rate of closure monitored. Management needs to focus attention of target cost achievement during design reviews and phase-gate reviews to communicate the importance of target costing to the organization.

KAIZEN COSTING

The process of continual cost reduction that occurs after a product design has been completed and is now in production. Cost reduction techniques can include working with suppliers to reduce the costs in their processes, implementing less costly re-designs of the product, or reducing waste costs. To better understand the activities through which a firm develops a competitive advantage and creates shareholder value, it is useful to separate the business system into a series of value-generating activities referred to as the value chain. In his 1985 book Competitive Advantage, Michael Porter introduced a generic value chain model that comprises a sequence of activities found to be common to a wide range of firms.

Porter identified primary and support activities as shown in the following diagram:

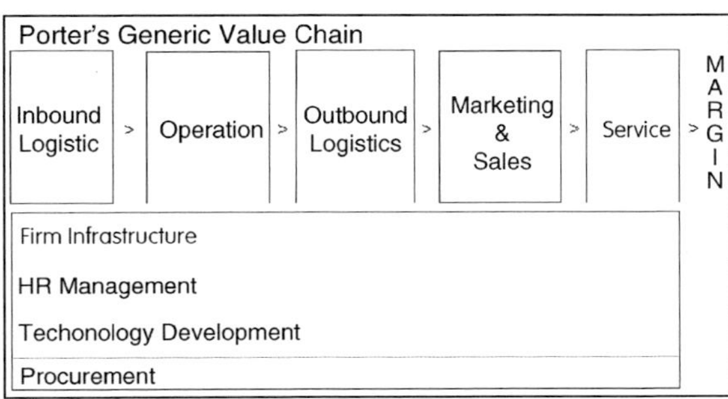

Fig. Porter's Generic Value Chain

The goal of these activities is to offer the customer a level of value that exceeds the cost of the activities, thereby resulting in a profit margin.

The primary value chain activities are:

- *Inbound Logistics*: The receiving and warehousing of raw materials, and their distribution to manufacturing as they are required.
- *Marketing and Sales*: The identification of customer needs and the generation of sales.
- *Operations*: The processes of transforming inputs into finished products and services.
- *Outbound Logistics*: The warehousing and distribution of finished goods.
- *Service*: The support of customers after the products and services are sold to them.

These primary activities are supported by:

- Human resource management: employee recruiting, hiring, training, development, and compensation.
- Procurement: purchasing inputs such as materials, supplies, and equipment.
- Technology development: technologies to support value-creating activities.
- The infrastructure of the firm: organizational structure, control systems, company culture, etc.

The firm's margin or profit then depends on its effectiveness in performing these activities efficiently, so that the amount that the customer is willing to pay for the products exceeds the cost of the activities in the value chain. It is in these activities that a firm has the opportunity to generate superior value. A competitive advantage may be achieved by reconfiguring the value chain to provide lower cost or better differentiation.

The value chain model is a useful analysis tool for defining a firm's core competencies and the activities in which it can pursue a competitive advantage as follows:

- *Cost advantage*: By better understanding costs and squeezing them out of the value-adding activities.
- *Differentiation*: By focusing on those activities associated with core competencies and capabilities in order to perform them better than do competitors.

COST ADVANTAGE AND THE VALUE CHAIN

A firm may create a cost advantage either by reducing the cost of individual value chain activities or by reconfiguring the value chain. Once the value chain is defined, a cost analysis can be performed by assigning costs to the value chain activities. The costs obtained from the accounting report may need to be modified in order to allocate them properly to the value creating activities.

Porter identified 10 cost drivers related to value chain activities:

1. Capacity utilization
2. Degree of vertical integration
3. Economies of scale
4. Firm's policy of cost or differentiation
5. Geographic location
6. Institutional factors
7. Interrelationships among business units
8. Learning
9. Linkages among activities
10. Timing of market entry

A firm develops a cost advantage by controlling these drivers better than do the competitors. A cost advantage also can be pursued by reconfiguring the value chain. Reconfiguration means structural changes such a new production process, new distribution channels, or a different sales approach. For example, FedEx structurally redefined express freight service by acquiring its own planes and implementing a hub and spoke system.

DIFFERENTIATION AND THE VALUE CHAIN

A differentiation advantage can arise from any part of the value chain. For example, procurement of inputs that are unique and not widely available to competitors can create differentiation, as can distribution channels that offer high service levels. Differentiation stems from uniqueness. A differentiation advantage may be achieved either by changing individual value chain activities to increase uniqueness in the final product or by reconfiguring the value chain.

Porter identified several drivers of uniqueness:

- Institutional factors
- Integration
- Interrelationships
- Learning
- Linkages among activities
- Location
- Policies and decisions
- Scale
- Timing

Many of these also serve as cost drivers. Differentiation often results in greater costs, resulting in tradeoffs between cost and differentiation. There are several ways in which a firm can reconfigure its value chain in order to create uniqueness. It can forward integrate in order to perform functions that once were performed by its customers. It can backward integrate in order to have more control over its inputs. It may implement new process technologies or utilize new distribution channels. Ultimately, the firm may need to be creative in order to develop a novel value chain configuration that increases product differentiation.

TECHNOLOGY AND THE VALUE CHAIN

Because technology is employed to some degree in every value creating activity, changes in technology can impact competitive advantage by incrementally changing the activities themselves or by making possible new configurations of the value chain.

Various technologies are used in both primary value activities and support activities:

- Inbound Logistics Technologies
  - Transportation
  - Material handling
  - Material storage
  - Communications
  - Testing
  - Information systems
- Operations Technologies
  - Process
  - Materials
  - Machine tools
  - Material handling
  - Packaging
  - Maintenance
  - Testing
  - Building design and operation
  - Information systems
- Outbound Logistics Technologies
  - Transportation
  - Material handling
  - Packaging
  - Communications
  - Information systems
- Marketing and Sales Technologies
  - Media
  - Audio/video
  - Communications
  - Information systems
- Service Technologies
  - Testing
  - Communications
  - Information systems

Note that many of these technologies are used across the value chain. For example, information systems are seen in every activity. Similar technologies are used in support activities. In addition, technologies related to training, computer-aided design, and software development frequently are employed in support activities. To the extent that these technologies affect cost drivers or uniqueness, they can lead to a competitive advantage.

LINKAGES BETWEEN VALUE CHAIN ACTIVITIES

Value chain activities are not isolated from one another. Rather, one value chain activity often affects the cost or performance of other ones. Linkages may exist between primary activities and also between primary and support activities. Consider the case in which the design of a product is changed in order to reduce manufacturing costs.

Suppose that inadvertantly the new product design results in increased service costs; the cost reduction could be less than anticipated and even worse, there could be a net cost increase. Sometimes however, the firm may be able to reduce cost in one activity and consequently enjoy a cost reduction in another, such as when a design change simultaneously reduces manufacturing costs and improves reliability so that the service costs also are reduced. Through such improvements the firm has the potential to develop a competitive advantage.

ANALYZING BUSINESS UNIT INTERRELATIONSHIPS

Interrelationships among business units form the basis for a horizontal strategy. Such business unit interrelationships can be identified by a value chain analysis. Tangible interrelationships offer direct opportunities to create a synergy among business units. For example, if multiple business units require a particular raw material, the procurement of that material can be shared among the business units.

This sharing of the procurement activity can result in cost reduction. Such interrelationships may exist simultaneously in multiple value chain activities. Unfortunately, attempts to achieve synergy from the interrelationships among different business units often fall short of expectations due to unanticipated drawbacks. The cost of coordination, the cost of reduced flexibility, and organizational practicalities should be analysed when devising a strategy to reap the benefits of the synergies.

OUTSOURCING VALUE CHAIN ACTIVITIES

A firm may specialize in one or more value chain activities and outsource the rest. The extent to which a firm performs upstream and downstream activities is described by its degree of vertical integration. A thorough value chain analysis can illuminate the business system to facilitate outsourcing decisions. To decide which activities to outsource, managers must understand the firm's strengths and weaknesses in each activity, both in terms of cost and ability to differentiate.

Managers may consider the following when selecting activities to outsource:

- Whether the activity can be performed cheaper or better by suppliers.

- Whether the activity is one of the firm's core competencies from which stems a cost advantage or product differentiation.
- The risk of performing the activity in-house. If the activity relies on fast-changing technology or the product is sold in a rapidly-changing market, it may be advantageous to outsource the activity in order to maintain flexibility and avoid the risk of investing in specialized assets.
- Whether the outsourcing of an activity can result in business process improvements such as reduced lead time, higher flexibility, reduced inventory, etc.

THE VALUE CHAIN SYSTEM

A firm may specialize in one or more value chain activities and outsource the rest. The extent to which a firm performs upstream and downstream activities is described by its degree of vertical integration. A thorough value chain analysis can illuminate the business system to facilitate outsourcing decisions. To decide which activities to outsource, managers must understand the firm's strengths and weaknesses in each activity, both in terms of cost and ability to differentiate.

Managers may consider the following when selecting activities to outsource:

- Whether the activity can be performed cheaper or better by suppliers.
- Whether the activity is one of the firm's core competencies from which stems a cost advantage or product differentiation.
- The risk of performing the activity in-house. If the activity relies on fast-changing technology or the product is sold in a rapidly-changing market, it may be advantageous to outsource the activity in order to maintain flexibility and avoid the risk of investing in specialized assets.
- Whether the outsourcing of an activity can result in business process improvements such as reduced lead time, higher flexibility, reduced inventory, etc.

A firm's value chain is part of a larger system that includes the value chains of upstream suppliers and downstream channels and customers.

Porter calls this series of value chains the value system, shown conceptually below:

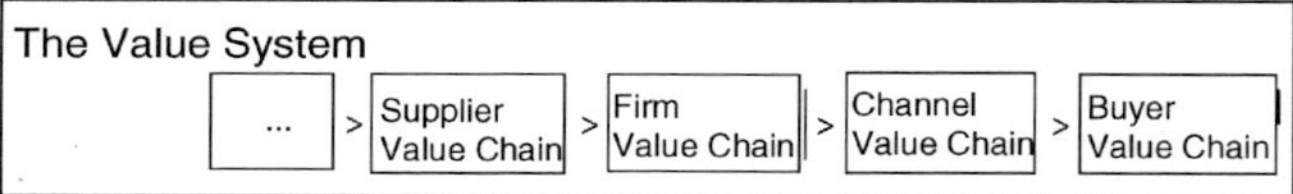

Linkages exist not only in a firm's value chain, but also between value chains. While a firm exhibiting a high degree of vertical integration is poised to better coordinate upstream and downstream activities, a firm having a lesser degree of vertical integration nonetheless can forge agreements with suppliers and channel partners to achieve better coordination. For example, an auto manufacturer may have its suppliers set up facilities in close proximity in order to minimize transport costs and reduce parts inventories. Clearly, a firm's success in developing and sustaining a competitive advantage depends not only on its own value chain, but on its ability to manage the value system of which it is a part.

LIFE-CYCLE COST ANALYSIS

ENERGY EFFICIENCY AND LIFE-CYCLE COST ANALYSIS

Life-cycle cost (LCC) analysis is the most rational, objective method for selecting the optimum HVAC system for a laboratory facility. Through LCC analysis, all factors that influence total system cost can be identified and quantified. Subjective factors such as fuel cost adjustments, component reliability, and maintenance costs are also included. LCC analysis can be used to assess the economic consequences of any decision by comparing two or more alternatives.

Annual Cost Comparison

Review of the annual cost of space conditioning for a laboratory or cleanroom shows the high impact of energy costs. A Class 10,000 cleanroom system costs five to 10 times as much to operate annually as the conditioning system for the facility's office spaces; a Class 100 laboratory cleanroom system will cost 50 times as much.

In either case, however, the contributions to total cost are:

- Capital costs, *i.e.* interest plus depreciation, contributing 15 to 25 per cent;
- Energy costs, contributing 65 to 75 per cent; and
- Maintenance costs, contributing 10 per cent.

A life-cycle cost analysis does not need to be extremely complex to yield reasonably accurate figures for first and operational costs. A modified LCC, similar to a simple payback, does not account for inflation or cost of money; this modified LCC can give an order-of-magnitude appraisal to help determine whether or not to add an EEM to a system. If LCC computations are easily understood, the analysis is more likely to be used by design teams and accepted by researchers/owners. One approach to simplifying life-cycle cost analysis is to convert facility operating costs to an equivalent annual expense per fume hood. This number can serve as a common denominator for comparing the composite performances of various system designs and for examining the sensitivity of each design alteration. The energy engineer should concentrate on determining realistic values for the most sensitive design factors before selecting the HVAC system type.

LCC Factors

LCC factors that influence a laboratory's HVAC system design can be broken into three categories: design factors, economic factors, and performance factors. Sometimes other factors must be considered; for example, a functional-use factor may be developed based on efficiency studies of personnel in the operations of different laboratory systems or components. Because laboratory personnel LCCs are very high, the more functional a design or system is, the more LCC savings are possible. An example is the workspace flexibility and reduced costs of space planning that can be afforded by a raised floor system.

JUST-IN-TIME

Just-in-time (JIT) is an inventory strategy that strives to improve a business's return on investment by reducing in-process inventory and associated carrying costs. To meet JIT objectives, the process relies on signals or Kanban between different points in the process, which tell production when to make the next part. Kanban are usually 'tickets' but can be simple visual signals, such as the presence or absence of a part on a shelf. Implemented correctly, JIT can improve a manufacturing organization's return on investment, quality, and efficiency. Quick notice that stock depletion requires personnel to order new stock is critical to the inventory reduction at the center of JIT. This saves warehouse space and costs.

However, the complete mechanism for making this work is often misunderstood. For instance, its effective application cannot be independent of other key components of a lean manufacturing system or it can "...end up with the opposite of the desired result.". In recent years manufacturers have continued to try to hone forecasting methods , however some research demonstrates that basing JIT on the presumption of stability is inherently flawed.

ACTIVITY-BASED MANAGEMENT

Activity-based management (ABM) is a method of identifying and evaluating activities that a business performs using activity-based costing to carry out a value chain analysis or a re-engineering initiative to improve strategic and operational decisions in an organization. Activity-based costing establishes relationships between overhead costs and activities so that overhead costs can be more precisely allocated to products, services, or customer segments. Activity-based management focuses on managing activities to reduce costs and improve customer value. Kaplan and Cooper. Cost and effect: Using integrated cost systems to drive profitability and performance. (Boston: Harvard Business School Press.)

Divide ABM into operational and strategic:

- Operational ABM is about "doing things right", using ABC information to improve efficiency. Those activities which add value to the product can be identified and improved. Activities that don't add value are the ones that need to be reduced to cut costs without reducing product value.

- Strategic ABM is about "doing the right things", using ABC information to decide which products to develop and which activities to use. This can also be used for customer profitability analysis, identifying which customers are the most profitable and focusing on them more.

A risk with ABM is that some activities have an implicit value, not necessarily reflected in a financial value added to any product. For instance a particularly pleasant workplace can help attract and retain the best staff, but may not be identified as adding value in operational ABM. A customer that represents a loss based on committed activities, but that opens up leads in a new market, may be identified as a low value customer by a strategic ABM process. Managers should interpret these values and use ABM as a "common, yet neutral, ground ... this provides the basis for negotiation". ABM can give middle managers an understanding of costs to other teams to help them make decisions that benefit the whole organisation, not just their activities' bottom line.

COST-VOLUME-PROFIT ANALYSIS

Cost-volume-profit (CVP) analysis expands the use of information provided by breakeven analysis. A critical part of CVP analysis is the point where total revenues equal total costs (both fixed and variable costs). At this breakeven point (BEP), a company will experience no income or loss. This BEP can be an initial examination that precedes more detailed CVP analyses. Cost-volume-profit analysis employs the same basic assumptions as in breakeven analysis.

The assumptions underlying CVP analysis are:

- All units produced are sold.
- Changes in activity are the only factors that affect costs.
- Costs can be classified accurately as either fixed or variable.
- The behaviour of both costs and revenues in linear throughout the relevant range of activity.
- When a company sells more than one type of product, the sales mix will remain constant.

INTERNAL RATE OF RETURN

The Internal Rate of Return (IRR) is the discount rate that generates a zero net present value for a series of future cash flows. This essentially means that IRR is the rate of return that makes the sum of present value of future cash flows and the final market value of a project equal its current market value. Internal Rate of Return provides a simple 'hurdle rate', whereby any project should be avoided if the cost of capital exceeds this rate. Usually a financial calculator has to be used to calculate this IRR, though it can also be mathematically calculated using the following formula:

$$CF_o + \frac{CF_1}{(1+r)^1} + \frac{CF_2}{(1+r)^2} + \frac{CF_3}{(1+r)^3} + \frac{CF_n}{(1+r)_n} + \frac{CF_n}{(1+r)^n} = 0$$

CF is the Cash Flow generated in the specific period. IRR, denoted by 'r' is to be calculated by employing trial and error method. Internal Rate of Return is the flip side of Net Present Value (NPV), where NPV is the discounted value of a stream of cash flows, generated from an investment. IRR thus computes the break-even rate of return showing the discount rate, below which an investment results in a positive NPV. A simple decision-making criteria can be stated to accept a project if its Internal Rate of Return exceeds the cost of capital and rejected if this IRR is less than the cost of capital. However, it should be kept in mind that the use of IRR may result in a number of complexities such as a project with multiple IRRs or no IRR. Moreover, IRR neglects the size of the project and assumes that cash flows are reinvested at a constant rate.

The Modified Internal Rate of Return (MIRR) is an other financial measure used to determine the attractiveness of an investment. In IRR calculations, positive cash flows are assumed to be 'paid' instantly to the investor who can use them immediately to reinvest on a new project. But in reality, the positive cash flows are not paid instantly to the investors, but rather kept by the 'project management entity' until the end of the project. The Modified Internal Rate of Return assumes that the positive cash flows are immediately re-invested until the end of the project. To make these calculations, it is common practice to use the weighted average cost of capital as interest rate on the positive cash flows.

ASPECTS OF DECISION-MAKING

AVERAGE COST

In economics, average cost is equal to total cost divided by the number of goods produced. It is also equal to the sum of average variable costs plus average fixed costs. Average costs may be dependent on the time period considered. Average costs affect the supply curve and are a fundamental component of supply and demand.

$$AC = \frac{TC}{Q}$$

Average cost is distinct from the price, and depends on the interaction with demand through elasticity of demand and elasticity of supply. In cases of perfect competition, price may be lower than average cost due to marginal cost pricing. Average cost will vary in relation to the quantity produced unless fixed costs are zero and variable costs constant. A cost curve can be plotted, with cost on the y-axis and quantity on the x-axis. Marginal costs are often shown on these graphs, with marginal cost representing the cost of the last unit produced at each point; marginal costs are the first derivative of total or variable costs. A typical average cost curve will have a U-shape, because fixed costs are all incurred before any production takes place and marginal costs are typically increasing, because of diminishing marginal productivity.

In this "typical" case, for low levels of production there are economies of scale: marginal costs are below average costs, so average costs are decreasing as quantity increases. An increasing marginal cost curve will intersect a U-shaped average cost curve at its minimum, after which point the average cost curve begins to slope upward.

This is indicative of diseconomies of scale. For further increases in production beyond this minimum, marginal cost is above average costs, so average costs are increasing as quantity increases. An example of this typical case would be a factory designed to produce a specific quantity of widgets per period: below a certain production level, average cost is higher due to under-utilised equipment, while above that level, production bottlenecks increase the average cost.

RELATIONSHIP TO MARGINAL COST

When average cost is declining as output increases, marginal cost is less than average cost. When average cost is rising, marginal cost is greater than average cost. When average cost is neither rising no average cost.

Other special cases for average cost and marginal cost appear frequently:

- Constant marginal cost/high fixed costs: each additional unit of production is produced at constant additional expense per unit. The average cost curve slopes down continuously, approaching marginal cost. An example may be hydroelectric generation, which has no fuel expense, limited maintenance expenses and a high up-front fixed cost. Industries where fixed marginal costs obtain, such as electrical transmission networks, may meet the conditions for a natural monopoly, because once capacity is built, the marginal cost to the incumbent of serving an additional customer is always lower than the average cost for a potential competitor. The high fixed capital costs are a barrier to entry.
- Minimum efficient scale/maximum efficient scale: marginal or average costs may be non-linear, or have discontinuities. Average cost curves may therefore only be shown over a limited scale of production for a given technology. For example, a nuclear plant would be extremely inefficient for production in small quantities; similarly, its maximum output for any given time period may essentially be fixed, and production above that level may be technically impossible, dangerous or extremely costly. The long run elasticity of supply will be higher, as new plants could be built and brought on-line.

- Low or zero fixed costs / constant marginal cost: since there is no economy of scale, average cost will be close to or equal to marginal cost. Examples may include buy and celling of commodities etc.

Relationship Between AC, AFC, AVC and MC

- The Average Fixed Cost curve starts from a height and goes on declining continuously as production increases.
- The Average Variable Cost curve, Average Cost curve and the Marginal Cost curve start from a height, reach the minimum points, then rise sharply and continuously.
- Marginal Cost curve is the determining curve, while the rest are determined curves.
- The movement in the Marginal Cost curve determines the movement and direction of the other curves.
- The Average Fixed Cost curve nears the Average Cost curve initially and then moves away from it. The Average Variable Cost Curve is never parallel or intersects the Average Cost curve due to the existence of the Average Fixed Cost in all units of production.
- The Marginal Cost curve always passes through the minimum points of the Average Variable Cost and Average Cost curves, though the Average Variable Cost curve attains the minimum point prior to that of the Average Cost curve.

AVERAGE FIXED COST

Average fixed cost is an economics term used to describe the total fixed costs divided by the quantity (Q) of units produced.

$$AFC = \frac{TFC}{Q}$$

Average fixed cost is a per-unit measure of fixed costs. As the total number of goods produced increases, the average fixed cost decreases because the same amount of fixed costs are being spread over a larger number of units. Average variable cost plus average fixed cost equals average total cost.

$$ATC = AVC + AFC$$

AVERAGE VARIABLE COST

Average variable cost (AVC) is an economics term to describe a firm's variable costs divided by the quantity (Q) of total units of output. It is a cost that a firm must generate from its business if it must continue business because firm must incur it whether it makes profit or not.

$$AVC = \frac{TVC}{Q}$$

Where:

- TVC = Total Variable Cost
- AVC = Average Variable Cost
- Q = Quantity of Units Produced

Average variable cost plus average fixed cost equals average total cost:

$$AVC + AFC = ATC.$$

COST-MINIMIZATION ANALYSIS

Cost-minimization is the simplest of the pharmaco-economics tools and is applied when comparing two drugs of equal efficacy and equal tolerability. Therapeutic equivalence must be referenced by the author conducting the study and should have been done prior to the cost-minimization work. Since equal efficacy and equal tolerability is already demonstrated, there is no requirement to find a common efficacy denominator as would be the case when conducting a cost-effectiveness study. The author is not precluded from doing so through the use of "cost/cure" or "cost/year of life gained". If efficacy and tolerability is demonstrated, however, then a simple comparison of "cost/ course of treatment" can suffice for the purpose of comparing two or more therapeutically equivalent treatment alternatives.

How ever when doing so you do run the risk of confusing possible target markets due to the issue of severity of possible deaths occurring. This was the case in New York in 2004 with the well known case 'Murpheys Law' which is now a well known case study for cost minisation. This was all due to severe cost cutting leading to 'Murpheys' death due to a large back lash from his employees resulting in his death! Cost minimisation should be carefully considered before being implomented. When conducting a cost-minimization study, the author needs to measure all costs inherent to the delivery of the therapeutic intervention and that are relevant to the pharmacoeconomic perspective.

COST/BENEFIT ANALYSIS

You may have been intensely creative in generating solutions to a problem, and rigorous in your selection of the best one available. However, this solution may still not be worth implementing, as you may invest a lot of time and money in solving a problem that is not worthy of this effort. Cost Benefit Analysis or CBA is a relatively* simple and widely used technique for deciding whether to make a change.

As its name suggests, you simply add up the value of the benefits of a course of action, and subtract the costs associated with it. Costs are either one-off, or may be ongoing. Benefits are most often received over time. We build this effect of time into our analysis by calculating a payback period. This is the time it takes for the benefits of a change to repay its costs. Many companies look for payback on projects over a specified period of time *e.g.* three years.

How to Use the Tool

In its simple form, cost-benefit analysis is carried out using only financial costs and financial benefits. For example, a simple cost benefit ratio for a road scheme would measure the cost of building the road, and subtract this from the economic benefit of improving transport links. It would not measure either the cost of environmental damage or the benefit of quicker and easier travel to work. A more sophisticated approach to building a cost benefit models is to try to put a financial value on intangible costs and benefits.

This can be highly subjective - is, for example, a historic water meadow worth $25,000, or is it worth $500,000 because if its environmental importance? What is the value of stress-free travel to work in the morning? These are all questions that people have to answer, and answers that people have to defend. The version of the cost benefit approach we explain here is necessarily simple. Where large sums of money are involved project evaluation can become an extremely complex and sophisticated art. The fundamentals of this are explained in Principles of Corporate Finance by Richard Brealey and Stewart Myers - this is something of an authority on the subject.

Example

A sales director is deciding whether to implement a new computer-based contact management and sales processing system. His department has only a few computers, and his salespeople are not computer literate. He is aware that computerized sales forces are able to contact more customers and give a higher quality of reliability and service to those customers. They are more able to meet commitments, and can work more efficiently with fulfillment and delivery staff.

His financial cost/benefit analysis is shown below:

Costs:

- 10 network-ready PCs with supporting software @ $2,450 each
- 1 server @ $3,500
- 3 printers @ $1,200 each
- Cabling and Installation @ $4,600
- Sales Support Software @ $15,000

Training costs:

- Computer introduction - 8 people @ $400 each
- Keyboard skills - 8 people @ $400 each
- Sales Support System - 12 people @ $700 each

Other costs:

- Lost time: 40 man days @ $200 / day
- Lost sales through disruption: estimate: $20,000
- Lost sales through inefficiency during first months: estimate: $20,000

Benefits:

- Tripling of mail shot capacity: estimate: $40,000 / year
- Ability to sustain telesales campaigns: estimate: $20,000 / year

- Improved efficiency and reliability of follow-up: estimate: $50,000 / year
- Improved customer service and retention: estimate: $30,000 / year
- Improved accuracy of customer information: estimate: $10,000 / year
- More ability to manage sales effort: $30,000 / year

COST-EFFECTIVENESS ANALYSIS

Cost-effectiveness analysis (CEA) is a technique for selecting among competing wants wherever resources are limited. Developed in the military, CEA was first applied to health care in the mid-1960s and was introduced with enthusiasm to clinicians by Weinstein and Stason in 1977:

- "If these approaches were to become widely understood and accepted by the key decision makers in the health-care sector, including the physician, important health benefits or cost savings might be realised."

Regardless of whether this hope was realised, CEA has since become a common feature in medical literature.

THE BASICS OF CEA

CEA is a technique for comparing the relative value of various clinical strategies. In its most common form, a new strategy is compared with current practice in the calculation of the cost-effectiveness ratio:

$$\text{CE ratio} = \frac{\text{cos t}_{\text{new strategy}} - \text{cos t}_{\text{currentpractice}}}{\text{effect}_{\text{new strategy}} - \text{effect}_{\text{current pratice}}}$$

The result might be considered as the "price" of the additional outcome purchased by switching from current practice to the new strategy. If the price is low enough, the new strategy is considered "cost-effective." It's important to carefully consider exactly what that statement means. If a strategy is dubbed "cost-effective" and the term is used as its creators intended, it means that the new strategy is a good value. Note that being cost-effective does not mean that the strategy saves money, and just because a strategy saves money doesn't mean that it is cost-effective.

Also note that the very notion of cost-effective requires a value judgment—what you think is a good price for an additional outcome, someone else may not. It's also worthwhile to recognize that CEA is only relevant to certain decisions. The various way a new strategy might compare with an existing approach. Note that a CEA is relevant only if a new strategy is *both* more effective and more costly.

TRANSACTION COSTS

Transaction costs are commissions and processing charges incurred as part of a business transaction. In some cases, this transaction cost is a percentage of the total sale. In other cases, it may be a flat fee. In general, the money spent on the transaction costs is often referred to as a *spread*. Understanding transaction costs is very important for anyone who is looking to buy or sell any financial product, whether it is stocks, bonds, currency or valuable metals. It does not matter whether you are buying or selling assets, transaction costs can be incurred in a number of different situations. It is important to read all policies and agreements of the company executing the transaction in order to have full awareness of which transaction costs you may incur. One of the most common types of transaction costs is the buy/sell spread.

While they can go by several different names, spreads are the costs that an investment manager charges to execute a transaction. To provide a real-world example, let's assume the currency exchange rate is $2 US Dollar for every 1 Euro. Though someone may expect to get 5 Euros if they pay $10 USD, it is likely that he will receive somewhat less than that. Why is it that a trader may get less than the published rate? Because of the buy/sell spread. The person or agency executing the trade takes out a cut in order to provide the service. The amount charged for that service will likely be different, depending on the person or firm.

Some firms will actually use their transaction costs as an incentive to attract customers. If an investment firm has a competitive rate in their transaction costs, this can lead to a substantial cost savings for an investor, especially if that investor executes a large number of trades as a general practice. Though it is not as prevalent as it once was, several trading firms specializing in online trades advertise their transaction costs regularly.

TOTAL COST

In economics, and cost accounting, total cost describes the total economic cost of production and is made up of variable costs, which vary just as to the quantity of a good produced and include inputs such as labour and raw materials, plus fixed costs, which are independent of the quantity of a good produced and include inputs that cannot be varied in the short term, such as buildings and machinery. Total cost in economics includes the total opportunity cost of each factor of production in addition to fixed and variable costs. The rate at which total cost changes as the amount produced changes is called marginal cost. This is also known as the marginal unit variable cost. If one assumes that the unit variable cost is constant, as in cost-volume-profit analysis developed and used in cost accounting by the accountants, then total cost is linear in volume, and given by: total cost = fixed costs + unit variable cost * amount.

ABSORPTION COSTING

Absorption costing is a method for appraising or valuing a firm's total inventory by including all the manufacturing costs incurred to produce those goods. These manufacturing costs include.

Product Costs

- *Direct Materials*: These are the raw materials such as wood, metal, bricks, etc that are used in order to create a finished usable good which will be demanded by the market.
- *Direct Labour*: Direct Labour is the manwork and total factory hours put behind assembling the raw materials, creating the finished good, etc.
- *Fixed Manufacturing Overhead*: This includes expenses such as rent of factory where the raw materials are turned into finished goods, amortization of factory building, utilities, etc.
- *Variable Manufacturing Overhead*: These are the general and administrative expenses in the manufacturing process.

Absorption costing is different from the other costing methods because it takes into account fixed manufacturing overhead. It is hard to factor in the fixed manufacturing overhead expenses into calculating the per unit price of goods, therefore other methods such as Variable Costing do not take it into account. One drawback of absorption costing is that managers can increase production levels without taking into account total sales. With higher production levels, this year's expenses can be deferred to next year, thus lowering this year's costs. What does this mean? The managers get a fat bonus and pay raises thanks to more "profits."

Inventory Production and Absorption Costing

When beginning inventory and ending inventory levels are different, profit calculations using the Absorption costing can be difficult. Here are the effects of fluctuating inventory levels:

- If Beginning Inventory = Ending Inventory, then Absorption Costing = Variable Costing
- If Inventory Levels = Low, then Variable Costing Profit > Absorption Costing Profit
- If Inventory Levels = High, then Absorption Costing Profit >Variable Costing Profit

SUNK COSTS

Sunk costs are sums that have already been spent and can not be recovered. The concept is important because sunk costs are irrelevant to financial decisions. Many people tend to feel instinctively that because an investment has been made it is necessary to get a return on it. This can lead to people rejecting one course of action in favour of another that actually generates smaller cash flows. This can happen to business, portfolio investment and personal decisions. Suppose a hotel has calculated that their cost for providing a room is £100 per night, of which £50 covers their rental of the building and £20 covers their other fixed costs and £30 covers the costs that result from having an extra guest. Now suppose the market rate for hotel rooms goes down and they are only able to charge £50 per night. The hotel is committed to remaining open. It appears that the hotel will make a £50 loss on each night per guest so they should not accept bookings until prices rise. Of course this is wrong as the rent and other fixed costs are already committed to and have to be paid anyway.

The hotel should accept bookings at any price it can get above £30, as these make a positive contribution. A common mistake made by investors is reluctance to sell securities at a loss. It does not matter what you paid for shares, if the market price has fallen you have already made that loss. It is a sunk cost and should be forgotten about. What matters is whether the shares are worth holding or not at the current market price. A key question is whether the shares would still be worth buying at current prices. If not, they are probably not worth holding.

SEMI-VARIABLE COSTS

Semi-variable costs are those that have both fixed cost and variable cost elements. For example, a manufacturer's electricity bill may include elements that are fixed and elements that are variable.

SEARCH COST

Search costs are one facet of transaction costs or switching costs. Rational consumers will continue to search for a better product or service until the marginal cost of searching exceeds the marginal benefit. Search theory is a branch of microeconomics that studies decisions of this type. The costs of searching are divided into external and internal costs. External costs include the monetary costs of acquiring the information, and the opportunity cost of the time taken up in searching. External costs are not under the consumer's control. All they can do is choose whether or not to incur them. Internal costs include the mental effort given over to undertaking the search, sorting the incoming information, and integrating it with what the consumer already knows. Internal costs are determined by the consumer's ability to undertake the search, and this in turn depends on intelligence, prior knowledge, education and training. These internal costs are the background to the study of bounded rationality. The Internet was expected to eliminate search costs. For example, electronic commerce was predicted to cause disintermediation as search costs become low enough for end-consumers to incur them directly instead of employing retailers to do this for them. This would in turn lead to lower prices and less variation between prices quoted by different sellers.

REPUGNANCY COSTS

Repugnancy costs are costs borne by an individual or entity as a result of a stimulus that goes against that individual or entity's cultural mores. The cost could be emotional, physical, mental or figurative. The stimulus could be anything from food to people to an idea. These costs are perspective-dependent and individual. These costs may be different for different groups of people; countries, states, ethnicities, etc. The term allows for a clear and understandable way of representing the concept of contextual stigma in a literal and applicable sense.

QUALITY COST

Quality cost is the sum of all costs a company invests into the release of a quality product. When developing a software product, there are four types of quality costs: prevention costs, appraisal costs, internal failure costs, and external failure costs.

1. Prevention costs represent everything a company spends to prevent software errors, documentation errors, and other product-related errors. These include requirements and usability analysis, for example. Dollars spent on prevention costs are the most effective quality dollars, because preventing errors from getting into the product is much cheaper than fixing errors later. If there is an error in a requirement or the intended usability, and money is spent on developing the software to the erroneous requirement, the costs of identifying the error, determining how to fix it, and then developing new code to correct it will arise later.
2. Appraisal costs include the money spent on the actual testing activity. Any and all activities associated with searching for errors in the software and associated product materials falls into this category. This includes all testing: by the developers themselves, by an internal test team, and by an outsourced software test organization. This also includes all associated hardware, software, labour, and other costs. Once a product is in the coding phases, the goal is to do the most effective appraisal job, so that internal failure work is streamlined and well-managed and prevents skyrocketing external failure costs.
3. Internal failure costs are the costs of coping with errors discovered during development and testing. These are bugs found before the product is released. The further in the development process the errors are discovered, the more costly they are to fix. So the later the errors are discovered, the higher their associated internal failure costs will be.
4. External failure costs are the costs of coping with errors discovered after the product is released. These are typically errors found by your customers. These costs can be much higher than internal failure costs, because the stakes are much higher. These costs include post-release customer and technical support. Errors at this stage can also be costly in terms of your company's reputation and may lead to lost customers.

The Four Categories of Quality Costs

All the costs can be effectively reduced through smarter test efforts that include a high degree of test automation. Test automation when done right leads to greater test coverage, resulting in higher-quality products. Higher-quality products require less technical support, fewer patches, and lead to greater customer satisfaction. Smarter automated testing also speeds up the release process and incrementally reduces the manual test costs.

But most of all, more test coverage gives you and your customers more confidence in your product. You will feel more comfortable knowing that there are not bugs lurking in your software that have not been exposed yet because of insufficient test coverage. You will also not have to scramble at the last minute to deal with a problem and fix it to your customer's satisfaction in a rush. The solution to quality cost problems is to get a better understanding of your investment in product quality and manage your costs better. The first place most organizations look for a better understanding is in the highest cost area: the software test effort or lack thereof. For example, if you do not test at all, your testing or appraisal cost is low.

You will ship on time but your external failure costs will skyrocket. Your prevention and appraisal costs will result in finding errors that can be corrected while they are still internal failures, where they are cheaper to deal with than when they are external failures. The goal of understanding quality costs is to analyse where you spend your time and money to get the most bang for the buck.

It is well known that it is faster and cheaper to find and fix a bug during unit testing done by developers early in the development cycle. Should we then spend most of our time/budget on unit testing? No. here are many limitations to unit testing. Unit testing is not capable of finding many varieties of bugs, including graphical user interface (GUI) bugs, usability problems, end-to-end bugs, and configuration bugs.

For most organizations, getting a better unit test effort will help you release a better product sooner. It is not a replacement for the test effort done by skilled software testers, but it may reduce the time that test effort takes. Understanding quality costs will hopefully help you shift some of your test effort to the most cost-effective places.

The total quality cost is shown in the upper bathtub-shaped curve. On the bottom axis is the quality of performance, ranging from totally defective to zero defects. On the left axis is the cost per good unit of product. You can see that with highly defective software, your prevention and appraisal costs are very low, but your failure costs are very high, yielding a high total quality cost. With zero defect software, likewise, your failure costs are very low, but your prevention and appraisal costs are very high. To optimize your total quality costs, you want to be between these extremes, at the bottom of the bathtub curve.

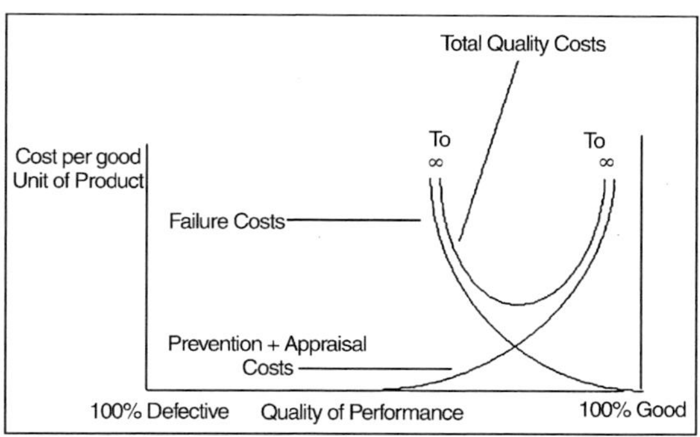

The Oretical Model of Optimum Quality Cost

This offers two challenges: First, a sufficiently sophisticated accounting system allowing a typical mid-sized company to track the total cost of quality has yet to be developed. To optimize total quality cost, you need to have the appropriate categories in your accounting system and keep track of the related costs. Second, you need to be able to track your external quality costs. You may not even have enough information from customers on why the software is not working for them.

How are you going to know what to book into your accounting system for external failure costs? The point here is that while capturing this data is difficult and expensive, you know that the benefit is reducing your overall cost of quality. You need to determine if the benefits of tracking your total quality cost will give you enough of a return on investment to make setting up the appropriate accounting system and paying for the implementation of the programme worthwhile.

ECONOMIC COST

The economic cost of a decision depends on both the cost of the alternative chosen and the benefit that the best alternative would have provided if chosen. Economic cost differs from accounting cost because it includes opportunity cost. As an example, consider the economic cost of attending college. The accounting cost of attending college includes tuition, room and board, books, food, and other incidental expenditures while there. The opportunity cost of college also includes the salary or wage that otherwise could be earning during the period. So for the two to four years an individual spends in school, the opportunity cost includes the money that one could have been making at the best possible job.

The economic cost of college is the accounting cost plus the opportunity cost. Thus, if attending college has a direct cost of $20,000 dollars a year for four years, and the lost wages from not working during that period equals $25,000 dollars a year, then the total economic cost of going to college would be $180,000 dollars ($20,000 x 4 years + $25,000 x 4 years).

EXPLICIT COST

An explicit cost is an easily accounted cost, such as wage, rent and materials. It can be transacted in the form of money payment and is lost directly, as opposed to monetary implicit costs. Explicit cost are those which the entrepreneur has to pay from his own pocket. Explicit costs require an outlay of money by the firm.

Implicit Costs, Explicit Costs, and Total Costs

Implicit cost + explicit cost = total cost. Implicit cost is not equal to total cost, but a component of it. A simple example: Sean builds a cabinet. He spends 2 hours building the cabinet. He could have been working instead and normally makes $25/hour at his job. Since he was building a cabinet he wasn't paid for this time.

The materials to make the cabinet cost him $20;

- His Explicit Costs are: $20 in materials
- His Implicit Costs are: $25/hr x 2 hrs= $50 of foregone pay
- His Total Costs are: $20 in materials + $50 of foregone pay = $70 Total Costs

INDIRECT COSTS

Indirect costs are costs that are not directly accountable to a cost object. Indirect costs may be either fixed or variable. Indirect costs include taxes, administration, personnel and security costs, and are also known as overhead.

Indirect vs. Direct Costs

Direct costs are those for activities or services that benefit specific projects, *e.g.*, salaries for project staff and materials required for a particular project. Because these activities are easily traced to projects, their costs are usually charged to projects on an item-by-item basis. Indirect costs are those for activities or services that benefit more than one project. Their precise benefits to a specific project are often difficult or impossible to trace. For example, it may be difficult to determine precisely how the activities of the director of an organization benefit a specific project.

It is possible to justify the handling of almost any kind of cost as either direct or indirect. Labour costs, for example, can be indirect, as in the case of maintenance personnel and executive officers; or they can be direct, as in the case of project staff members. Similarly, materials such as miscellaneous supplies purchased in bulk—pencils, pens, paper—are typically handled as indirect costs, while materials required for specific projects are charged as direct costs.

ISOCOST

In economics an isocost line represents a combination of inputs which all cost the same amount. Although similar to the budget constraint in consumer theory, the use of the isocost pertains to cost-minimization in production, as opposed to utility-maximization. The typical isocost line represents the ratio of costs of labour and capital, so the formula is often written as.

$$rK + wL = C$$

Where w represents the wage of labour, and r represents the rental rate of capital.

The slope is:

$$-w / r$$

or the negative ratio of wages divided by rental fees.

The isocost line is combined with the isoquant line to determine the optimal production point.

The Cost Function for a Firm with Two Variable Inputs

Consider a firm that uses two inputs and has the production function F. This firm minimizes its cost of producing any given output y if it chooses the pair (z1, z2) of inputs to solve the problem Min z1,z2w1s conditional input demand functions. The firm's minimal cost of producing the output y is w1z1*(y,w1, w2) + w2z2*(y,w1, w2) (the value of its total cost for the values of z1 and z2 that minimize that cost). The function TC defined by

$$TC(y,w1,w2) = w1z1 * (y,w1,w2) + w2z2 * (y,w1,w2)$$

Which is called the firm's (total) cost function. (Note that the hard part of the problem is finding the conditional input demands; once you have found these, then finding the cost function is simply a matter of adding the conditional input ogether with the weights w1 and w2.). An Isocost line shows all the combinations of capital and labour that can be bought for a given total cost"

LOCK-IN (DECISION-MAKING)

Lock-in can be seen as the escalating commitment of decision-makers to an ineffective course of action. It concerns institutional lock-in as compared to technical lock-in of which the QWERTY keyboard is a famous example. The decision-making process is characterised by various informal and formal decision-making moments and decision-makers can become committed to the project before the formal decision to build was taken. The formation of commitment is not necessarily bad, but when commitment turns into lock-in, it has by definition a negative influence on the project performance. Lock-in can occur at the decision-making level or at the project level. There are possibilities to avoid lock-in when decision-makers can be made aware of this phenomenon. However, lock-in can also be used intentionally, in which case, it is much more difficult to prevent and hence manage cost overruns.

Decision Making Process

The decision-making process of large infrastructure projects is marked by the formal decision to build the project. However, there are several possible moments in the decision-making process before the formal decision is taken at which decision-makers are committed to the project. The extent of which decision-makers are committed to the project is of importance here. Early commitment, commitment to the project before the formal decision to build has been taken, is in itself not necessarily negative. It could be advantageous to the decision-making process as it could enforce a decision.

This eventually could limit delay and contribute to the projects' performance. Early commitment can result in negative outcomes once the commitment turns into escalating commitment and lock-in. As lock-in is based on escalating commitment, it has, by definition, a negative influence on project performance. Lock-in has the potential to explain the large cost overruns in large scale transportation infrastructure projects.

Formation

Lock-in with respect to decision-making is created when sub-optimal policies are used as a consequence of *e.g.* path dependency, even though a better alternative is present. The term refers to the escalating commitment of decision-makers to an ineffective course of action. Escalating commitment itself refers to the style of psychological coping associated with the inability to withdraw from obligations. The process of escalating commitment is also known as "entrapment" , the "sunk-cost effect" , the "knee-deep in the big muddy" effect , and the "too-much-invested-to-quit" effect.

Occurrence

Lock-in can occur both at the decision-making level and can influence the extent of overruns in two ways:

1. The first involves the "methodology" of calculating cost overruns just as to the "formal decision to build". Due to lock-in, however, the "real decision to build" is made much earlier in the decision-making process and the costs estimated at that stage are often much lower than those that are estimated at a later stage in the decision-making process, thus increasing cost overruns.
2. The second way that lock-in can affect cost overruns is through "practice". Although decisions about the project need to be made, lock-in can lead to inefficient decisions that involve higher costs. Sunk costs in terms of both time and money, the need for justification, escalating commitment , and inflexibility and the closure of alternatives are indicators of lock-in.

Prevention

There are different types of lock-in; conscious/unconscious and intentional/unintentional lock-in. Some of these types of lock-in can be avoided. Decision-makers can be made conscious about their behaviour, for example by confronting them with the lack of sufficient alternatives. When these decision-makers are willing to change their behaviour and consider other alternatives, they are less likely to become committed to one project alternative and hence, the chance for lock-in can be partly avoided. However, other types of lock-in are more difficult to control, especially intentional lock-in. Intentional lock-in is the result of specific behaviour of parties that act deliberately in the interest of their project. Cost overruns may thus be partly unnecessary or avoidable if such deliberate creation of lock-in had not taken place, and be partly unavoidable due to the incapacity of decision-makers to make optimal decisions.

MARGINAL COST OF CAPITAL SCHEDULE

Marginal Cost of Capital (MCC) Schedule is a graph that relates the Cost of Capital (MCC) Schedule is a graph that relates the firm's weighted average cost of each dollar of capital to the total amount of new capital raised. The WACC is the minimum rate of return allowable, and still meeting financial obligationts such as debt, interest payments, dividends etc... Therefore, the WACC averages the required returns from all long-term financing sources. The WACC is based on cash flows, which are after-tax. By the same notion then, the WACC should be calculated on an after-tax basis.

MARGINAL COST

In economics and finance, marginal cost is the change in total cost that arises when the quantity produced changes by one unit. That is, it is the cost of producing one more unit of a good. Mathematically, the marginal cost (MC) function is expressed as the first derivative of the total cost (TC) function with respect to quantity (Q). Note that the marginal cost may change with volume, and so at each level of production, the marginal cost is the cost of the next unit produced.

$$MC = \frac{dTC}{dQ}$$

In general terms, marginal cost at each level of production includes any additional costs required to produce the next unit. If producing additional vehicles requires, for example, building a new factory, the marginal cost of those extra vehicles includes the cost of the new factory. In practice, the analysis is segregated into short and long-run cases, and over the longest run, all costs are marginal.

At each level of production and time period being considered, marginal costs include all costs which vary with the level of production, and other costs are considered fixed costs. A number of other factors can affect marginal cost and its applicability to real world problems. Some of these may be considered market failures. These may include information asymmetries, the presence of negative or positive externalities, transaction costs, price discrimination and others.

Cost Functions and Relationship to Average Cost

In the simplest case, the total cost function and its derivative are expressed as follows, where Q represents the production quantity, VC represents variable costs, FC represents fixed costs and TC represents total costs.

$$MC = \frac{dTC}{dQ} = \frac{d(FC + VC)}{dQ} = \frac{dVC}{dQ}$$

Since fixed costs do not vary with production quantity, it drops out of the equation when it is differentiated. The important conclusion is that marginal cost is not related to fixed costs. This can be compared with average total cost or ATC, which is the total cost divided by the number of units produced and does include fixed costs.

$$ATC = \frac{FC + VC}{Q}$$

For discrete calculation without calculus, marginal cost equals the change in total cost that comes with each additional unit produced. For instance, suppose the total cost of making 1 shoe is $30 and the total cost of making 2 shoes is $40. The marginal cost of producing the second shoe is $40 - $30 = $10.

Economies of Scale

Production may be subject to economies of scale. Increasing returns to scale are said to exist if additional units can be produced for less than the previous unit, that is, average cost is falling. This can only occur if average cost at any given level of production is higher than the marginal cost. Conversely, there may be levels of production where marginal cost is higher than average cost, and average cost will rise for each unit of production after that point.

This type of production function is generally known as diminishing marginal productivity: at low levels of production, productivity gains are easy and marginal costs falling, but productivity gains become smaller as production increases; eventually, marginal costs rise because increasing output becomes more expensive. For this generic case, minimum average cost occurs at the point where average cost and marginal cost are equal; this point will not be at the minimum for marginal cost if fixed costs are greater than zero.

Externalities

Externalities are costs that are not borne by the parties to the economic transaction. A producer may, for example, pollute the environment, and others may bear those costs. A consumer may consume a good which produces benefits for society, such as education; because the individual does not receive all of the benefits, he may consume less than efficiency would suggest.

Alternatively, an individual may be a smoker or alcoholic and impose costs on others. In these cases, production or consumption of the good in question may differ from the optimum level.

Negative Externalities of Production

Much of the time, private and social costs do not diverge from one another, but at times social costs may be either greater or less than private costs. When marginal social costs of production are greater than that of the private cost function, we see the occurrence of a negative externality of production.

Productive processes that result in pollution are a textbook example of production that creates negative externalities. Such externalities are a result of firms externalising their costs onto a third party in order to reduce their own total cost.

As a result of externalising such costs we see that members of society will be negatively affected by such behaviour of the firm. In this case, we see that an increased cost of production on society creates a social cost curve that depicts a greater cost than the private cost curve. In an equilibrium state we see that markets creating negative externalities of production will overproduce that good. As a result, the socially optimal production level would be lower than that observed.

Positive Externalities of Production

When marginal social costs of production are less than that of the private cost function, we see the occurrence of a positive externality of production. Production of public goods are a textbook example of production that create positive externalities. An example of such a public good, which creates a divergence in social and private costs, includes the production of education.

It is often seen that education is a positive for any whole society, as well as a positive for those directly involved in the market. We see that such production creates a social cost curve that is less than that of the private curve.

In an equilibrium state we see that markets creating positive externalities of production will under produce that good. As a result, the socially optimal production level would be greater than that observed.

Social Costs

Of great importance in the theory of marginal cost is the distinction between the marginal private and social costs. the marginal private cost shows the cost associated to the firm in question. it is the marginal private cost that is used by business decision makers in their profit maximization goals, and by individuals in their purchasing and consumption choices. marginal social cost is similar to private cost in that it includes the cost functions of private enterprise but also that of society as a whole, including parties that have no direct association with the private costs of production. It incorporates all negative and positive externalities, of both production and consumption. hence, when deciding whether or how much to buy, buyers take account of the cost to society of their actions if private and social marginal cost coincide. the equality of price with social marginal cost, by aligning the interest of the buyer with the interest of the community as a whole is a necessary condition for economically efficient resource allocation.

4

Marginal Costing

MARGINAL AND ABSORPTION COSTING

CHARACTERISTICS

Marginal costing is also termed as variable costing, a technique of costing which includes only variable manufacturing costs, in the form of direct materials, direct labour, and variable manufacturing overheads while determining the cost per unit of a product. Where as Absorption costing, is a costing technique that includes all manufacturing costs, in the form of direct materials, direct labour, and both variable and fixed manufacturing overheads, while determining the cost per unit of a product. It is also referred to as the full- cost technique.

In the costing of product/service, a marginal costing technique considers the behavioural characteristics of costs (segregations of costs into fixed and variable elements), because per unit variable cost is fixed and total costs are variable in nature, where as total fixed costs are fixed and per unit fixed cost is variable in nature and furthermore variable costs are controllable in nature, while total fixed costs are un-controllable in nature.

Marginal costing is useful for short-term planning, control and decision-making, particularly in a business where multi-products are produced. In marginal costing technique, the contribution is calculated after deducting variable costs from sales value with reference to each product or service, in order to calculate the total contribution from all products/services which are made towards the total fixed costs incurred by the business. As the fixed costs are treated as period costs, are deducted from total contribution to arrive at net profit. In the context of costing of a product/service, an absorption costing considers a share of all costs incurred by a business to each of its products/ services. In absorption costing technique; costs are classified according to their functions. The gross profit is calculated after deducting production costs from sales and from gross profit, costs incurred in relation to other business functions are deducted to arrive at the net profit.

Absorption costing gives better information for pricing products as it includes both variable and fixed costs. Marginal costing may lead to lower prices being offered if the firm is operating below capacity. Customers may still expect these lower prices as demand/capacity increases.

Profit Statements

The net profit shown by marginal costing and absorption costing techniques may not be the same due to the different treatment of fixed manufacturing overheads. Marginal costing technique treats fixed manufacturing overheads as period costs, where as in absorption costing technique these are absorbed into the cost of goods produced and are only charged against profit in the period in which those goods are sold. In absorption costing income statement, adjustment pertaining to under or over-absorption of overheads is also made to arrive at the profit.

TERMS

Product and Period Costs

- *Product costs*: The costs of manufacturing the products;
- *Period costs*: These are the costs other than product costs that are charged to, debited to, or written off to the income statement each period.

A Case Example on Marginal and Absorption Costing:

Table. Data for a Quarter for a Manufacturing Company

Level of Activity	60%	100%
Sales and Production(Units)	36,000	60,000
	₹. ('000)	₹. ('000)
Sales	432	720
Production costs: (Variable and fixed)	366	510
Sales, distribution and administration costs (Variable and fixed)	126	150

The normal level of activity for the current year is 60,000 units, and fixed costs are incurred evenly throughout the year. There were no stocks of the product at the start of the quarter, in which 16,500 units were made and 13,500 units were sold. Actual fixed costs were the same as budgeted. Then, various calculations regarding Absorption vs. Marginal costing can be worked out as under:

	Production Costs (Rs.)	Sales etc costs (Rs.)
Total costs of 60,000 units (fixed plus variable)	5,10,000	1,50,000
Total costs of 36,000 units (fixed plus variable)	3,66,000	1,26,000
Difference = variable costs of 24,000 units	1,44,000	24,000
Variable costs per unit	Rs.6	Re.1
	Production Costs (Rs.)	Sales etc. Costs (Rs.)
Total costs of 60,000 units	5,10,000	1,50,00 0
Variable costs of 60,000 units	3,60,000	60,000
Fixed costs	1,50,000	90,000

The rate of absorption of fixed production overheads will therefore be:

₹.1,50,000 ÷ 60,000 = ₹. 2.50 per unit.

- The fixed production overhead absorbed by the products would be 16,500 units produced × ₹. 2.50 = ₹. 41,250
- Budgeted annual fixed production overhead = ₹.1,50,000

	Rs.
Actual quarterly fixed production overhead = budgeted quarterly fixed production overhead (1,50,000 ÷ 4)	37,500
Production overhead absorbed into production [see (i) above]	41,250
Over -absorption of fixed production overhead	3,750

- Profit statement for the quarter, using Absorption Costing

	Rs.	Rs.	Rs.
Sales (13,500× Rs.12)			1,62,000
Costs of production (no opening stocks)			
Value of stocks produced (16,500 × Rs. 8.50)		1,40,250	
Less value of closing stock			
(3,000 units × full production cost of Rs. 8.50)		(25,500)	
		1,14,750	
Sales etc costs			
Variable (13,500 × Re. 1)	13,500		
Fixed (1/4 of Rs. 90,000)	22,500		
		36,000	
Total cost of sales		1,50,750	
Less over-absorbed production overhead		3,750	
			1,47,000
Profit			15,000

– Profit statement for the quarter using Marginal Costing

	Rs.	Rs.
Sales (13,500×Rs.12)		1,62,000
Variable costs of production (16,500 × Rs. 6)	99,000	
Less value of closing stocks (3,000 × Rs. 6)	18,000	
Variable production cost of sales	81,000	
Variable sales etc. costs (13,500 × Re.1)	13,500	
Total variable cost of sales (13,500 × Rs. 7)		94,500
Contribution (13,500 × Rs. 5)		67,500
Fixed Costs: Production	37,500	
Sales etc.	22,500	
		60,000
Profit		7,500

ABSORPTION AND MARGINAL COSTING SYSTEMS

A popular topic for examination at Foundation Level has been the preparation of profit statements in both absorption and marginal costing formats, and the reconciliation of the profits reported by the two systems.

Example: A company sells a single product at a price of £14 per unit. Variable manufacturing costs of the product are £6.40 per unit. Fixed manufacturing overheads, which are absorbed into the cost of production at a unit rate (based on normal activity of 20,000 units per period), are £92,000 per period. Any over-absorbed or under-absorbed fixed manufacturing overhead balances are transferred to the profit and loss account at the end of each period, in order to establish the manufacturing profit.

Sales and production (in units) for two periods are as follows:

	Period 1	Period 2
Sales	15,000	21,600
Production	18,000	21,000

Required:

- Prepare a trading statement to identify the manufacturing profit for Period 2 using the existing absorption costing method.
- Determine the manufacturing profit that would be reported in Period 2 if marginal costing was used.
- Explain, with supporting calculations, why the manufacturing profit in.

ABSORPTION COSTING PRINCIPLES

In product/service costing, an absorption costing system allocates or apportions a share of all costs incurred by a business to each of its products/services. In this way, it can be established whether, in the long run, each product/service makes a profit. This can only be a guide. Arbitrary assumptions have to be made about the apportionment of many of the costs which, given that some costs will tend to remain fixed during a period, will also be dependent on the level of activity. An absorption costing system traditionally classifies costs by function. Sales less production costs (of sales) measures the gross profit (manufacturing profit) earned. Gross profit less costs incurred in other business functions establishes the net profit (operating profit) earned.

Using an absorption costing system, the profit reported for a manufacturing business for a period will be influenced by the level of production as well as by the level of sales. This is because of the absorption of fixed manufacturing overheads into the value of work-in-progress and finished goods stocks. If stocks remain at the end of an accounting period, then the fixed manufacturing overhead costs included within the stock valuation will be transferred to the following period.

ABSORPTION COSTING PROFIT STATEMENT

The first stage in the preparation of absorption costing profit statements is the measurement of the gross profit (manufacturing profit) earned. This requires the calculation of unit production costs, including the establishment of absorption rates for manufacturing overheads. Referring to the example being used for illustration in this article (see earlier), variable manufacturing costs per units are given in the question (at £6.40 per unit). Fixed manufacturing overheads of £92,000 per period are to be absorbed at a unit rate (based on normal production activity of 20,000 units per period). The fixed manufacturing overhead absorption rate is therefore £4.60 per unit (£92,000 ¸ 20,000 units) giving a total manufacturing cost of £11.00 per unit (£6.40 + £4.60).

The use of normal activity as the basis for overhead absorption is similar to the use of budgeted activity. It is to be expected that actual activity (and indeed actual expenditure also) will be different to normal/budget thus giving rise to overhead over or under absorption. It is important that this is highlighted in profit statements. The use of normal (or budgeted) activity and expenditure to establish the absorption rate not only helps to focus attention on overhead recovery but also has the effect of 'normalising' per unit product/service costs.

Referring again to the example, fixed manufacturing overheads will be over-absorbed in Period 2 because the actual production of 21,000 units exceeds the normal activity, the basis used to establish the absorption rate, by 1,000 units. The extent of the over-absorption (the balance remaining in the fixed manufacturing overhead account) is, therefore, £4,600 (1,000 units at £4.60 per unit). This amount will be transferred to the profit and loss account in order to establish the manufacturing profit. It will have a positive effect (i.e., it will be added to profit) because more manufacturing overhead has been absorbed into stock in the period than has been incurred (see the entries in the fixed manufacturing overhead account demonstrated later in examples).

The Examiner's Report for the June 2000 Paper 3 noted that the over-absorption of fixed manufacturing overhead caused problems for many candidates. It was frequently not identified. Where it was calculated, it was at times described as 'under-absorbed' or was at least treated as such in terms of its impact on the manufacturing profit. Other candidates wrongly calculated the over/under- absorption based upon the difference between sales and production quantities, rather than upon the difference between actual production and normal production. Preparation of the remainder of the trading statement (to identify the manufacturing profit for Period 2 using absorption costing) should be straightforward (see Example 2). The manufacturing cost of sales (the transfer out of the finished goods stock account) is simply the 21,600 units sold in the period (which at a selling price of £14.00 per unit yields total sales for the period of £302,400) multiplied by the unit manufacturing cost of £11.00.

Example:

Period 2 Trading Statement:	£000	
Sales	302.4	(21,600 units at £14.00 per unit)
Manufacturing cost of goods sold	237.6	(21,600 units at £11.00 per unit)
Manufacturing profit (before adjustment)	64.8	(21,600 units at £3.00 per unit)
Fixed manufacturing overhead over-absorbed	4.6	(1,000 units at £4.60 per unit)
Manufacturing profit (after adjustment)	69.4	

The Examiner's Report noted that there were many examples (in the examination scripts marked) of candidates matching the cost of the goods produced in the period (not the manufacturing cost of the goods sold) with sales.

Many examination candidates also got into difficulty because they attempted to introduce stock into the profit statement. There is generally no requirement to do this (unless opening and closing stocks are valued at a different rate per unit) but such an approach should (but often did not) lead to the same profit result.

In this example, no details of stock are provided in the question, but it could be assumed, for example, that 3,000 units were in stock at the end of Period I (production of 18,000 units less sales of 15,000 units). Finished goods stock at the end of Period 2 would then be 2,400 units due to the excess of sales over production of 600 units in that period.

Example:

A trading statement including stock would be.		
Period 2 Trading Statement	£000	
Sales	302.4	
Manufacturing cost of goods sold:		
Opening stock of finished goods	33.0	(3,000 units at £11.00 per unit)
Cost of goods produced	231.0	(21,000 units at £11.00 per unit)
Closing stock of finished goods	(26.4)	(2,400 units at £11.00 per unit)
	237.6	
Manufacturing profit (before adjustment)	64.8	
Fixed manufacturing overhead over-absorbed	4.6	

In the adapted question used for illustration is no information provided about costs incurred in other business functions (selling, administration, distribution) and thus it is not possible to complete the profit statement. If information on other costs was available, the costs incurred in the period would simply be deducted from the adjusted manufacturing profit to arrive at net profit.

MARGINAL COSTING PRINCIPLES

In product/service costing, a marginal costing system emphasises the behavioural, rather than the functional, characteristics of costs. The focus is on separating costs into variable elements (where the cost per unit remains the same with total cost varying in proportion to activity) and fixed elements (where the total cost remains the same in each period regardless of the level of activity).

Whilst this is not easily achieved with accuracy, and is an oversimplification of reality, marginal costing information can be very useful for short-term planning, control and decision-making, especially in a multi-product business. In a marginal costing system, sales less variable costs (regardless of function) measures the contribution that individual products/ services make towards the total fixed costs incurred by the business.

The fixed costs (regardless of function) are treated as period costs and, as such, are simply deducted from contribution in the period incurred to arrive at net profit.

MARGINAL COSTING PROFIT STATEMENT

Referring back to Example 1, as there is no information regarding non-manufacturing costs, it may be assumed that sales less variable manufacturing costs measures contribution. NB.

If any variable costs are incurred in non-manufacturing functions then they would also be deducted from sales in the measurement of contribution. The trading statement for Period 2, assuming that a marginal costing system was in place instead.

Example:

Period 2 Trading Statement:	£000	
Sales	302.40	
Variable cost of goods sold	138.24	(21,600 units at £6.40 per unit)
Contribution	164.16	(21,600 units at £7.60 per unit)
Fixed manufacturing overhead	92.00	
Manufacturing profit	72.16	

Costing approach is more straightforward. The Examiner's Report noted that candidates generally had rather more success with the marginal costing statement in part (b) than with the absorption costing statement in part (a), although some confusion between the two was demonstrated.

In practice, the marginal costing profit statement would be completed by the further deduction of fixed costs incurred in other functions.

PROFIT RECONCILIATION

The net profit reported by absorption and marginal costing systems may not be the same owing to the differing treatment of fixed manufacturing overheads.

As has been demonstrated above, whilst marginal costing systems treat fixed manufacturing overheads as period costs (i.e. a charge against profit in the period incurred), in absorption costing systems they are absorbed into the cost of goods produced and are only charged against profit in the period in which those goods are sold.

As a result, if quantities produced and sold in a period are not the same (i.e., if the levels of work-in-progress or finished goods stock change) a different profit will be reported by the two systems. The differing profits can be reconciled, and the difference explained, by an analysis of the product of the stock change and the fixed manufacturing overhead absorption rate. Thus, in answer to part (c) of Example 1:

Period 2 finished goods stock reduction 600 unitsx fixed manufacturing overhead absorption rate, £4.60 per unit = £2,760 difference in profit i.e., the difference between the absorption costing manufacturing profit of £69,400 and the marginal costing manufacturing profit of £72,160. Absorption costing has a lower profit because more goods are being taken out of stock (including a charge for fixed manufacturing overhead) than are going into stock. This is demonstrated by the entries in the respective cost accounting systems.

Example: In the absorption costing system.

Table. Fixed Manufacturing Overhead Account

Incurred	**£92,000**	**Absorbed into Finished Goods**	**£96,600** —
Over-absorbed – to P&L A/c (1,000 units at £4.60/unit)	£4,600	(21,000 units at £4.60/unit)	
	£96,600	£96,600	

Table. Finished Goods Stock Account

Fixed mfg o'hd absorbed (21,600 units at £4.60/unit)	£96,600	Cost of sales (fixed mfg o'hd only)	£99,360

Table. The Total Fixed Manufacturing Overhead Charged Against Profit in the Period =

Overhead in cost of sales	£99,360
Less over-absorption	£4,600
	£94,760

Table. In the Marginal Costing System

	Fixed Manufacturing	Overhead Account
Incurred	£92,000	P&L A/c-period cost £92,000

Absorption costing £94,760 less marginal costing £92,000 =£2,760 more fixed manufacturing overheads and less profit in absorption costing. The difference in profit between absorption and marginal costing systems is nothing to do with overhead over/under absorption, a popular misconception amongst examination candidates.

Despite an over-absorption of £4,600, which is a positive adjustment to the absorption costing profit, the profit was nevertheless less than the marginal costing profit. *To emphasise again*: The difference in reported profit demonstrated above, which can only be a timing difference, is due to changes in the level of finished goods stock which in an absorption costing system moves overhead, and therefore profit, from one period to another.

As a general rule: If production quantity > sales quantity then absorption costing profit > marginal costing profit. If production quantity < sales quantity then absorption costing profit <marginal costing profit. Many candidates, when answering examination questions on this topic, do appreciate that the different treatment of fixed manufacturing overhead is the reason for profit differences but they are rarely able to reconcile the profits.

COST VOLUME PROFIT ANALYSIS

LEARNING OBJECTIVES

After you have read and studied this chapter, you should be able to:

- Discuss the assumptions underlying the conventional linear cost-volume-profit (CVP) model.
- Explain the implications of relaxing each of these assumptions in terms of the theoretical cost- volume-profit model.
- Explain the meaning of a series of graphic illustrations for both the linear and nonlinear CVP models including production functions, revenue functions and cost functions.
- Discuss the difference between performing a "what-if" analysis and converting from the linear model to the theoretical nonlinear model.
- Solve a variety of linear CVP problems for single product companies in either units or sales dollars.
- Define and use the margin of safety.
- Solve a variety of linear CVP problems for multiproduct companies in either units or sales dollars.
- Solve similar problems on a cash flow basis.
- Discuss the controversy concerning the compatibility of the contribution margin approach with activity based costing and the lean enterprise concepts of just in time and the theory of constraints.

ANALYSIS OF CVP

Conceptually, conventional linear cost-volume-profit (CVP) analysis is a simplified, short term planning technique that evolved as a practical version of the theoretical model of the firm described in economics textbooks. From an accounting perspective it is compatible with the direct, or variable costing method of inventory valuation. To use the CVP model, a company must separate total costs into fixed and variable categories using one of the methods. Recall from our earlier discussions of these terms that variable costs are those costs that vary with changes in the level of activity. The only activities that are allowed to affect variable costs in traditional cost-volume-profit analysis are production output and sales. Remember that fixed costs are those costs that do not vary with changes in the activity level.

Conceptually, fixed costs are not constant. By definition, fixed simply means that these costs are not driven by short run changes in production or sales volume. Although explicit recognition of non production volume related cost drivers is a key concept in activity based costing, the idea is ignored in the conventional linear CVP model. Finally, it is important to recognize that the concept of fixed and variable costs is a short run concept. All costs tend to vary in the long run as the company adds to its' capacity to produce and distribute products and services. Therefore, the short run emphasis of CVP analysis tends to conflict with the long run emphasis of activity based costing and the lean enterprise concepts of JIT and TOC. This creates another thought provoking controversial issue.

The purpose of this chapter is to describe the assumptions and techniques of the conventional linear cost-volume-profit approach as well as the controversy concerning the compatibility of CVP analysis with ABC and the continuous improvement concepts. The chapter is divided into five main sections. The first section addresses the underlying assumptions of the conventional linear model and the implications of relaxing these assumptions. This section is mainly conceptual and is illustrated with a series of graphs.

The second section illustrates the basic planning techniques for a single product company that provide the foundation for more realistic problems. The third section extends the basic analysis to multiproduct companies. Both sections two and three are more mechanical than conceptual and are mainly illustrated with a series of related equations. The fourth section is fairly short, but illustrates how to convert the analysis to a cash flow basis. The last section introduces the controversy associated with the CVP approach as it relates to the newer concepts of ABC, JIT and TOC. Since the CVP methodology is closely related to direct or variable costing, this chapter helps provide a better foundation for the more detailed comparison of direct and absorption costing presented in.

ASSUMPTIONS OF CONVENTIONAL LINEAR CVP ANALYSIS

Conventional linear cost volume profit analysis is based on five assumptions as follows:

- Constant sales price.
- Constant variable cost per unit.

- Constant total fixed cost.
- Constant sales mix.
- Units sold equal units produced.

Note that these are the same assumptions that are applicable to the master budget, with the exception of number five. Now we will examine the implications of each assumption.

Constant Sales Price

To assume that the sales price is constant implies that the company is facing a horizontal demand function as illustrated in Figure below. The implications of a horizontal demand function are that the company can sell any number of units at a constant sales price. Another way to describe this is to say that consumers are willing and able to buy any quantity the company offers for sale at a constant price. Average revenue (AR) is constant and equal to the sales price, (i.e., AR = PX÷X = P) as illustrated in Figure.

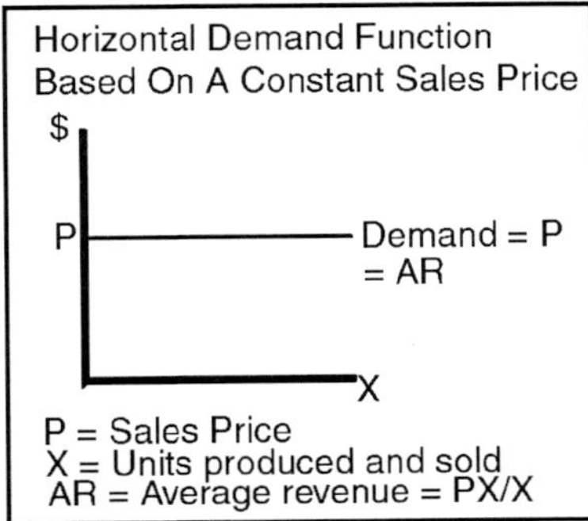

The slope of the total revenue function (see Figure 11-2) is equal to the sales price. When the company sells one additional unit, total revenue increases by an amount equal to the sales price of that unit. The fact that the sales price is constant causes the slope of the total revenue function to be constant which results in a linear total revenue function. Another way to describe this is to say that total revenue increases at a constant rate as additional units are sold.

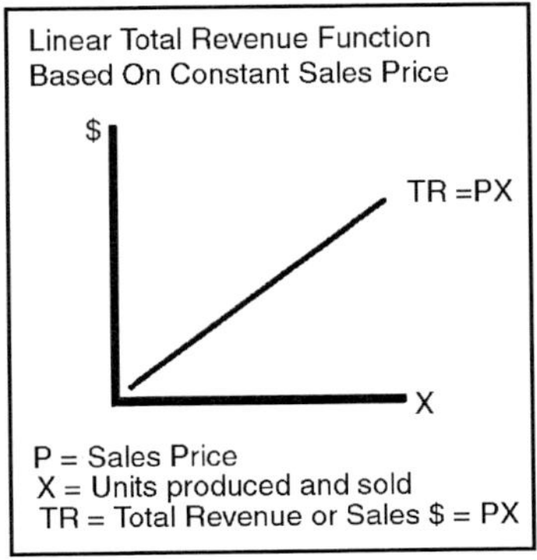

A more realistic down sloping demand function (see Figure below) illustrates what economists refer to as the law of demand. This law describes the fundamental idea that consumers are willing and able to buy more at a lower price than a higher price.

When the price is decreased from P1 to P2, the quantity purchased, or demanded, increases from X1 to X2. The total revenue function based on the law of demand is nonlinear as illustrated in Figure. Total revenue increases at a decreasing rate as additional units are sold. This is because the sale of additional units requires that the company reduce the sales price. Each price corresponds to a specific sales quantity. Thus, average revenue (AR) will be decreasing, rather than constant.

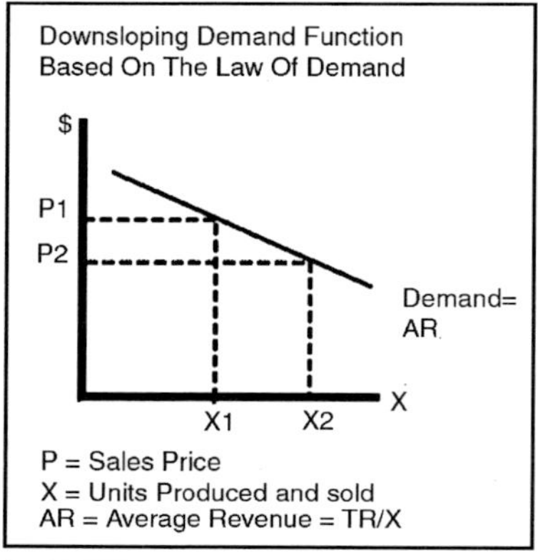

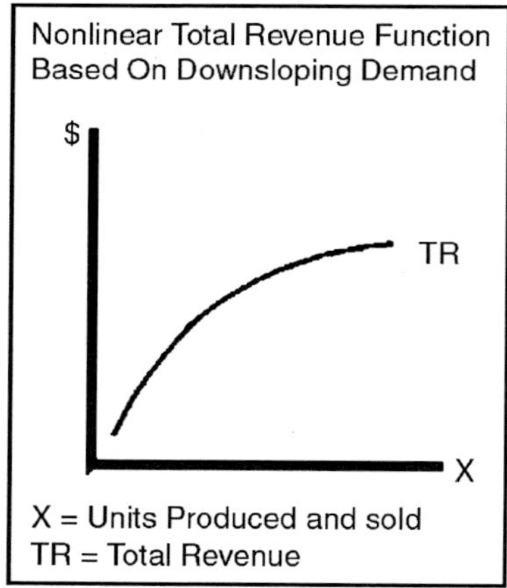

Although the assumption of a constant sales price is not realistic, it is defended as a practical way to expedite the planning process within a fairly narrow range of sales activity. The idea that most products are subject to a down sloping demand curve is intuitively obvious, but applying the concept is simply not practical. Most companies sell too many products in a constantly changing economic environment. Today's demand curve is very likely to be obsolete tomorrow.

Constant Variable cost per unit

The second assumption of the conventional linear cost-volume-profit approach is that the variable cost per unit of output is constant. This includes two important underlying assumptions: a) input prices are assumed to be constant for all variable inputs such as direct material, direct labour, and the various types of indirect resources represented by variable factory overhead costs and variable selling and administrative expenses, and b) the firm experiences constant productivity, i.e., constant output per variable input.

Constant productivity is illustrated in Figure 11-5. When productivity is constant, each new unit of output requires an equal amount of input and thus each unit of output will cost the same amount. This causes both the production function to be linear (see Figure below) and the average variable cost function to be horizontal. Output (X) is placed on the vertical axis because output is the dependent variable, i.e., inputs drive outputs. Output is on the horizontal axis in the other graphs because cost is the dependent variable, i.e., output drives cost.

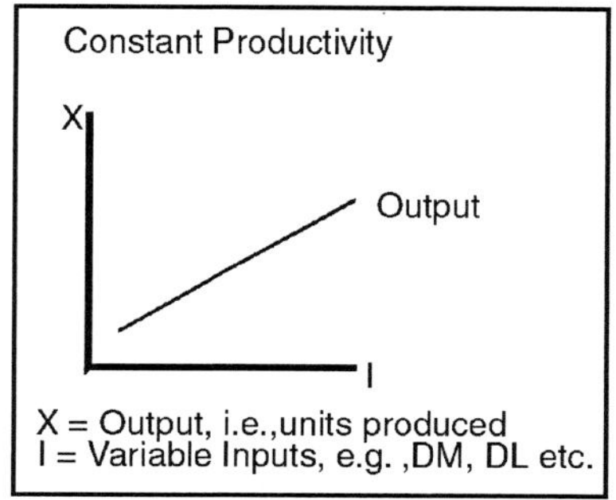

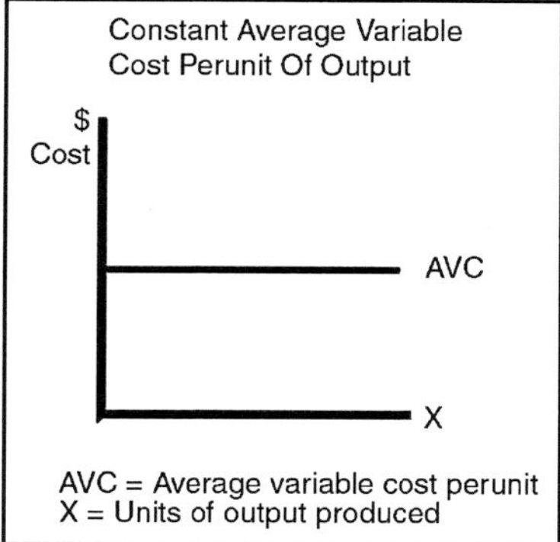

Although it is convenient to assume constant productivity for short run planning purposes, other types of production functions are more realistic when the whole range of production possibilities is considered. When a company begins to expand output from a low volume startup level to a medium volume level, productivity might be expected to increase due to the effects of increased specialization, experience and learning. When productivity is increasing, output increases at an increasing rate (see Figures below). As variable inputs are added to production, each input generates more output than the previous input. When productivity is increasing, average variable cost per unit will be decreasing.

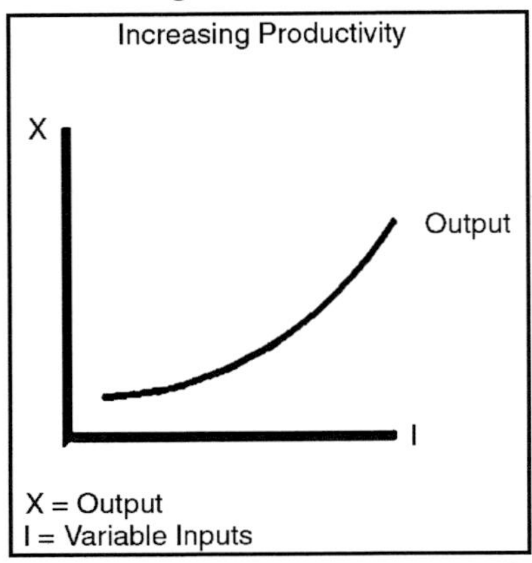

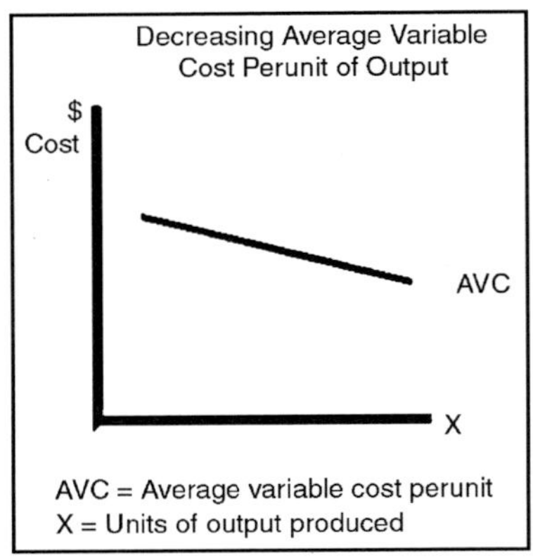

If the company increased production from a medium volume level to a high volume level by continuing to add variable inputs to a fixed size facility, productivity would be expected to decrease as indicated in Figures. This is because at high volume production levels, the inputs (labour, materials etc.) would become excessive relative to the size of the fixed facility. In the case of decreasing productivity, average variable cost per unit will be increasing as illustrated in Figures. Each unit will cost more because it requires more inputs to produce.

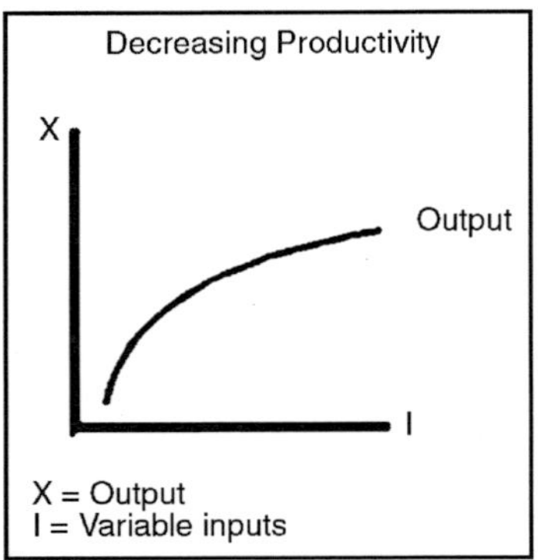

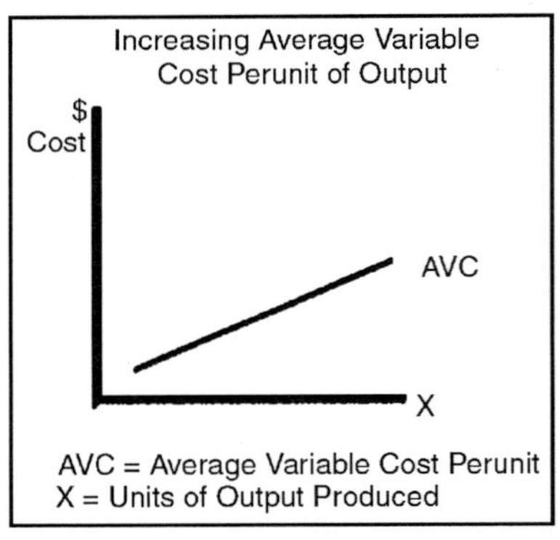

Theoretically, the production and average variable cost functions for the entire range of short run production possibilities will be similar to those illustrated in Figures. The point where the production function changes directions from increasing to decreasing productivity and the average variable cost function changes from decreasing to increasing cost per unit is referred to as the point of diminishing returns. Output continues to increase beyond this point, but at a decreasing rate.

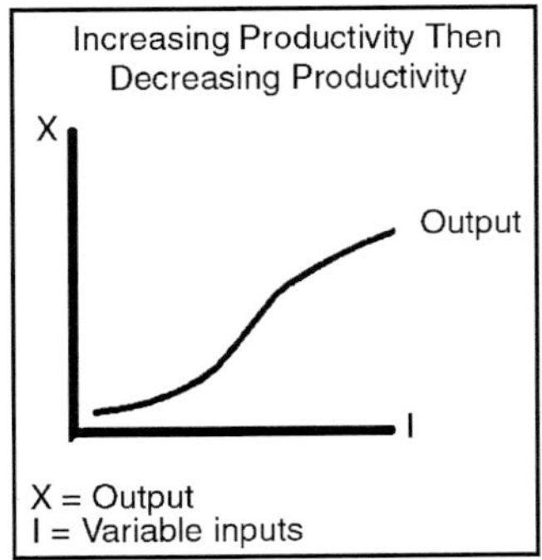

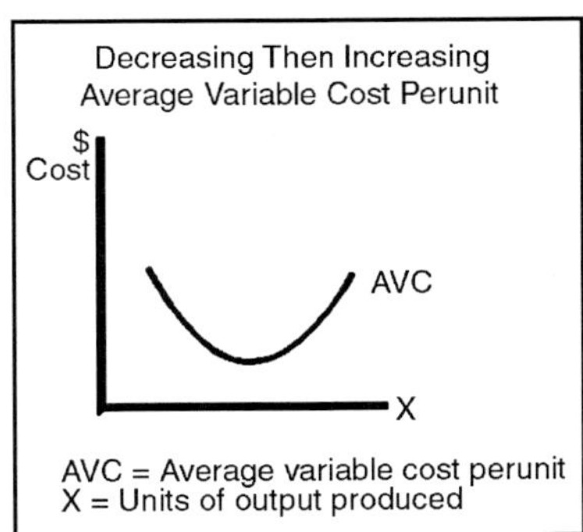

Constant Fixed Costs

A family of total cost functions for the conventional linear model is presented in Figures. The total variable cost and total cost functions are linear, i.e., they increase at a constant rate, because productivity is assumed to be constant. The total fixed cost function is represented by a horizontal line because of assumption three which eliminates the possibility of a non-output related change in fixed costs during the planning period. No changes in the company's fixed factors of production can occur. The total cost and total variable cost functions are vertically parallel and separated by the amount of total fixed costs.

A comparable family of total cost functions for the theoretical economic model appears in Figures below. The total variable cost and total cost functions increase at a decreasing rate at first in response to increasing productivity. When the inputs are becoming more productive, additional outputs cost less per unit because they require less input.

However, when productivity begins to decrease, the total cost and total variable cost functions begin to increase at an increasing rate. In the case of decreasing productivity, the inputs are generating less output per input, thus the unit cost of additional outputs is increasing. The total cost functions are also parallel and separated vertically by the amount of total fixed costs.

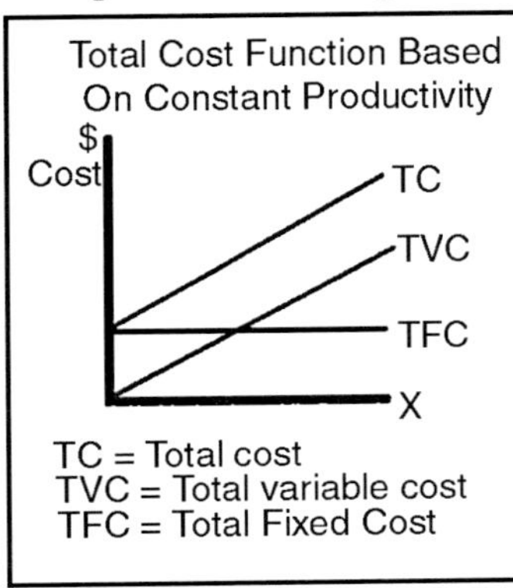

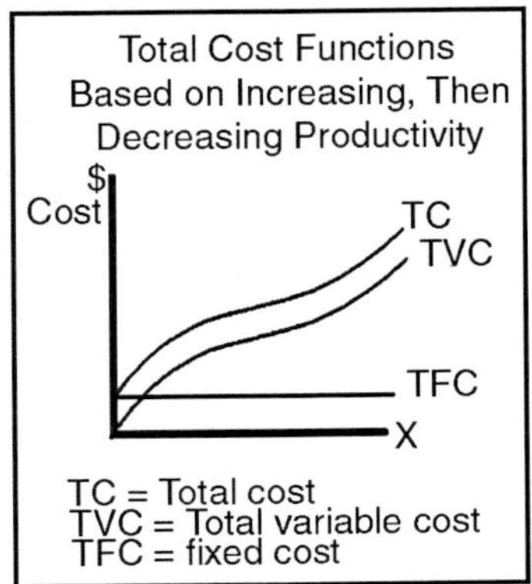

Constant Sales Mix and Inventory Level

The last two assumptions of the conventional linear cost-volume-profit model are more easily understood than the previous assumptions. The fourth assumption is that the sales mix will remain constant during the planning period for a multiproduct company. Sales mix proportions may be stated in terms of either units or dollars as explained in the illustrations below.

The fifth and last assumption is that units produced are equal to units sold. This means that there will be no changes in beginning or ending inventory levels to complicate the analysis. This assumption along with the assumption concerning constant fixed cost will be relaxed in the following chapter where we will use the conventional linear CVP model to consider the differences between direct costing and full absorption costing.

CONVENTIONAL AND THEORETICAL MODELS

Graphic summaries of the two models are presented in Figures below. In the linear model there is one break-even point (BEP) where total revenue is equal to total cost. Since the total revenue and total cost functions are linear, the profit function is also linear. This is because the slope of the profit function is equal to contribution margin per unit which is automatically constant when the sales price and variable cost per unit are constant.

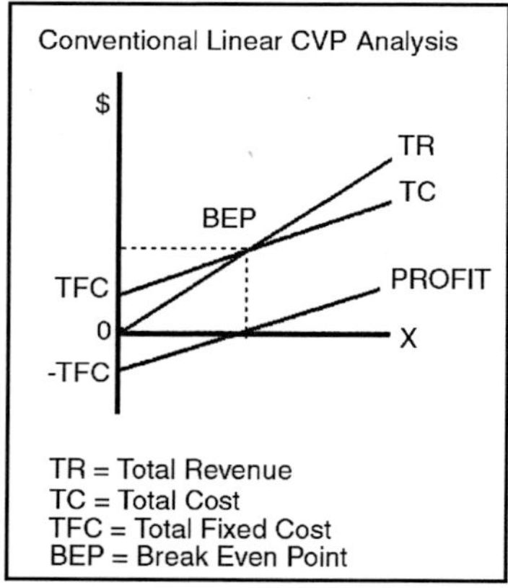

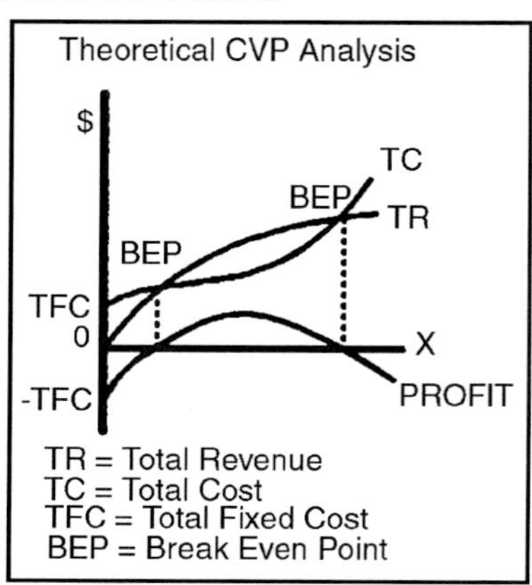

The theoretical model summarized in Figure above conveys a very different picture. There are two break-even points where total revenue and total cost are equal. The theoretical profit function intersects the horizonal axis at the two break-even points and reaches a maximum level at the point where the vertical distance between TR and TC is the greatest.

In the linear model illustrated in Figure 11-15, the area to the left of the break-even point represents a loss area and the area to the right of this point represents a profit area that continuously grows larger as additional units are produced and sold. In the linear model the company maximizes profit where production and sales are at maximum capacity. However, in the theoretical model, there are two loss areas, one to the left of the first BEP and one to the right of the second BEP. The profit area is between the two break-even points, thus trying to achieve the maximum level of production and sales will produce losses rather than increased profits.[3] For this reason, some critics of the conventional linear model argue that it represents a naive and dangerous view of a firm's economic environment.

On the other hand, advocates of the linear model contend that short term planning does not require a theoretical model of the entire range of production possibilities. Although the concepts underlying the theoretical model are important, the model does not provide a practical approach for short term planning. However, the linear model is a practical and adequate alternative for planning within the normal relevant range of production and sales alternatives.

Analysis Versus Changing the Model

For any given linear CVP analysis, we can ask a whole set of "what-if" questions about how increases and decreases in the sales price, unit variable costs, sales mix and fixed costs would affect the outcome. However, when we do that we are simply changing from one set of static assumptions to another set. This means that we are changing from one conventional linear problem to a somewhat different conventional linear problem. If the first two assumptions are relaxed to allow the sales price and unit variable costs to change continuously in response to the forces of supply and demand, we are not asking a "what if" question, we are changing the analysis from the practical linear approach to the theoretical nonlinear approach.

TECHNIQUES FOR SOLVING CVP PROBLEMS

The following symbols are used below to illustrate the various techniques used in cost-volume-profit analysis.

P = Sales price.

V = Variable costs per unit.

Note: This is not inventory cost because it includes both variable manufacturing costs as well as variable selling and administrative expenses.

X = The number of units produced and sold. A unit is a common way to describe an output, but an output may be expressed in pounds, gallons, board feet, cubic feet, etc.

TR = S = Total revenue, or sales dollars.

TVC = Total variable costs = VX

TFC = Total fixed costs.

TC = Total costs = TFC + TVC.

P-V = Contribution margin per unit. This is the amount of sales revenue that each unit provides towards covering the fixed costs and providing a profit, i.e., what's left over after the variable costs associated with the unit have been covered.

TCM = Total contribution margin = (P – V)(X).

CMR = (P-V) ÷ P = (TR – TVC) ÷ TR = (PX – VX) ÷ PX = 1 – (V ÷ P)

These are just different ways to define the contribution margin ratio. They all work because the functions are linear.

There are many algebraic equations illustrated on the next several pages that may appear to require memorization. However, every equation is simply a variation of the following basic concepts:

Total Revenue = Total Cost + Profit
TR = TC + NIBT
TR = TFC + TVC + NIBT
TR – TVC = TFC + NIBT
TCM = TFC + NIBT

Total revenue, or sales dollars, less total variable costs equals total contribution margin. Contribution margin is the revenue over and above the variable costs that contributes towards covering the fixed costs and also towards providing a profit after the fixed costs have been covered. Practically any cost-volume-profit problem can be solved with the last equation stated above and an understanding of the concepts involved.

Solving Single Product CVP Problems in Units

A summary of the cost volume profit equations for single product problems is presented below. All five equations are variations of the basic conceptual equation stated above. To reinforce the concept, each equation is developed and illustrated below.

Single product cvp problems in units number equation used to determine:

- (P-V)X = TFC Units needed to break-even.
- (P-V)X = TFC + NIBT Units needed to generate a target net income before taxes.
- (P-V)X = TFC + [NIAT ÷ (1-T)] Units needed to generate a target net income after taxes.
- (P-V)X = TFC + (R)(PX) Units needed to generate a target NIBT stated as a proportion (R) of sales dollars (PX).
- (P-V)X = TFC + [(R)(PX) ÷ (1-T)] Units needed to generate a target NIAT stated as a proportion (R) of sales dollars (PX).

UNITS NEEDED TO BREAK-EVEN

We can derive the break-even equation by starting with the fact that total revenue equals total cost at the break-even point. Then the equation is restated in terms of unit sales, unit prices and unit cost and then rearranged into the more convenient format presented in Equation.

TR = TC
TR = TFC + TVC
PX = TFC + VX
PX – VX = TFC
(P – V)X = TFC or TCM = TFC
X = TFC ÷ (P – V)

Equation above shows that the break-even point is where total contribution margin (P – V)(X) is equal to total fixed costs, i.e., this level of production and sales provides just enough revenue to cover all the cost.

UNITS NEEDED FOR TARGET NET INCOME BEFORE TAXES

This equation can be derived from scratch in the same manner used to develop Equation 1. Notice however that Equation 2 may be obtained by simply adding the desired amount of net income to the right hand side of Equation.

TR = TFC + TVC + TARGET NIBT
PX = TFC + VX + NIBT
PX – VX = TFC + NIBT
(P – V)X = TFC + NIBT
X = (TFC + NIBT) ÷ (P – V)

Equations simply indicates that total contribution margin is equal to the total fixed costs plus the desired net income before taxes. These relationships are illustrated graphically in Figure below which is similar to present.

Figure below shows that the break-even point is where the two lines representing total revenue and total cost intersect. To the left of this intersection, the vertical difference between the total revenue and total cost functions represents a net loss. To the right of the break-even point, the vertical difference between the two functions represents net income before taxes. The lower part of the graph shows that the break-even point can also be found by plotting the before tax profit function.

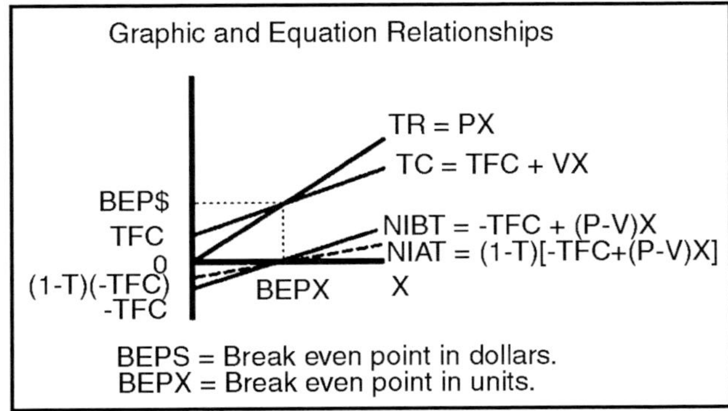

When the number of units produced and sold equals zero, the loss is equal to total fixed costs. When the firm produces a positive number of units, the loss is reduced by an amount equal to the contribution margin per unit multiplied by the number of units produced and sold. The slope of NIBT is contribution margin per unit. When enough units are produced and sold to cover the fixed costs, the company reaches the break-even point. This is the point on the graph where the profit function intersects the horizontal axis and it is directly below the point where the total revenue and total cost functions intersect.

UNITS NEEDED FOR NET INCOME

If T = the tax rate, and NIAT = desired net income after taxes, then

(1-T)(NIBT) = NIAT therefore NIBT = NIAT ÷ (1-T)

Substituting NIAT÷(1-T) for NIBT in Equation 2, provides Equation 3, which allows us to solve for units needed to generate a desired amount of net income after taxes.

$$(P - V)\ X = TFC + [NIAT \div (1 - T)]$$

$$X = [TFC + [NIAT \div (1 - T)]] \div (P - V)$$

The after tax relationships are also illustrated graphically in Figure above. The after tax profit function begins at a point equal to (1 – T)(–TFC) assuming the tax benefits of a loss can be used in a prior period or perhaps in some other segment of the company. The slope of the after tax profit function is (1 – T)(P – V), therefore the function is not as steep as the before tax profit function. The break-even point is the same however, and the vertical difference between the two profit functions is equal to the amount of the tax involved.

When target net income before taxes is stated as a % of sales $. If we use R to define the desired rate of return on sales, i.e., R = NIBT/TR, then we can substitute R(PX) for the desired net income before taxes in Equation.

$$(P - V)X = TFC + (R)(PX)$$

$$X = [TFC + (R)(PX)] \div (P - V)$$

Since PX equals sales dollars, then R multiplied by PX will provide the desired profit before taxes. Although the desired profit is often stated as a percentage, R is a proportion, i.e, it ranges from 0 to 1.

When target net income after taxes is stated as a percentage of sales $. If the target rate of return is stated as an after tax rate, i.e., R = NIAT/TR, then the following approach is used. Substituting R(PX)÷(1-T) for R(PX) in Equation.

$$(P - V)X = TFC + [(R)(PX) \div (1 - T)]$$

X = [TFC + [(R)(PX) ÷ (1 þ T)]] ÷ (P – V)

When solving CVP problems, it is less confusing visually and more convenient for computational purposes to leave (P – V) on the left-hand side of the equations initially. It is best to simplify the expressions on both sides of the equation first, rather than attempt to divide every element on the right-hand side by P – V. The Cal Company produces pocket size calculators that are sold for $10 per unit.

The costs associated with each unit are as follows:

- Direct material = $3.00,

- Direct labour = \$.25,
- Variable overhead = \$2.00,
- Variable selling and administrative cost = \$.75.

Total fixed costs are \$100,000 for manufacturing and \$20,000 for the selling and administrative functions. The company's tax rate is 40%. In a recent meeting, the board of directors asked the following questions. How many calculators do we need to produce and sell to accomplish each of the following requirements?

- Break-even.
- Earn net income before taxes of \$40,000.
- Earn net income after taxes of \$24,000.
- Earn a 20% return on sales before taxes.
- Earn a 12% return on sales after taxes.

To answer these questions, we start by calculating the contribution per unit as follows:

Contribution margin per unit,

$$= P - V = 10\ 2\ (3 + .25 + 2 + .75) = 10 - 6 = 4.$$

Then, the five questions are answered by using the equations in Exhibit 11-1.

- Break-even.
  Using Equation [1] 4X = 120,000
  X = \$120,000 ÷ 4 = 30,000 units.
- Earn net income before taxes of \$40,000.
  Using Equation [2] 4X = 120,000 + 40,000
  X = 160,000 ÷ 4 = 40,000 units.
- Earn net income after taxes of \$24,000.
  Using Equation [3] 4X = 120,000 + [24,000 ÷ (1-.4)]
  4X = 120,000 + 40,000
  X = 160,000 ÷ 4 = 40,000 unit.

  A graphic solution to Example is illustrated in Figure below.

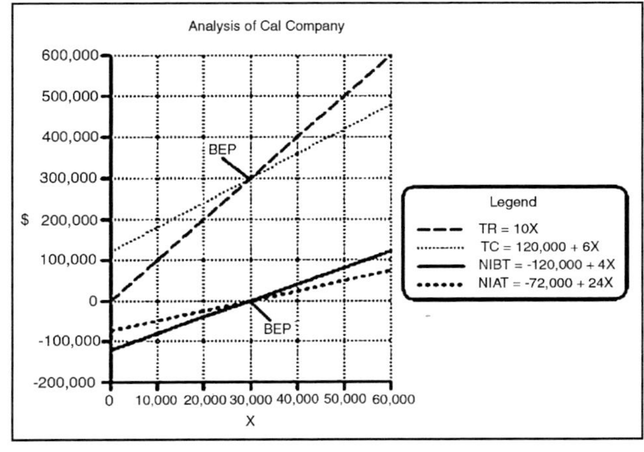

- Earn a 20% return on sales before taxes.
  Using Equation [4] 4X = 120,000 +.2(10X)
  4X = 120,000 + 2X
  2X = 120,000
  X = 120,000 ÷ 2 = 60,000 units.
- Earn a 12% return on sales after taxes.
  Using Equation [5] 4X = 120,000 + [.12(10X) ÷ (1-.4)]
  4X = 120,000 +.2(10X)
  4X = 120,000 + 2X
  2X = 120,000
  X = 120,000 ÷ 2 = 60,000 units.

After Tax Equations

The equation for NIAT that appears in the graph is found by multiplying the equation for NIBT by (1-T), i.e., (1-.4)(-120,000 + 4X) = -72,000 + 2.4X. Rearranging this equation we have 2.4X = 72,000 + NIAT. This revised equation indicates that the contribution margin after taxes ($2.4X) is equal to fixed costs after taxes ($72,000) plus the desired after tax income. It provides an alternative way to find the answers to questions 3 and 5 as illustrated below.

- Earn net income after taxes of $24,000.
  - 2.4X = 72,000 + NIAT desired
  - 2.4X = 72,000 + 24,000
  - 2.4X = 96,000
  - X = 96,000 ÷ 2.4 = 40,000 units.
- Earn a 12% return on sales after taxes.
  - 2.4X = 72,000 + NIAT desired
  - 2.4X = 72,000 +.12(10X)
  - 2.4X = 72,000 + 1.2X
  - 1.2X = 72,000
  - X = 72,000 ÷ 1.2 = 60,000 units.

Checking the Solutions

The accuracy of linear cost-volume-profit calculations can be verified easily. For example, the answers to the questions above can be verified as follows:

- Is 30,000 units the break-even point? Yes, since total contribution margin is equal to total fixed cost of 120,000, i.e., (4)(30,000) = $120,000.
- Will 40,000 units generate a before tax profit of $40,000? Yes, because total contribution margin is (4)(40,000) = $160,000 and this amount is 160,000 - 120,000 = $40,000 above total fixed costs.
- Will 40,000 units generate an after tax profit of $24,000? Yes, since (1-.4)($40,000 NIBT) = $24,000.

- Will 60,000 units provide a 20% return on sales before taxes? Yes, since the NIBT is TCM - TFC or (4)(60,000) - 120,000 = \$120,000. Sales equals PX or (\$10)(60,000) = \$600,000. R = 120,000 ÷ 600,000 =.20 or 20%.
- Will 60,000 units provide a 12% return on sales after taxes. Yes, (1-.4)(.2) =.12 or 12%. For an alternative check (1-.4)(120,000) = \$72,000 NIAT. Therefore, the after tax rate of return is 72,000 ÷ 600,000 =.12 or 12%.

SINGLE PRODUCT CVP PROBLEMS

A summary of the cost volume profit equations for solving single product problems in dollars is presented. These five equations are also variations of the basic conceptual equation stated in the first part of this chapter. Each of these equations is developed and illustrated below.

Table. Single Product Cvp Problems In Dollars

Number	Equation	Used To Determine
1	(CMR)(S) = TFC	Sales \$ at break-even point
2	(CMR)(S) = TFC + NIBT	Sales \$ for target NIBT
3	(CMR)(S) = TFC + [NIAT ÷ (1 – T)]	Sales \$ for target NIAT
4	(CMR)(S) = TFC + (R)(S) or sales \$	Sales \$ for target NIBT stated as a proportion (R)
5	(CMR)(S) = TFC + [(R)(S) ÷ (1 – T)] of sales \$	Sales \$ for target NIAT stated as a proportion (R)

BREAK-EVEN POINT

The equation for the break-even point in sales dollars may also be derived by equating total revenue and total cost. It is more convenient to use the single symbol S for sales dollars, rather than TR for total revenue.

$$TR = TC$$

$$S = TFC + TVC$$

Since the variable cost ratio (V÷P) multiplied by sales dollars (S) equals total variable cost, we can substitute (V ÷ P)(S) for variable cost in the equation above as follows.

$$S = TFC + (V \div P)(S)$$

Then subtracting variable cost from both sides of the equation provides the basic break-even point equation in sales dollars.

$$S - (V \div P)(S) = TFC$$

Stated in words, the equation indicates that total revenue, less total variable costs, equals total contribution margin, and the break even point is where total contribution margin is equal to total fixed cost. Since the contribution margin ratio (CMR = 1- V÷P) multiplied by total revenue equals total contribution margin, it is more convenient for computational purposes to state the equation in the following manner.

$$(1 - V \div P)(S) = TFC$$

$$(CMR)(S) = TFC$$

$$S = TFC \div CMR$$

Total revenue needed for target net income before taxes: Although we could derive this equation from scratch, the fact that total contribution margin must be equal to the total fixed costs plus the desired net income before taxes allows us to develop.

$$(CMR)(S) = TFC + NIBT$$

$$S = (TFC+NIBT) \div CMR$$

Total revenue needed for target net income after taxes: Solving for total revenue needed to generate a target net income after taxes involves substituting NIAT ÷ (1 – T) for NIBT in the equation for Sales dollars needed before taxes (i.e., Equation). This provides Equation 3.

$$(CMR)(S) = TFC + [NIAT \div (1 - T)]$$

$$S = [TFC + [NIAT \div (1 - T)]] \div CMR$$

Total revenue needed when target nibt is stated as a percentage of sales $: To solve a problem in sales dollars, when the desired net income is stated as a percentage of sales dollars, substitute (R)(S) into Equation for NIBT as follows.

$$(CMR)(S) = TFC + (R)(S)$$

$$S = [TFC + (R)(S)] \div CMR$$

Total revenue needed when target niat is stated as a percentage of sales $: When the desired net income is stated as an after tax rate (R), the equation needed is developed by simply dividing (R)(S) in Equation by (1 – T).

$$(CMR)(S) = TFC + [(R)(S) \div (1 - T)]$$

$$S = [TFC + [(R)(S) \div (1 - T)]] \div CMR$$

To emphasize a point made earlier, it is less confusing visually and also more convenient for computational purposes to leave CMR on the left-hand side of each of the 5 equations initially. Simplify the expressions first, rather than attempting to divide every element on the right-hand side by CMR.

The Cal Company example can be restated in the following manner. Variable costs (including both manuf-acturing and selling and administrative costs) represent sixty per cent of sales dollars. Total fixed costs are $120,000. Assume the board of directors wants the answers to their questions provided in sales dollars rather than units. What amount of sales in dollars does the company need to accomplish each of the following requirements? 1. Break-even. 2. Earn net income before taxes of $40,000. 3.

Earn net income after taxes of $24,000. 4. Earn a 20% return on sales before taxes. 5. Earn a 12% return on sales after taxes. To answer these questions, we need the contribution margin ratio.

The ratio is,

$$CMR = 1 - V/P = 1 - .6 = .4$$

Then, the answers to the five questions are easily obtained as follows:

- Break even.
  Using Equation .4S = 120,000
  S = 120,000 ÷ .4 = $300,000
- Earn net income before taxes of $40,000.
  Using Equation .4S = (120,000 + 40,000)
  S = 160,000 ÷ .4 = $400,000
- Earn net income after taxes of $24,000.
  Using Equation .4S = 120,000 + (24,000 ÷ .60)
  .4S = 120,000 + 40,000
  S = 160,000 ÷ .4 = $400,000
- Earn a 20% return on sales before taxes.
  Using equation .4S = 120,000 +.2S
  .2S = 120,000
  S = 120,000 ÷ .2 = $600,000
- Earn a 12% return on sales after taxes.
  Using equation .4S = 120,000 + (.12S ÷.6)
  .4S = 120,000 +.2S
  .2S = 120,000
  S = 120,000 ÷ .2 = $600,000

A graphic analysis of this example is also illustrated in Figure 11-18 since we are simply solving the problem in dollars rather than units. The graph is also useful for comparing the two approaches. Example 11 – 1 places emphasis on the horizontal axis (units) while Example 11 – 2 places emphasis on the vertical axis (dollars).

MARGIN OF SAFETY

Before we move on to multiproduct companies, there is a handy concept referred to as the margin of safety that you might find useful. The margin of safety (MS) for any sales level represents the amount of sales dollars above or below the break-even point. Mathematically, the margin of safety is:

MS = Sales$ – Break-even sales$

When sales are above the break-even point, the margin of safety is positive. When sales are below the break-even point, the margin of safety is negative. After determining the MS for a particular sales level, Equations can be used to make some quick calculations.

$$NIBT = (MS)(CMR)$$

Solving Equation 6 provides the amount of contribution margin above the break-even point (when MS is positive) and this amount represents the net income (or loss if the MS is negative) before taxes.

Why? Because after the total fixed costs have been covered, additional contribution margin represents the before tax profit. Before the fixed cost have been covered the additional contribution needed represents the before tax loss.

The equation for after tax profit is,

$$NIAT = (MS)(CMR)(1 - T)$$

Suppose we are in a board of directors meeting and a board member asks how much income would Cal Company generate at a particular sales level. For convenience let's say $1,000,000.

Using the margin of safety we can answer this question quickly. Since we already know the break-even point is $300,000, then the margin of safety is 1,000,000 - 300,000 = $700,000.

Using Equation,

$$NIBT = (700{,}000)(.4) = \$280{,}000.$$

Using Equation,

$$NIAT = (700{,}000)(.4)(.6) = \$168{,}000.$$

To show that the margin of safety calculations work on either side of the break-even point, consider another example. Suppose someone ask, how much income would Cal Company generate when total revenue is only $200,000?

$$MS = 200{,}000 - 300{,}000 = -100{,}000, \text{ i.e., } \$100{,}000 \text{ below the BEP}$$

Using Equation NIBT = (–100,000)(.4) = –40,000 net loss before taxes, or Using Equation NIAT = (–40,000)(.6) = –24,000 net loss after taxes. Solving Multiple Product Cvp Problems In Units Some additional symbols are needed to illustrate the algebraic techniques applicable to multiple product problems.

The following symbols are used below:

- i = The number designating a particular product.
- Pi = The price of product i.
- Vi = The variable cost per unit of product i.
- X = Total mixed units sold, i.e., includes all products.
- Xi = Units of product i sold.
- Mi = The mix ratio for product i, i.e., the proportion that product i represents out of the total number of units sold.
- E = Sigma or summation sign which means "the sum of".

- W = Weighted average contribution margin per unit = E [(Pi-Vi)(Mi)]
- Y = The weighted average price = E (Pi)(Mi)

A summary of the cost volume profit relationships for multiproduct problems is presented in Exhibit 11-3. The five equations are comparable to the single product equations presented in Exhibit 11-1, but are somewhat more involved.

Each equation is developed and illustrated below,

EXHIBIT 11-3

Summary Equations For Solving

Multiple Product Cvp Problems In Units

Number	Equation	Used To Determine
[1]	WX = TFC	Total mixed units at the BEP.
[2]	WX = TFC + NIBT	Total mixed units for target NIBT.
[3]	WX = TFC + [NIAT ÷ (1-T)]	Total mixed units for target NIAT.
[4]	WX = TFC + (R)(YX)	Total mixed units for target NIBT stated as a proportion (R) of sales $.
[5]	WX = TFC + [(R)(YX) ÷ (1-T)]	Total mixed units for target NIAT stated as a proportion (R) of sales $.
	Xi = X(Mi)	The number of units of each product after X is obtained.

BREAK-EVEN POINT FOR MULTIPLE PRODUCTS

The same logic used to solve single product problems is applicable to multiple product problems. At the break-even point, total contribution margin is equal to total fixed costs. However, in multiple product situations, total contribution margin is found by multiplying the weighted average contribution margin per unit by the total number of mixed units produced and sold.

The weighted average contribution margin per unit is calculated by multiplying each product's contribution margin per unit (Pi – Vi) by the mix ratio applicable to that product (Mi) and then summing the results. The mix ratios (Mi's) represent the weights. The equation is,

$$W = E\ [(Pi-Vi)(Mi)]$$

The break-even equation for mixed units (X) is stated in the following manner.

$$WX = TFC$$

After the total mixed units (X) have been determined, then the number of units of the individual products are found by multiplying the total mixed units by each product's mix ratio.

$$Xi = X(Mi)$$

Units Needed For Target Net Income Before Taxes: The equation for mixed units needed to generate a desired amount of net income before taxes is developed by simply adding NIBT to the right hand side of Equation.

$$WX = TFC + NIBT$$

Units needed for target net income after taxes: The equation for mixed units needed to generate a desired after tax profit is developed by substituting NIAT ÷ (1 – T) for NIBT.

$$WX = TFC + [NIAT \div (1 - T)]$$

When Target Net Income Before Taxes Is Stated As A Percentage Of Sales $

Using R to represent the target rate of return on sale dollars before taxes, i.e., R = NIBT÷TR, the following equation can be used to find the mixed units needed.

$$WX = TFC + (R)(YX)$$

Sales dollars are represented by the term YX. Since total sales dollars are mixed, we must multiply the total mixed units (X) by a weighted average price (Y) to find the total mixed sales dollars. Then, multiplying the term YX by R represents the desired NIBT. The weighted average price (Y) is found by multiplying the price of each product (Pi) by the product mix ratios (Mi) and then summing the results, i.e., Y = E (Pi)(Mi).

When Target Net Income After Taxes Is Stated As A Percentage Of Sales $

The appropriate equation for after tax net income is found by dividing the term [(R)(YX], in Equation 4, by 1 – T.

$$WX = TFC + [(R)(YX) \div (1 - T)]$$

Remember that it is usually best for computational purposes to leave the amount represented by W on the left hand side in each of the equations until the expression on the right hand side has been simplified. Also remember that the units for individual products (Xi) are always found by multiplying the total mixed units (X) by the mix ratios (Mi) for each product.

The Sandlot Cap Company produces baseball caps in two categories referred to as regular logo and special logo. Caps in the regular logo category are high volume products that display familiar names of universities and professional sports teams.

Caps in the special design category are typically created for a particular customer to promote special events such as the Olympics, or the opening of a unique museum exhibit. For convenience we will refer to the regular logo caps as product X1 and the special logo caps as product X2. Sales prices and variable costs are provided below.

Product	Price	Variable Cost PerUnit	Mix Ratio Based on Units
X1	$4	$3	.75
X2	8	5	.25

The variable costs for each product include direct materials and conversion costs of $2. Marketing costs account for an additional $1 for regular logo caps and $3 for special logo caps. As indicated above, three quarters of the company's unit sales are represented by regular logo caps, while the other one quarter represents special logo caps. The company's total fixed costs are $300,000. Sandlot Cap Company management wants to know how many caps need to be produced and sold to accomplish the following:

- Break even.
- Earn desired net income before taxes of $60,000.
- Earn desired net income after taxes of $36,000 given the tax rate is 40%.
- Earn desired net income before taxes equal to 15% of sales dollars.
- Earn a desired net income after taxes equal to 9% of sales dollars.

To solve this problem we need to calculate the weighted average contribution margin per unit, i.e., the contribution margin per mixed unit.

$$W = (4-3)(.75) + (8-5)(.25) = 1.5$$

The mix ratios (.75 and.25) are used as the weights to reflect the fact that the company normally sells three times as many X1's as X2's. After obtaining the weighted average contribution of $1.50, then 1.5X represents the total contribution margin on the lefthand side of each equation.

1. To break-even.
   - Using Equation 1.5X = 300,000
   - X = 300,000 ÷ 1.5 = 200,000 Total mixed units.
   - X1 = (200,000)(.75) = 150,000 units
   - X2 = (200,000)(.25) = 50,000 units
2. To earn $60,000 net income before taxes.
   - Using Equation 1.5X = 300,000 + 60,000
   - 1.5X = 360,000
   - X = 360,000 ÷1.5 = 240,000 mixed units
   - X1 = (240,000)(.75) = 180,000 units
   - X2 = (240,000)(.25) = 60,000 units
3. To earn $36,000 net income after taxes.
   - Using Equation 1.5X = 300,000 + (36,000 ÷ .6)
   - 1.5X = 300,000 + 60,000
   - X = 360,000 ÷1.5 = 240,000 mixed units
   - X1 = (240,000)(.75) = 180,000 units
   - X2 = (240,000)(.25) = 60,000 units

In the last two requirements, income is stated as a percentage of sales dollars. Therefore, we need the YX measure of total mixed sales dollars to indicate the desired amount of income. Total mixed sales dollars is the weighted average price Y, multiplied by the mixed units X. To calculate Y we must use the unit mix ratios as weights to reflect the importance of each product in the price.

$$Y = 4(.75) + 8(.25) = \$5$$

Then, \$5 represents the weighted average price and 5X represents the total mixed sales dollars.

4. To earn before tax net income equal to 15% of sales dollars, we substitute.15(5X) in the equation for desired income, i.e., R(YX).
   - Then using Equation
   - 1.5X = 300,000 + .15(5X)
   - 1.5X = 300,000 + .75X
   - .75X = 300,000
   - X = 300,000 ÷ .75 = 400,000 mixed units
   - X1 = .75(400,000) = 300,000 units
   - X2 = .25(400,000) = 100,000 units
5. To earn after tax net income equal to 9% of sales dollars, the desired income is,
   - (R)(YX) ÷ 1 – T, or (.09)(5X) ÷ (1 – .4).
   - Then using Equation
   - 1.5X = 300,000 + [(.09)(5X) ÷ (1 – .4)]
   - 1.5X = 300,000 + [.45X ÷ .6]
   - 1.5X = 300,000 + .75X
   - .75X = 300,000
   - X = 300,000 ÷ .75 = 400,000 mixed units
   - X1 = .75(400,000) = 300,000 units
   - X2 = .25(400,000) = 100,000 units

After Tax Equations As An Alternative

A graphic analysis of the Sandlot Cap Company example appears in Figure.

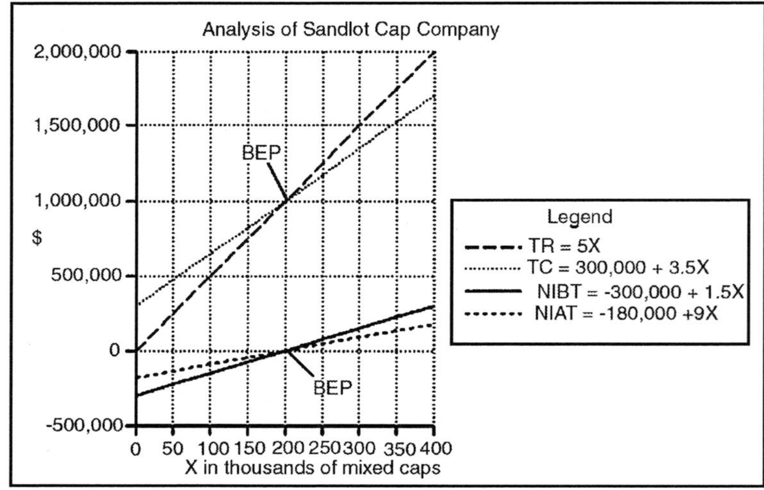

The equation for NIAT illustrated in the graph is found by multiplying the equation for NIBT by (1-T), i.e., (1-.4)(-300,000) + (1-.4)(1.5X) = -180,000

+.9X. Rearranging this equation we have.9X = 180,000 + NIAT where.9X is the weighted average contribution margin after taxes. We can use this equation as an alternative way to find the answers to question 3 and 5 as follows.

3. Earn desired net income after taxes of $36,000.
   - .9X = 180,000 + 36,000
   - .9X = 216,000

   X = 216,000 ÷ .9 = 240,000 mixed units
5. Earn desired net income after taxes equal to 9 per cent of sales dollars.
   - .9X = 180,000 + .09(5X)
   - .9X = 180,000 + .45X
   - .45X = 180,000
   - X = 180,000 ÷ .45 = 400,000 mixed units

Solving Multiple Product Cvp Problems In Dollars

The following additional symbols are used to develop this section:

- S = Total mixed sales dollars.
- Si = Sales dollars for product i.
- CMRi = Contribution margin ratio for product i.
- M$i = The mix ratio for product i based on sales dollars. Note, these ratios are not equal to the mix ratio based on units.
- WCMR = The weighted average contribution margin ratio = E(CMRi)(M$i)

Number	Equation	Used To Determine
[1]	WCMR(S) = TFC	Sales $ at break-even point.
[2]	WCMR(S) = TFC + NIBT	Sales $ for target NIBT.
[3]	WCMR(S) = TFC + [NIAT ÷ (1-T)]	Sales $ for target NIAT.
[4]	WCMR(S) = TFC + (R)(S)	Sales $ for target NIBT stated as a proportion (R) of sales $.
[5]	WCMR(S) = TFC + [(R)(S) ÷ (1-T)]	Sales $ for target NIAT stated as a proportion (R) of sales $.
	Si = S(M$i)	Sales dollars for each product after S is obtained.

Break-even Point In Sales Dollars For Multiple Products: The same basic conceptual logic used in the previous sections is used to develop the equations in this section. The firm breaks even when total contribution margin is equal to total fixed costs.

(WCMR)(S) = TFC

The difference between the equations for single product and multiproduct situations is that we must use a weighted average contribution margin ratio,

WCMR = E(CMRi)(M$I) to find the total mixed sales dollars. Then sales dollars for the individual products are found by multiplying the total mixed sales dollars (S) by the mix ratios for each product, Si = (S)(M$I)

Total Revenue Needed For Target Net Income Before Taxes Equation is developed in the usual manner by simply adding the desired amount of NIBT to the right hand side of Equation.

$$(WCMR)(S) = TFC + NIBT$$

Total Revenue Needed For Target Net Income After Taxes

Revising the previous equation to include after tax profit we have:

$$(WCMR)(S) = TFC + [NIAT \div (1 - T)]$$

When Target Net Income Before Taxes Is Stated As A Percentage Of Sales $ If R is used as the before tax target rate of return on sales, i.e., NIBT÷S, then the equation needed to achieve the target return before taxes is:

$$(WCMR)(S) = TFC + (R)(S)$$

When Target Net Income After Taxes Is Stated As A Percentage Of Sales $ If R is used as the after tax target rate of return on sales, i.e., NIAT÷S, the equation becomes,

$$(WCMR)(S) = TFC + [(R)(S) \div (1 - T)]$$

Suppose the Sandlot Cap Company information is provided to you in the following format.

Product	**Contribution Margin Ratios**	**Mix Ratios Based on Sales Dollars**
X1	.25	.6
X2	.375	.4

TFC = $300,000.

Sandlot Cap Company management wants to know the amount of sales dollars needed for each product to accomplish the same five objectives.

- Break even.
- Earn desired net income before taxes of $60,000.
- Earn desired net income after taxes of $36,000. Assume the tax rate is 40%.
- Earn desired net income before taxes equal to 15% of sales dollars.
- Earn a desired net income after taxes equal to 9% of sales dollars.

To find the answers we need to start by calculating the weighted average contribution margin ratio.

$$WCMR = (.25)(.60) + (.375)(.40) = .30$$

The mix ratios stated in dollars are used as the weights.

Then the solutions are obtained as follows:

1. To break even. Using Equation .3S = 300,000
   - S = 300,000 ÷ .3 = $1,000,000

- S1 = (1,000,000)(.6) = $600,000
- S2 = (1,000,000)(.4) = 400,000

2. To earn $60,000 before taxes. Using Equation .3S = 300,000 + 60,000
   - S = 360,000 ÷ .3 = $1,200,000
   - S1 = (1,200,000)(.6) = $720,000
   - S2 = (1,200,000)(.4) = 480,000
3. To earn $36,000 after taxes. Using Equation .3S = 300,000 + (36,000 ÷ .6)
   - S = 360,000 ÷ .3 = $1,200,000
   - S1 = ($1,200,000)(.6) = $720,000
   - S2 = ($1,200,000)(.4) = 480,000
4. To earn desired NIBT of 15% of sales dollars. Using Equation
   - .3S = 300,000 + .15S
   - .15S = 300,000
   - S = 300,000 ÷ .15 = $2,000,000
   - S1 = ($2,000,000)(.6) = $1,200,000
   - S2 = ($2,000,000)(.4) = 800,000
5. To earn desired NIAT of 9% of sales dollars. Using Equation
   - .3S = 300,000 + (.09S ÷.6)
   - .15S = 300,000
   - S = 300,000 ÷.15 = $2,000,000
   - S1 = ($2,000,000)(.6) = $1,200,000
   - S2 = ($2,000,000)(.4) = 800,000

The solutions to these five questions are also illustrated in Figure since we simply changed our emphasis from the horizontal axis (units) to the vertical axis (dollars). The mix ratios determine whether the emphasis is on units or dollars and the manner in which the answers must be obtained. If the mix ratios are stated in units, as in Example 11-4, then the solutions must be obtained in units. If the mix ratios are stated in dollars, as in Example 11-5, then the solutions must be obtained in dollars. Why? To see why we cannot use the mix ratios interchangeably, suppose the Sandlot Cap Company data were stated in the following manner.

Product	**Price**	**Variable Cost per Unit**	**Mix Ratios Based on Sales Dollars**
X1	$4	$3	.6
X2	8	5	.4

Total fixed costs = $300,000. Now, find the break-even point in units. Try this, at least mentally before you look at the solution in the footnote below.[4] Now suppose Sandlot Cap Company management gave you following information and asks for the break-even point. TFC is still $300,000. What would you do?

Product	**Contribution MarginRatios**	**Mix Ratios Based on Units**
X1	.25	.75
X2	.375	.25

Think about it and then consult the footnote below. *The Cash Flow Break-even Point*: Since some of the fixed costs do not require cash payments (e.g., depreciation), the cash flow break-even point will be below the conventional accrual accounting break-even point. The following

Cash Flow Break-even Before Taxes: The cash flow break-even point is where the cash inflows before taxes are equal to the cash outflows before taxes. This is presented in equation form below.

$$PX = TFC + VX - \text{Non cash Fixed Costs}$$

$$PX - VX = TFC - \text{Non cash Fixed Costs}$$

$$(P - V)\,X = TFC - \text{Non cash Fixed Costs}$$

The equation above is based on the assumption that all other costs are paid for during the period and that all sales dollars are collected during the period.

Cash Flow Break-even After Taxes: The cash flow break-even point after taxes is where the cash inflows after taxes are equal to the cash outflows after taxes. We simply convert the contribution margin and total fixed costs to an after tax basis by multiplying by 1-T.

The equation is as follows:

$$(1 - T)(P - V)X = (1\ 2\ T)(TFC) - \text{Non cash Fixed Costs}$$

Example: Cal Company's specifics from Example 11-1 are P = \$10, V = \$6, total fixed costs = \$120,000 and the tax rate is 40%. If depreciation is \$24,000 and there are no other non cash fixed costs, then the cash flow break-even point after taxes is:

$$(1 - .4)(4X) = (1 - .4)(120{,}000) - 24{,}000$$

$$2.4X = 72{,}000 - 24{,}000$$

$$X = 48{,}000 \div 2.4 = 20{,}000 \text{ units}$$

The solution is verified in Figure below.

Income Statement Showing Cal Company's Cash Flow Break-even Point

Sales	
(20,000)(\$10)	\$200,000
Variable Costs (20,000)(\$6)	120,000
Contribution Margin	80,000
Less Total Fixed Costs	120,000
Net Loss	(40,000)
Add Tax Reduction(.4)(40,000)	16,000
Add back Depreciation	24,000
Cash Flow after taxes	0

We can also use the equation above to calculate the number of units needed to generate a desired amount of net cash inflow after taxes. Just add the desired amount and solve for X. For example, suppose management desires a net cash inflow after taxes of \$36,000.

2.4X = 48,000 + 36,000

X = 84,000 ÷ 2.4 = 35,000 units

Check: (35,000units)($4) = 140,000 contribution margin. Subtract fixed cost of $120,000, then multiply by.6 and we have $12,000 NIAT. Add back depreciation of 24,000 to obtain $36,000.

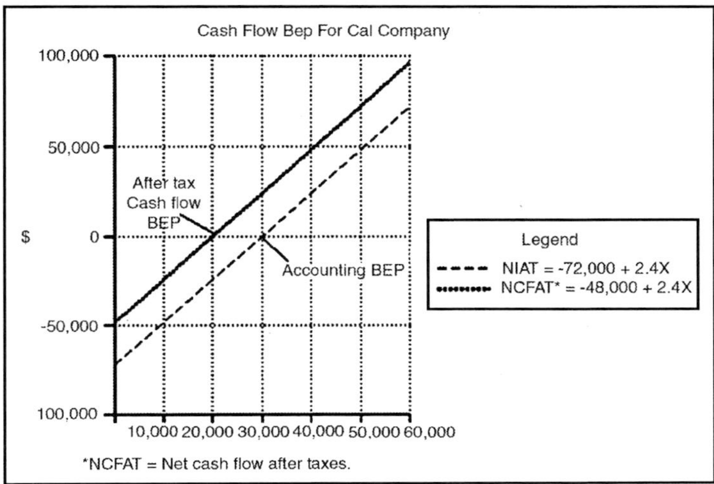

The Controversy Over The Contribution Margin Approach. There are two issues that involve the contribution margin approach and the closely related direct (or variable) costing inventory valuation method. The first issue is a relatively old controversy over whether direct costing or full absorption costing is the most useful way to present accounting information. The second issue questions the compatibility of the contribution margin approach to activity based costing and the lean enterprise concepts of just-in-time and the theory of constraints.

The second issue questions the wisdom of separating costs into fixed and variable categories.[7] The following discussion concentrates on the second controversy. We will return to the first issue in the next chapter.

The Case Against

From the activity based costing perspective, critics of the contribution margin approach argue that the costs traditionally defined as fixed costs have been increasing faster than the costs traditionally defined as variable costs. As a result, the CVP model does not reflect the cost structure of complex, multiproduct organizations.

Although the CVP model may be useful for some short term forecasting and optimization decisions, it is misleading for decisions such as product introduction, product pricing, product mix and make versus buy. The so-called fixed costs are not explained by output volume, but by the diversity and complexity of the company's products, services, customers, distribution channels and product lines. The CVP approach is flawed because it assumes that the volume of production is the only cost driver. As a result, the model motivates managers to produce as much as possible to lower total unit cost. It encourages managers to add new products and services ignoring the "overhead creep" that inevitably results It supports the misguided view that the company should never drop a part of the business as long as that part generates a positive contribution margin.

But this signal to constantly expand is a trap because the costs that are assumed to be constant, increase rapidly instead, in response to the greater demands that are placed on the various support activities. As the so-called fixed costs rise, the manager attempts to add more volume to lower unit cost again. The process is somewhat analogous to a dog chasing it's tail.

From the lean enterprise, or continuous improvement perspective, the contribution margin approach emphasizes maximizing output with a static set of constraints, rather than emphasizing the continuous improvement of the company's value creating processes and activities. The contribution margin approach has the same basic defect as any other constrained optimization technique. It promotes short run optimization within a static system.

However, from the viewpoint of the lean enterprise concepts of just-in-time and the theory of constraints, becoming competitive and maintaining competitiveness in the long run requires a dynamic learning organization. The emphasis should be on relentlessly eliminating waste, removing constraints, re-engineering processes when necessary and increasing customer value, not on maximizing output in an attempt to minimize short run unit costs.

THE CASE FOR

Defenders of the contribution margin approach argue that the concepts of contribution margin and related techniques are useful for short term planning and for performing a variety of special relevant cost studies. Although production volume is not the only cost driver, it is still the major cost driver. Production volume based systems and techniques such as direct costing and CVP analysis still provide reasonably accurate information for a fraction of the cost of elaborate ABC systems. Another advantage of these methods is that income statements based on the contribution margin approach (i.e., direct costing) are much easier for managers to understand than statements based on either traditional full absorption costing or activity based costing.

In addition, direct costing reduces the full cost behavioral bias towards over production by eliminating the production volume variance and the inventory change effect that increases net income when production exceeds sales. The contribution margin approach is neutral, or nearly neutral, because it does not encourage management to produce anything that cannot be sold. The argument that the contribution margin approach promotes overproduction is not warranted. In fact, full absorption costing creates a much stronger motivation to overproduce and ABC is just an expanded form of that same methodology. In addition, CVP analysis does not discourage continuous improvement. It is just a quantitative tool that can be used or misused like any other tool. The CVP approach can complement the plan-do-check-action (PDCA) continuous improvement cycle by providing a way to estimate the financial consequences of proposed changes in the system.

A Possible Reconciliation With Abc

A possible reconciliation between ABC and the contribution margin approach is provided by Robin Cooper's levels of cost variability. The idea is to combine ABC with the contribution margin approach to reveal contributions at the unit, batch, product, distribution and customer levels to review these terms). This expanded information will indicate which products, distribution channels and customers really are profitable and perhaps help avoid the potential trap set by the contribution margin logic that keeps companies from ever dropping anything.

- The economic, or theoretical cost-volume-profit model was developed by a number of theorist between 1800 and 1930. The classical economists (e.g., Adam Smith, David Ricado, Thomas Malthus, Jeremy Bentham and Jean Baptiste Say) believed that the cost of production (supply) determined the market price. The marginalist (e.g., Herman Gossen, William Jevons) believed that demand was the primary determinant of market price. Around 1890, the neoclassical economist, Alfred Marshall argued that the interaction of supply and demand determines the price using his famous scissors analogy (i.e., both supply and demand are needed, just as both blades of a pair of scissors are needed to cut a piece of paper). Later, around 1930, Edward Chamberlin and others developed the theoretical model described in this chapter. Joel Dean presented the linear model as a practical alternative. See Marshall, A. 1890. *Principles of Economics*. The Macmillan Company; Chamberlin, E. H. 1946. *The Theory of Monopolistic Competition*. Harvard University Press; and Dean, J. 1951. *Managerial Economics*: Prentice-Hall, Inc.: 326-347. for some examples of non-production volume related drivers and measurements.
- In the theoretical model, profits are maximized where marginal revenue is equal to marginal cost. Solving for this point requires using calculus. Marginal revenue is the rate of change in total revenue and can be found by taking the first derivative of the total revenue function. Marginal cost is the rate of change in total cost and can be determined by taking the first derivative of the total cost function. Upper level microeconomics textbooks show this in considerable detail using quadratic and cubic equations.

- Although you may be tempted to multiply P-V for each product by the mix ratios to obtain the weighted average contribution margin per unit, that step will produce the wrong answer. Note that (1)(.6) + (3)(.4) = 1.8 and we know from Example 11-4 that W is 1.5 not 1.8. We must solve the problem in dollars first and then convert to units. Therefore, we need to calculate the contribution margin ratios (4-3)÷4 =.25 and (8-5)÷8=.375 and then solve for sales dollars as in Example 11-5, question 1 above. We calculate the weighted average contribution margin ratio, i.e., (.25)(.60) + (.375)(.4) =.30. Then solve for mixed sales dollars at the break-even point, i.e., S= $300,000 ÷.30 = $1,000,000. Find the sales dollars for each product, S1 = (1,000,000)(.6) = $600,000 and S2 = (1,000,000).4) = $400,000. Then we divide by the sales prices to find the break-even point in units, i.e., X1 = $600,000 ÷ $4 = 150,000 caps and X2 = $400,000 ÷ $8 = 50,000 caps.
- Multiplying the contribution margin ratios by the mix ratios and summing the results we get.28125. Comparing this number to W and WCMR (1.50 and.30 from examples 11-4 and 11-5) reveals that.28125 is not a recognizable piece of information. Any attempt to use it will produce the wrong answer. Since there is no way to find the contribution margin per unit for each product, or the mix ratios in dollars, you would need to ask for additional information to answer the question.
- The first issue started back around 1936. See Harris, J. 1936. What did we earn last month? *NACA Bulletin* (January 15): 501-526. Harris used the term direct costing rather than variable costing.
- A long list of references could be provided here, but the edited version of a 1989 panel discussion by Robert Kaplan, John Shank, Charles Horngren and Germain Boer provides the best single reference. See
- This is essentially an argument that any model that recognizes the distinction between fixed and variable costs will create a bias towards overproduction. This is because total unit cost decreases as the average fixed cost per unit decreases when additional units are produced, i.e., unit fixed cost = TFC÷ X.
- The theoretical economic model is also flawed for the same reason. Although changes in productivity are considered in the model, the problem referred to as "overhead creep" is not considered. In other words, in the theoretical model, productivity affects the rate of change in variable costs, but fixed costs remain constant.
- The controversy over the usefulness of constrained optimization techniques is a broader issue since a long list of techniques fall into

this category. The economic order quantity and economic batch size models, linear programming and standard costing provide a few examples.

- See Johnson, H. T. 1989. Professors, customers and value: Bringing a global perspective to management accounting education.*Proceedings* of the Third Annual Management Accounting Symposium.

P/V RATIO ANALYSIS

RATIO ANALYSIS

The Profit Volume (PV) Ratio is the ratio of Contribution over Sales. It measures the Profitability of the firm and is one of the important ratios for computing profitabilty. The Contribution is the extra amount of sales over variable cost. Contribution is also Fixed cost plus profit.

Profit = Sales – Variable Cost – Fixed Cost.

Thus Contribution is:

Profit + Fixed Cost = Sales - Variable Cost.

Therefore PV Ratio = (Contribution/Sales)X100. (This as a percentage of sales) Inventory ratio analysis model is easy to follow financial template to calculate vital Inventory ratios for current year.

***The model includes*:**

- Roll forward Inventory Balance Sheet Schedule;
- 12 mo Cost of Goods Sold;
- 12 mo Inventory additions;
- 12 mo Avg Inventory additions
- 12 mo Avg Net Inventory

INVENTORY TURNOVER RATIO

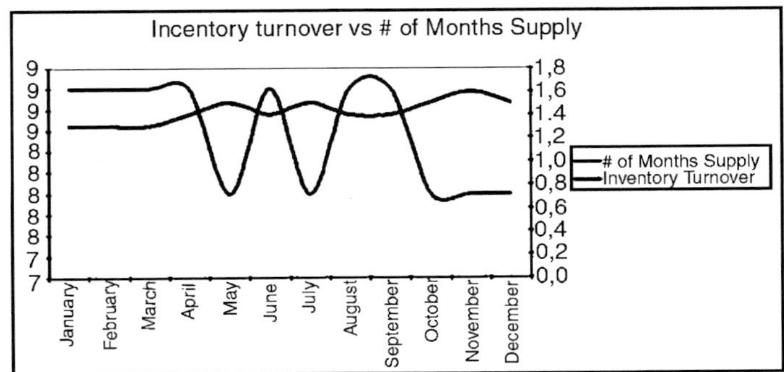

How many times Inventory is over during 12 months period; the ratio is activity ratio that shows company effectiveness in managing its inventory levels; A low turnover ration may indicate overstocking, obsolescence, or low market demand for the product. High turnover ration may indicate inadequate inventory level and potential inability to answer customer depend on time. However, you always need to compare your company Inventory Turnover ration to that of the industry that your company is in.

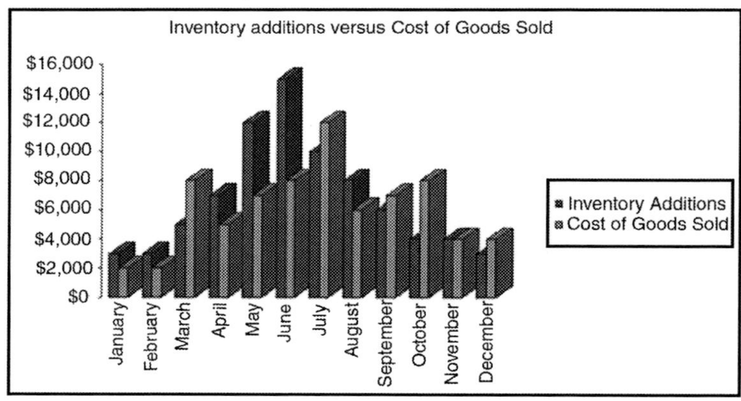

PV LOSS RATIO

This column represents the Present Value of the Loss Ratio to date at the end of the policy year. The definition of the Loss Ratio is controlled by the Loss Ratio Definitionswitch in PRICING ASSUMPTIONS. The rate that is used for the PV calculation is specified in the cell in the Rate for PV of loss ratio field in PRICING ASSUMPTIONS.

All Loss Ratio calculations are done on a Gross basis, i.e. before reinsurance. The PV of the loss ratio is calculated by first determining the PV of the numerator values to date and then dividing by the PV of the denominator values to date. The calculation is demonstrated in the following example:

Example:

Assume:

- Loss Ratio Definition switch is set to (paid claims + change in DLR)/premium
- Rate for PV of loss ratio is set to 6%

Policy Year	Premium	Paid Claim	Increase in DLR	Loss Ratio	PV Loss Ratio
1	435.38	31.750	68.063	22.92517	22.92517
2	368.30	48.363	34.909	22.60974	22.78517
3	323.390	49.362	28.838	24.18139	23.16050

Policy Year 1

PV Loss Ratio = Loss Ratio = (Paid claim + Inc in DLR)/Premium = 22.925%

Policy Year 2

$$\text{PV Loss Ratio} = \frac{\text{(Paid claim Y2/1.06 + Inc in DLR Y2/1.06 + Paid claim Y1 + Inc in DLR Y1)}}{\text{(Prem Y2/1.06 + Prem Y1)}}$$

= (48.363/1.06 + 34.909/1.06 + 31.750 + 68.063)/(368.301/1.06 + 435.388)

=22.785%

IMPLICATION

DEFINITION

In any discipline one seeks to establish facts and to draw conclusions based on observations and theories. One can do so deductively or inductively. In inductive reasoning, one starts with many observations and formulates an explanation that seems to fit.

In deductive reasoning, one starts with premises and, using the rules of logical inference, draws conclusions from them. In disciplines such as mathematics, deductive reasoning is the predominant means of drawing conclusions. In fields such as psychology, inductive reasoning predominates, but once a theory has been formulated, it is both tested and applied through the processes of deductive thinking. It is in this that logic plays a role. Basic to deductive thinking is the word "implies," symbolized by "=>." A statement p⇒q means that whenever p is true, q is true also. For example, if p is the statement, "x is in Illinois," and q is the statement "x is in the United States," then p⇒q is the statement, "If x is in Illinois, then x is in the United States."

In logic as well as in ordinary English, there are many ways of translating p⇒q into words: "If p is true, then q is true" "q is implied by p;" "p is true only if q is true;" "q is a necessary condition for p;" "p is a sufficient condition for q."

The implication p ⇒q has a truth table some find a little perplexing:

p	q	p=>q
T	T	T
T	F	F
F	T	T
F	F	T

The perplexing part occurs in the next to last line where a false value of p seems to imply a true value of q. The fact that p is false does not imply anything at all. The imolication says only that q is true whenever p is. It doesn't say what happens when p is false. In the example given earlier, replacing x with Montreal makes both p and q false, but the implication itself is still true. Implication has two properties which resemble the reflexive and transitive properties of equality. One, p⇒p, is called a "tautology." Tautologies, although widely used, do not add much to understanding. "Why is the water salty?" asks the little boy. The other property, "If p⇒q and q⇒r, then p=>r," is also widely used. In connecting two implications to form a third, it characterizes a lot of reasoning, formal and informal. "If we take our vacation in January, there will be snow. If there is snow, we can go skiing. Let's take it in January." This property is called a "syllogism."

A third property of equality 1 "If a = b, then b = a," called symmetry may or may not be shared by the implication p=>q. When it is, it is symbolized by the twoheaded arrow used earlier, "p q." p q means (p⇒q) Ë (q⇒p). It can be read "p and q are equivalent;" p is true if and only if q is true;" "p implies and is implied by q;" "p is a necessary and sufficient condition for q;" and "p implies q, and conversely."

In p⇒q, p is called the "antecedent" and q the "consequent." If the antecedent and consequent are interchanged, the resulting implication, q⇒p, is called the "converse." If one is talking about triangles, for example, there is a theorem, "If two sides are equal, then the angles opposite the sides are equal." The converse is, "If two angles are equal, then the sides opposite the angles are equal."

If an implication is true, it is never safe to assume that the converse is true as well. For example, "If x lives in Illinois, then x lives in the United States," is a true implication, but its converse is obviously false. In fact, assuming that the converse of an implication is true is a significant source of fallacious reasoning. "If the battery is shot, then the car won't start." True enough, but it is a good idea to check the battery itself instead of assuming the coverse and buying a new one.

Implications are involved in three powerful lines of reasoning. One, known as the Rule of Detachment or by the Latin *modus ponendo ponens,* states simply "If p⇒q and p are both true, then q is true."

This rule shows up in all sorts of areas. "If x dies, then y is to receive $100,000." When x dies and proof is submitted to the insurance company, y gets a check for the money. The statements p⇒q and p are called the "premises" and q the "conclusion." A second rule, known as *modus tollendo tollens,* says if p=>q is true and q is false, then p is false. "If x ate the cake, then x was home." If x was not at home, then someone else ate the cake. A third rule, *modus tollerdo ponens,* says that if p V q and p are true, then q is true.

Mary or Ann broke the pitcher. Ann did not; so Mary did. Of course, the validity of the argument depends upon establishing that both premises are true. It may have been the cat. Another type of argument is known as *reductio ad absurdum,* again from the Latin. Here, if one can show that ~p⇒(q Ë ~q), then p must be true. That is, if assuming the negation of p leads to the absurdity of a statement which is both true and false at the same time, then p itself must be true.

TAX IMPLICATION

The interest of the "Aam Aadmi" was taken care of in the Budget 2010-11. The finance minister in order to provide impetus to consumption has proposed a new personal income tax slab, which will result in higher savings and simulta-neously higher disposable income at the hands of individuals.

Table. Tax Implication for Individual Asessee

Income Slab	Old tax rate	Tax computed	New tax rate	Tax computed	Cumulative benefit
Upto Rs 160000	0%	-	Nil	-	-
Rs 160001-300000	10%	14,000.00	10%	14,000.00	-
Rs 300001-500000	20%	40,000.00	10%	20,000.00	20,000.00
Up to Rs.800000	30%	90,000.00	20%	60,000.00	50,000.00
Above Rs.800000	30%	60,000.00	30%	60,000.00	50,000.00
Total Tax Liability for					
Income upto Rs.10lac	**20%**	**204,000.00**	**15%**	**154,000.00**	**50,000.00**

Table. Tax Implication for Women Asessee v

Income Slab	Old tax rate	Tax computed	New tax rate	Tax computed	Cumulative benefit
Upto Rs 190000	0%	-	Nil	-	-
Rs 190001-300000	10%	11,000.00	10%	11,000.00	-
Rs 300001-500000	20%	40,000.00	10%	20,000.00	20,000.00
Up to Rs.800000	30%	90,000.00	20%	60,000.00	50,000.00
Above Rs.800000	30%	60,000.00	30%	60,000.00	50,000.00
Total Tax Liability for					
Income upto Rs.10lac	**20%**	**201,000.00**	**15%**	**151,000.00**	**50,000.00**

Table:Tax implication for Senior Citizen

Income Slab	Old tax rate	Tax computed	New tax rate	Tax computed	Cumulative benefit
Upto Rs 240000	0%	-	Nil	-	-
Rs 240001-300000	10%	6,000.00	10%	6,000.00	-
Rs 300001-500000	20%	40,000.00	10%	20,000.00	20,000.00
Up to Rs.800000	30%	90,000.00	20%	60,000.00	50,000.00
Above Rs.800000	30%	60,000.00	30%	60,000.00	50,000.00
Total Tax Liability for					
Income upto Rs.10lac	**20%**	**196,000.00**	**15%**	**151,000.00**	**50,000.00**

This we believe will help boosting consumption and will be beneficiary for Auto's, FMCG, Consumer Durables, Hotels & Hospitality

CONCEPT AND USES OF CONTRIBUTION

CONCEPT

The concept of the group contribution using Kihara intermolecular potentials with a spherical core is extended to perfluorinated *n*-alkanes (n = 1–6). The effective Kihara parameters for groups (CF_2, CF_3, CF_4) are estimated by fitting second virial coefficient B and dilute gas viscosity ç together. The assumption of regarding CF_4 molecule as a single group is preferable to other two approaches based on the principle of group additivity: a combination of F–(CF_3) and CF_3–(F) groups; a single C–$(F)_4$ group and four F–(C) groups.

Application of the model shows that second virial coefficients are represented with better results than those of the Tsonopoulos correlation, and are comparable to the correlation of Dymond's group and the Hohm correlation. Feasibility of the present method to calculate dilute gas viscosities is proved by comparison with the Lucas method, the Hohm correlation, the correlation of Yaws, and the Simsci Data Bank.

Mixture property calculations of the model are enhanced by including binary group interaction coefficients $k_{ij,gc}$, determined from second cross virial coefficient data, and are more reliable than other correlations for second cross virial coefficients and mixture viscosities. Prediction results of binary diffusion coefficients, not supplied to the parameter evaluations, are in significant agreement with experimental data and are compared well with values obtained by means of the Fuller method. Results studied here would be of use when extended to halogenated paraffins and their mixtures.

The methods based on the Group Contribution Concept usually fail when one attempts to estimate the physico-chemical properties of different branched isomers of a given compound. We present a new concept, the Group-Interaction Contribution Approach (GIC) which considers the contribution of the different interactions between groups present in a molecule instead of the contribution of structural groups. This approach allows differentiation between branched isomers, thus leading to different values of the physico-chemical properties. The GIC Approach can be easily implemented in current correlations based on the group contribution concept.

The estimates of enthalpy of formation, normal boiling temperature and critical temperature of a series of 51 saturated hydrocarbons showed clearly that the GIC concept leads to very good estimations for branched isomers. Earlier this year, I spent an intense half-day closeted in a room with the top 70 executives at Intuit. Our aim was to come up with ways that people outside the company could volunteer their time, energy, and expertise to make life better for our customers.

Sound odd? Well, if you're not conducting an exercise like that at your organization, you risk missing the boat on a sea change that's transforming business. Every day, millions of people make all kinds of vountary contributionsto companies–from informed opinions to computing resources – that create tremendous value for those firms' customers and, consequently, for their shareholders. When I first encountered this idea, several years ago, it struck me as unfathomable: Volunteerism was for charities, not for red-blooded, profit-making firms.

That was just my first surprise. I also began to see that user contributions are fueling some of the world's fastest-growing and most competitively advantaged organizations – in some cases revolutionizing the economics of entire industries by radically shrinking their cost structures. Think of eBay, which opened as an online store with no inventory, leaving it up to customers to fill its "shelves" with goods to sell. Or Wikipedia, which gutted the value proposition of 230-year old *Encyclopaedia Britannica* by offering a free encyclopedia written and updated frequently by unpaid amateurs.

In other cases, the contribution is not as obvious but just as central to the value proposition. Skype incursalmost no capital costs because its internet-based phone system is built on the unused processing capacity of its customers' personal computers.

Google, too, is built on user contributions: Its search engine relies on thealgorithmic aggregation of links created by others between websites, and its ad placement system relies ondata from people's click behaviour. OK, I'm not saying you can or should transform your company into a Google or a Skype whose business model is primarily based on user contributions.

But you should understand the power of the phenomenon and, as I have, learn from the growing number of companies in traditional industries – firms like Honda, Procter & Gamble, Best Buy, and Hyatt – that are tapping user contributions to improve products, better serve customers, generate new business, reduce costs, boost employee performance, and more. Contribution-driven results like those are achievable for pretty much any business.

The concept of user contribution isn't new. But the companies I've just mentioned – both the internet highfliers and the old-economy behemoths – have actively created something I call a *user contribution system*. That is, they've created methods for aggregating and leveraging people's contributions or behaviors in ways that are useful to other people.

The *users* can be customers, employees, sales prospects – or even people with no previous connection to the company. Their *contributions* can be active (work, expertise, or information) or passive and even unknowing (behavioral data that is gathered automatically during a transaction or an activity). The *system* is the method, usually internet-based, by which contributions are aggregated and automatically converted into something useful to others.

Although the company retains control of the system and may choose to modify its design, the system converts inputs into useful outputs in real time with little or no intervention by the company. Such a system creates value for a business as a consequence of the value it delivers to users – personalized purchase recommendations, connections between buyers and sellers of hard-to-find items, new personal or business relationships, lower prices, membership in a community, entertainment, information of all kinds.

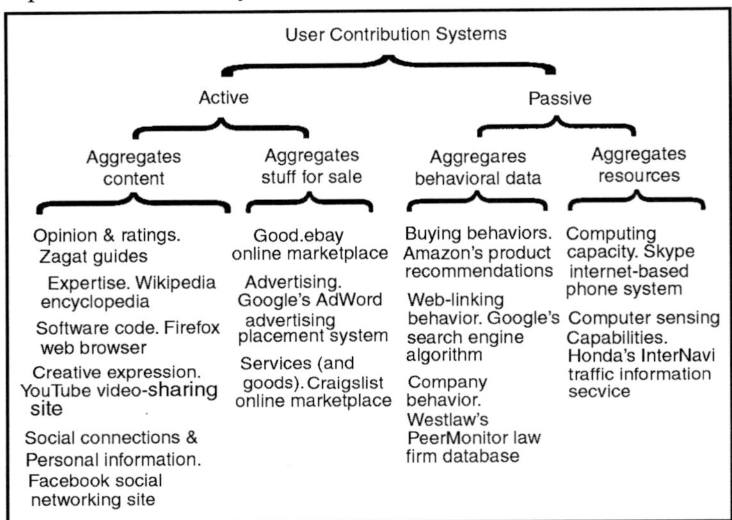

The challenge for executives is twofold. First, you must learn how to spot opportunities for creating value from user contributions. Second – and here's the difficult part – in acting on these opportunities, you must overcome natural organizational resistance to the idea of relinquishing significant control to people outside the company. The advice I offer here is based on my personal experience at Intuit – the successes and failures, the moments of exhilaration and the times when I had to conquer my own fear of putting so much power in the hands of users.

REVOLUTIONARY POTENTIAL

Though I didn't know it at the time, my interest in user contribution systems began in the early 1990s with a series of slim red books. The Zagat guides offered reviews with quantitative ratings based on sustained performance rather than on a single visit or two by one reviewer. And those recommendations originated not with paid experts but with regular diners like me. It was a decade, though, before I recognized the significance of the method to my own company. That "aha" came from watching the winners on the web.

The success of the leading internet firms has admittedly been touted ad nauseam by the media and business experts. Yet for better and for worse, the internet is a reflection of society and the preferences of hundreds of millions of people around the world. Like book best-seller lists, rankings of the most popular websites reflect what's winning the battle for people's attention. The companies joining the list of most popular websites in recent years include Wikipedia, YouTube, Facebook, Craigslist, and MySpace.

They have joined such older sites as Amazon, eBay, and Google. At first glance, these sites seem to have little in common, targeting unrelated areas of human endeavor: the cataloguing of information, video entertainment, social interaction, classified advertising, retail shopping, internet search. Some of the sites charge users; others are free. One's a nonprofit; another has one of the highest profit marginsamong public companies. Despite their differences, all these winning sites rely on – or are themselves – user contribution systems. Much of their success flows from inherent characteristics of contribution systems that create advantages, detailed here, of a magnitude rarely known in traditional business.

WHY CONTRIBUTORS CONTRIBUTE

Most contribution systems offer no financial compensation to contributors. In fact, payment can destroy participation by undermining a sense of collaboration and trust. Rather, they rely on motivations intrinsic to humanity – or involve contributions that require no motivation at all, because the user contributes without realizing it.

Contributing

Some systems collect participants' resources or data as a by-product of things people are doing for other purposes. As shoppers buy from Amazon, they automatically contribute toits recommendation engine, which suggests products based on the ratings and purchase decisions of other customers.

Practical Solutions

In some systems, participants contribute in order to get reasonably immediate rewards. For example, the site del.icio.usenables users to organize their bookmarks of websites. A byproduct of this activity is that, when aggregated, the bookmarks produce an index to the web that is valuable to others.

Social Reward

Many systems provide the benefits of interaction with others: being part of a community with a common interest, generating business prospects, getting a date – the drivers behind social networks like Facebook and LinkedIn.

Reputation

Contribution can be sparked by a desire for public recognition, like Amazon's badge for a "top 1,000 reviewer," or for the admiration of peers: Wikipedia articles carry no authorship credit, yet authors earn the respect of other contributors.

Altruism

Why would a person write a glowing online review of a restaurant – when it may become harder to get a table if others act on the opinion? Some people want to help local diners or reward superb restaurant owners. Others simply want the truth to be heard.

Cost Advantage

What does Wikipedia pay the authors and editors of its articles? What does Facebook or MySpace pay those who painstakingly fill in and update the personal profiles that make the site so valuable? Nothing. These sites enjoy free "raw materials," as users perform gratis work that companies typically have to pay for. People contribute for various reasons, some of them self-serving but all of them sufficient to make formal payment unnecessary.

Scalability Advantage

Craigslist's free classified advertising sites feature more than 30 million new offerings every month, and eBay's virtual shelves feature 120 million items, many times more than any other store on the planet can offer. Such scale doesn't require broad or deep contribution: Only a small percentage of users may contribute (about one user in 1,000 for Wikipedia) and active contributions may require little effort (as with Flickr, the photo-sharing site).

Competitive Advantage

Some contribution systems give companies a structural advantage over rivals because of network effects. That is, the more people who contribute to the system, the more useful it becomes, creating an upward spiral in which increasingly more people choose to use and contribute to it. Network effectsonce drove the winner-take-all market-share gains of Microsoft's Windows; today, they propel the success of sites like Wikipedia and Facebook.

Contribution systems won't displace most traditional products or businesses: I'm not expecting Wiki-Milk to displace real milk or the dairy industry. Still, given the power of user contributions, too many business leaders are failing to look for opportunities to leverage these systems in their industries. I think that's partly because of the novelty of the phenomenon, but it's also because of beliefs rooted in the past. All too often, executives mistakenly view user contribution as:

THREAT TO PROFIT BUSINESSES

But consider Schibsted, a 170-year-old Norwegian newspaper publisher that, instead of ignoring the online threat savaging much of the newspaper industry, started reinventing itself in the mid-1990s by embracing user contribution and becoming a leading European provider of online classified advertising.

Only for Tech Companies

But consider the Canadian grocery store chain Loblaws, which solicits online customer reviews and incorporates them in the marketing of new products.

Unreliable and Error-ridden

But consider the study in Nature that found volunteer-written Wikipedia to be, in general, about as accurate as expert-written articles in Encyclopaedia Britannica's online edition.

Lacking a Strong Business Case or Profit

But consider LinkedIn, whose social networking site for businesspeople now profits from numerous revenue streams: traditional ones, such as site advertising, upgrades to premium membership with more features, and paid job postings, along with more novel ones, such as tools that corporate HR departments can use to screen job candidates.

CONTRIBUTION

Even without knowing your business, I'd be willing to bet that contribution systems can address one or more of the business challenges you face better than the methods you currently use. To spur your thinking, let's look at some of the different ways that traditional companies are employing user contribution systems in a wide variety of business activities and functions.

Customer Service

Company-hosted online support forums, in which product users answer questions from other users free of charge, are commonplace among software and personal computer companies. I admit my initial surprise when I experienced firsthand how a user community can answer tough questions that even the manufacturer cannot. Now non-computer firms, such as AT&T, are beginning to follow this practice.

Troubleshooting is just one way to harness user contributions for service. Hyatt Hotels and Resorts has launched an online concierge service called Yatt'it that aggregates and lets users rate travel tips posted by Hyatt's customers and concierges. The aim is both to reduce the burden on concierges and to give travelers tailored, extensive city information in advance of their trip – and, if they've already arrived, without their having to wait in line.

Companies also use contribution systems to serve customers in ways that create a brand-new business. Westlaw, the legal research service, created a B2B contribution system that helps its customer base of law firms address important strategic issues. West PeerMonitor automatically aggregates anonymized financial and operating information from participating law firms.

The firms access the database to see how their performance compares with that of peers and how other markets compare with their own – data that may help a firm decide, for example, whether to expand geographically or whether a key practice area is operating efficiently. This customer service is valued so much that Westlaw charges handsomely for it.

Marketing

The power of contribution systems is now being tapped by traditional marketing powerhouses, including two of the giants: Procter & Gamble and Unilever. Procter & Gamble has created a website, BeingGirl, aimed at teen and preteen girls – a difficult group to reach in the marketing of its feminine-hygiene products because young girls are often uncomfortable viewing TV ads on the topic in the company of friends or family. The site originally consisted solely of information from experts.

But in 2005, P&G borrowed the contribution concept from tech websites, adding forums where girls could interact with one another. Now users can share their questions and personal experiences and get support and advice from other girls. This creation of a community around an important topic promotes engagement with the site – and with the Always and Tampax brands that it discreetly promotes. P&G says that as a marketing tool BeingGirl is now four times as effective as comparably priced television advertising.

The website In the Motherhood, cosponsored by Sprint and by Unilever's Suave line of personal-care products, also offers a community forum where users can share stories and offer tips – in this case on the subject of being a mom. In addition, mothers can submit stories (3,000 of them so far) that serve as potential plotlines for an online comedy series.

The community votes on the submissions, and those selected by the users are produced by professional directors and actors and subsequently posted to the site. (Several dozen have been produced so far, and cumulative views have passed the 20 million mark — it has been picked up for television by ABC.) Unilever research finds that the site increases users' intent to purchase a Suave product and engenders a feeling in customers that the makers of Suave really understand their lives.

Employee Support

Most company intranet sites are oneway streets, with management broadcasting the "company line" to employees. Best Buy, the U.S. retail chain, uses the opposite approach in a contribution system dubbed BlueShirt Nation. BlueShirt Nation allows employees to share and discuss their ideas and experiences: what works and what doesn't in carrying out a particular task or in interacting with customers, for example. The site, launched two years ago by two junior employees with no corporate IT support or funding, today has more than 20,000 registered employee users.

Best Buy has discovered that unfiltered information from colleagues can be more effective than memos from HR. For example, Blue Shirt Nation ran a contest in which employees submitted videos they had conceived and produced, with no company oversight, to spur employee adoption of 401(k) plans. The result of the buzz generated by the contest? A 30% increase in plan enrollment.

Capital Resources

Build a global telecommunications system with almost no capital equipment? Make free, high quality video calls anywhere in the world? Both once were unfathomable. But that's what Skype has done, thanks to a contribution system. Founded by Swedes and engineered in Estonia, Skype is the marquee example of how a company can reduce the cost of capital equipment to almost nothing by having users contribute the capital goods.

Skype's free software utilizes idle computing power on users' PCs to manage the calls – as many as 12 million simultaneously – for its 300 million customers. Its costs are so low that the company, which was acquired by eBay in 2006, can deliver high-quality voice and video computer-to-computer calls between subscribers at no charge. And it's profitable: revenue comes from calls made by Skype users to mobile phones and landlines, as well as from services such as voice mail.

Traditional companies, too, get customers to contribute needed capital. In Japan, Honda captures real-time traffic data from GPS systems that Honda owners buy from the company. Speed and location reports from each vehicle contribute to a data stream that Honda aggregates with other traffic data to provide information on traffic jams and other conditions to Honda drivers who subscribe to the company's InterNavi service. Users benefit from enhanced traffic updates; the company can offer a superior subscription service without having to pay for the capital infrastructure.

And there's more: Honda drivers also contribute reviews of local businesses and points of interest that other drivers can read from their InterNavi-equipped Hondas – an automotive version of a Zagat guide. Honda's system thus combines three user contributions – capital equipment, data about user location and vehicle speed, and reviews.

Design and Development

User contribution can tackle creative challenges from the technical to the artistic. The emblematic example of contribution in R&D is open source software, such as the Linux operating system and the Mozilla Foundation'sFirefox web browser, which is created and regularly upgraded by communities of unpaid volunteer developers. (This low-cost model makes Mozilla one of the rare nonprofits that is highly "profitable.")

In the creative arts, Thread less, a company that manufactures T-shirts, relies on a community of volunteer designers and artists to submit designs and a community of customers to select those that will go into production. Both of the user groups, as well as the company, benefit. The designers get free exposure for their work and a chance at monetary compensation: They receive $2,500 plus a percentage of sales if their design is chosen by Threadless customers.

Note that the Threadless user contribution system is subtly different from customer innovation approaches likecrowdsourcing, which are used with success by Dell, Starbucks, and other companies. Crowdsourcing is not a user contribution system in the pure sense, because the company stands between the input and the output. For example, it sifts through people's ideas for new products and services, selects ones to pursue, and then invests the time and expense needed to develop them.

Production

In some cases, organizations can "delegate" some or all of the production process to users. Wikipedia delegates all of it. The producers of Fox Television's American Idol delegate part of the process. The show relies on users (through their votes for performers) to make decisions traditionally reserved for television producers; it relies on amateur performers to offer entertainment usually provided by high-priced stars. The contributing singers benefit from a shot at stardom. Viewers, who contribute their opinions, benefit from compelling entertainment (if the show's high ratings are any indication) and a strong sense of engagement because their votes determine the show's content. Fox and its producers benefit from lower costs and fromadvertising revenue driven by the show's tremendous popularity – which results, in part, from the drama generated by the show's user-contributed surprises.

INTUIT AND USER CONTRIBUTION SYSTEMS

As a member of the boards of eBay and Amazon in the late 1990s, I was exposed to user contribution through the work of Jeff Bezos, Pierre Omidyar, and Meg Whitman. But the concept seemed rare and specialized, so I missed seeing its broader application and value. (I once told Jeff Bezos I thought his plan to supplement professional book reviews on Amazon with reviews written by anyone who felt like it was crazy:

Early success

At our annual off-site in 2005, I put this question to the company's top 300 executives: How might we leverage user contribution at Intuit, both to enhance existing businesses and to create new ones? Two executives in our Plano, Texas, division began to think about how to solve a common problem faced by professional tax preparers – getting answers to obscure questions. The result was a quickly cobbled-together wiki/forum site where tax preparers could contribute both questions and answers for the benefit of other tax preparers. Just 33 days after the executive off-site, TaxAlmanac was launched. Today, it has 170,000 pages, drawing on the collective expertise of thousands of tax professionals, and is used by 400,000 unique visitors – about equal to the number of tax preparers in the country. Tax preparers benefit from expertise that's free. Intuit benefits when visitors then buy our tax prep software – customer acquisition at almost zero cost. However, despite my evangelizing, the idea of contribution systems wasn't taking off elsewhere within the organization. TaxAlmanac was a small island in a sea of indifference.

A Major Setback

I then resurrected an idea that had been proposed several years before by an Intuit engineer: a website with user-generated reviews of local businesses to help folks find a good plumber, car dealer, or restaurant, linked to our Quicken financial software products. It seemed like a sure bet, so we put a big team on it, we launched Zipingo. But the site failed to attract a critical mass of users, and we shuttered it in August 2007. What went wrong? We made mistakes that stemmed from the difference between traditional products and contribution systems. User contribution is first of all about the users and their content. We failed to nurture and encourage early contributors, and we got distracted creating our own content – ancillary information like business addresses for the listings. Zipingo's failure hurt. I stopped pushing big team efforts to develop new contribution systems at Intuit. But even as I pulled back, small contribution-system projects started sprouting up

Gaining Traction

One of our engineering leaders conceived the idea of embedding a Q&A community into a product itself – that is, creating a user forum on every page of TurboTax, with questions and answers relevant to the topic of the particular page. Many were wary of the idea, and some were even hostile. I encouraged the group's efforts, but in an echo of my own skepticism about Amazon's user reviews years earlier, I wondered silently whether people striving to finish their own taxes would stop to answer some stranger's questions.

Working with the support of his division manager, the engineer's team of three built the system and tested it in the least popular version of TurboTax Online in January 2007. Just five weeks into the initial test, one-third of the questions posed already had answers. Crucially, our internal tax experts were pleased by the quality of the answers, which seemed to be self-correcting as other users refined them. TurboTax Live Community, as it's called, was the kind of clear success I'd been seeking. Live Community systems have spread to our other divisions and are inspiring more contribution experiments.

Yet wariness persists. This year, when the TurboTax marketing team decided to solicit and post all user reviews, unedited, on a prominent link from the product's home page, I blanched and took a deep breath. Again a surprise: The vast bulk of reviews are so positive that it looks as if we've posted only the good ones (which, I hasten to add, is not the case). Once again, we're learning from that most reliable of sources – our customers.

COMPANY WITH UCS

User contribution seems messy and scary; giving customers a public podium to comment freely about your products and company seems to violate the management canon "Don't hold me accountable for what I don't control." Naturally, adopting these methods is easier when competitors have beaten you to the punch and shown you where user contribution works in your industry. But what if you want to lead your rivals? Here's my advice for senior managers trying to create contribution systems in their companies.

Use Personal Experience to Move Mind-set

I've found that heads and hearts don't change until people participate in contribution systems themselves. To overcome wariness in inexperienced executives, ask enthusiasts to share stories of their personal experience with user contribution systems. To build awareness, have people count the user contribution systems found on an Amazon page and classify them by type. (If you look hard, you'll find 23 separate systems on a single Amazon product page.) Ask inexperienced executives to find and use contribution systems of personal interest to them – that helps develop a visceral feeling for how they work. Get sub-teams of leaders to brainstorm about contribution systems that might solve customer or employee problems and then ask them to sketch out prototypes they can present to a larger group.

Nurture Small Experiments

Encourage unofficial and "guerrilla" experiments. Challenge employees to create contribution systems that they are passionate about, without requiring them to get clearance from management. Experiment with small batches of employees or customers. (At Intuit, we tried one experiment on the TurboTax version that has the smallest sales volume, accounting for less than 1% of customers for that product.) Most of the experiments will fail; tell the organization in advance that this is OK. Communicate the value of the lessons learned from those failed experiments so that other teams benefit.

Ideas and Leadership

Expect ideas for contribution systems to emerge from those who use them the most. Often, these will be your youngest employees. Seek them out. Make them your mentors. Ask them to take the lead in creating ways for your company and customers to benefit from user contributions. Have them develop prototypes and show them directly to you; then help them act on some of the ideas that emerge.

Set Boundaries

I'm not advocating that you blow up your current business and completely reinvent it around a contribution system. Experiment at the edges of your business. Give experimenters a defined sandbox – spacious, perhaps, but defined – rather than an endless expanse of beach. Within those limits, though, make sure they aren't distracted by experts and that their experiments aren't smothered by larger initiatives with broader mandates.

Protect Experiments

Ceding some control of business processes to outsiders, even in a sandbox, will be scary for your organization. Leaders in certain functional areas – marketers and lawyers, for example – will feel especially anxious. (I can identify, having had to swallow hard a few times over things we were about to try at Intuit.) To counter the instinct to preserve control and the status quo, name a godfather or godmother with big-time clout to protect experiments and break through barriers when initiatives meet organizational resistance. (Three people, two division general managers and I, played this role in our early experiments at Intuit.)

Customer Base

Some new contribution systems face a chicken-or-egg problem – that is, they're empty and useless until folks begin contributing to them, but few visitors will be attracted to something that is empty and useless. Your company probably has advantages that start-ups can only dream of: existing customers, traffic to your website, accumulated behavioral data, and, sometimes, media that will find your experiments newsworthy.

Let users "vote," Early and Often

Customers are better than executives at picking winners in this arena, so get experiments into the hands of real customers as quickly as possible. Minimize or eliminate time lost to market research, lengthy analysis, PowerPoint presentations, or frequent reviews by management.(We've borrowed an idea from Google by creating a public webpage – intuitlabs.com – that displays our current experiments and gives experimenters a fast, direct path to customers, bypassing normal product-launch procedures.)

Seek Organizational

The guerrilla experiments are designed to get around organizational resistance. Ultimately, you want innovation in user contribution to become embedded in the organization's normal processes, but you'll most likely struggle to shift mindset until you can point to a successful experiment or two. The meeting earlier this year of Intuit's top executives to spur action on user contribution systems would have been a wasted effort two years ago.

Then, we had only begun to experiment. But with several successful initiatives now in operation, Intuit's newly promoted CEO, Brad Smith, and I felt the time was right to move the idea into the mainstream and talk about why user contribution is a focus of our evolving company strategy. I can't say everyone at that meeting bought into the concept. Some undoubtedly saw it as a distraction from their day jobs.

Still, there was real energy in the room that day. In the middle of the meeting, I stopped to ask whether folks had questions. Rather than answer them myself, I wrote the questions on the board and asked the entire group to tackle them. As I watched, people provided answers, better than the ones I would have given. (In fact, some of them became content for this article.) As we moved to take a break, I reminded our executives that we all had just experienced user contribution in action.

BREAK EVEN ANALYSIS

INTRODUCTION

Break-even analysis is a technique widely used by production management and management accountants. It is based on categorising production costs between those which are "variable" (costs that change when the production output changes) and those that are "fixed" (costs not directly related to the volume of production). Total variable and fixed costs are compared with sales revenue in order to determine the level of sales volume, sales value or production at which the business makes neither a profit nor a loss (the "break-even point").

THE BREAK-EVEN CHART

In its simplest form, the break-even chart is a graphical representation of costs at various levels of activity shown on the same chart as the variation of income (or sales, revenue) with the same variation in activity. The point at which neither profit nor loss is made is known as the "break-even point" and is represented on the chart below by the intersection of the two lines:

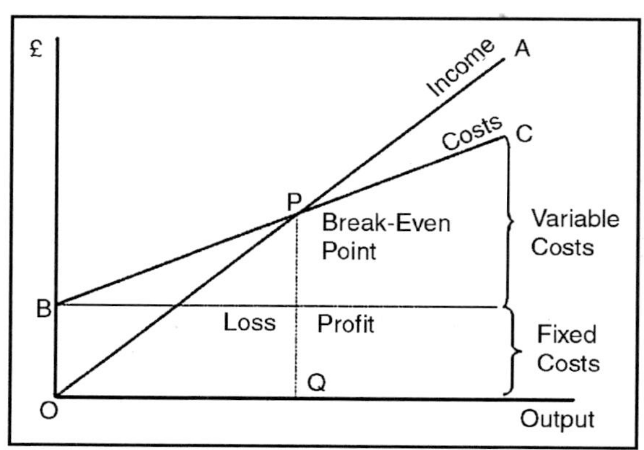

In the diagram above, the line OA represents the variation of income at varying levels of production activity ("output"). OB represents the total fixed costs in the business. As output increases, variable costs are incurred, meaning that total costs (fixed + variable) also increase. At low levels of output, Costs are greater than Income. At the point of intersection, P, costs are exactly equal to income, and hence neither profit nor loss is made.

FIXED COSTS

Fixed costs are those business costs that are not directly related to the level of production or output. In other words, even if the business has a zero output or high output, the level of fixed costs will remain broadly the same. In the long term fixed costs can alter - perhaps as a result of investment in production capacity (e.g. adding a new factory unit) or through the growth in overheads required to support a larger, more complex business.

Examples of fixed costs

- Rent and rates
- Depreciation
- Research and development
- Marketing costs (non- revenue related)
- Administration costs

Variable Costs

Variable costs are those costs which vary directly with the level of output. They represent payment output-related inputs such as raw materials, direct labour, fuel and revenue-related costs such as commission. A distinction is often made between "Direct" variable costs and "Indirect" variable costs. Direct variable costs are those which can be directly attributable to the production of a particular product or service and allocated to a particular cost centre. Raw materials and the wages those working on the production line are good examples. Indirect variable costs cannot be directly attributable to production but they do vary with output. These include depreciation (where it is calculated related to output - e.g. machine hours), maintenance and certain labour costs.

SEMI-VARIABLE COSTS

Whilst the distinction between fixed and variable costs is a convenient way of categorising business costs, in reality there are some costs which are fixed in nature but which increase when output reaches certain levels. These are largely related to the overall "scale" and/or complexity of the business. For example, when a business has relatively low levels of output or sales, it may not require costs associated with functions such as human resource management or a fully-resourced finance department. However, as the scale of the business grows (e.g. output, number people employed, number and complexity of transactions) then more resources are required. If production rises suddenly then some short-term increase in warehousing and/or transport may be required. In these circumstances, we say that part of the cost is variable and part fixed.

TYPES OF DECISION-MAKING

IRREVERSIBLE

This are those type of decisions, which, if made once cannot be unmade. Whatever is decided would than have its repercussions for a long time to come. It commits one irrevocably when there is no other satisfactory option to the chosen course. A manager should never use it as an all-or-nothing instant escape from general indecision.

REVERSIBLE

This are the decisions that can be changed completely, either before, during or after the agreed action begins. Such types of decisions allows one to acknowledge a mistake early in the process rather than perpetuate it. It can be effectively used for changing circumstances where reversal is necessary.

EXPERIMENTAL

This types of decisions are not final until the first results appear and prove themselves to be satisfactory. It requires positive feedback before one can decide on a course of action. It is useful and effective when correct move is unclear but there is a clearity regarding general direction of action.

TRIAL AND ERROR

In this type of decisions, knowledge is derived out of past mistakes. A certain course of action is selected and is tried out, if the results are positive, the action is carried further, if the results appear negative, another course is adopted and so on and so forth a trial is made and an error is occurred. Till the night combination this continues. It allows the manager to adopt and adjust plans continuously before the full and final commitment. It uses both, the positive and negative feedback before selecting one particular course of action.

MADE IN STAGES

Here the decisions are made in steps until the whole action is completed. It allows close monitoring of risks as one accumulates the evidence of outcomes and obstacles at every stage. It permits feedback and further discussion before the next stage of the decision is made.

CAUTIOUS

It allows time for contingencies and problems that may crop up later at the time of implementation. The decision-makers hedge their best of efforts to adopt the night course. It helps to limit the risks that are inherent to decision-making. Although this may also limit the final gains. It allows one to scale down those projects which look too risky in the first instance.

CONDITIONAL

Such types of decisions can be altered if certain foreseen circumstances arise. It is an 'either/or' kind of decision with all options kept open. It prepares one to react if the competition makes a new move or if the game plan changes radically. It enables one to react quickly to the ever changing circumstances of competitive markets.

DELAYED

Such decisions are put on hold till the decision–makers feel that the time is right. A go-ahead is given only when required elements are in place. It prevents one from making a decision at the wrong time or before all the facts are known. It may, at times result into forgoing of opportunities in the market that needs fast action.

BEING DECISIVE

The ability to take timely, clear and firm decisions is an essential quality of leadership, but the type of decision needed varies according to the circumstances. Learning to recognize the implications of taking each type of different decisions leads to error minimisation.

BEING POSITIVE

Taking decisive action does not mean making decisions on the spur of the moment. Although, it may be necessary in emergencies and also occasionally desirable for other reasons. A true leader approaches the decisions confidently, being aware of what must be taken into account and fully in command of the decision–making process.

MAKING FAST DECISIONS

It is important to be able to assess whether a decision needs to be made quickly or it can wait. Good decision-makers often do make instant decisions – but they then assess the long-term implications.

IDENTIFYING ISSUES

It is crucial to diagnose problems correctly. Before any decision is made identifying and defining the issue removes the criticality. This also means deciding who else needs to be involved in the issue, and analyzing what their involvement means.

PRIORITIZING FACTORS

While making a decision, a manager needs to prioritize on important factors. Some factors in a process are more important than others. The use of

Pareto's rule of Vital few and trivial many helps in setting up of the priorities. Giving every factor affecting a decision equal weight makes sense only if every factor is equally important, the Pareto rule concentrates on the significant 20 per cent and gives the less important 80 per cent lower priority.

USING ADVISERS

It is advisable to involve as many people as are needed in making a decision. In making collective decisions, specific expertise as well as experience of a person both can be used simultaneously. The decision-maker, having weighed the advice of experts and experienced hands, must then use authority to ensure that the final decision is seen through.

VETTING DECISIONS

If one does not have the full autonomy to proceed, it is advisable to consult the relevant authority – not just for the final go, but also for the input. It is always in the interest of the subordinate to have the plans vetted by a senior colleague whose judgment is trusted and is experienced. Even if there is no need to get the decision sanctioned, the top people are likely to lend their cooperation well if they have been kept fully informed all the way along the decision path.

SINGLE-PRODUCT PRICING

DEFINITION

Present a robust optimization approach to the problem of pricing a capacitated product over a finite time horizon in the presence of demand uncertainty. This technique does not require the knowledge of the underlying probability distributions, which in practice are difficult to estimate accurately, and instead models random variables as uncertain parameters belonging to a polyhedral uncertainty set.

A novelty of the proposed approach is that, instead of imposing an upper bound on the number of uncertain parameters that can reach their worst-case value, which is known as a budget-of-uncertainty constraint and has received much attention in the robust optimization literature, we introduce a budget of resource consumption by the uncertainty.

This budget limits the amount of the resource that can be used by the random part of the cumulative demand, and allows us to derive key insights on the structure of the optimal solution for a broad class of nominal demand functions. We establish the existence of a reference price for the product and show that this new parameter plays a crucial role in understanding the impact of uncertainty on the optimal prices.

In particular, it is not always optimal to decrease prices when demand is uncertain. Whether it is optimal or not will instead depend on whether the price at a given time period is above or below the reference price, and whether the maximal amount of uncertainty at that time exceeds a threshold. We compare the optimal solution in the cases of additive and multiplicative uncertainty and analyse the problem with linear nominal demand in detail. Numerical results are encouraging.

MULTI PRODUCT PRICING

INVESTIGATION

This dissertation investigates a number of related topics in dynamic multiproduct pricing arising in a competitive setting in markets with memory-sensitive consumers. The first problem is concerned with simultaneous pricing of a line of several products, both complementary products and substitutes, with a number of distinct price differentiation classes for each product.

A game-theoretic problem extension where the product line demand is sensitive to prices of outside competitors' products is also considered. The second problem features a number of firms simultaneously competing in price and inventory level decisions, and considers the effect of excess demand, where the firm faces part of the demand its competitors could not satisfy because of stockout.

An iterative relaxation algorithm is proposed to solve the problems stated, and sufficient conditions for convergence of the algorithm are proven. Extensive computational examples and a case study are included to illustrate solutions' practical applications. The third problem is concerned with profit-maximizing product innovation and pricing for firms that produce and sell short life-cycle products in a competitive environment. We incorporate the effects reference innovation level and reference price have on profits, and model consumers in the market with two attributes: their sensitivity to product innovation levels and their sensitivity to product prices.

We characterize both open-loop and closed-loop Nash equilibria for competition among firms that execute different types of product innovation and pricing strategies. The fourth problem deals with a firm's decision on the product introduction timing and pricing for successive product generations in the presence of consumer memory.

We analyse the case where a firm introduces multiple generations of a product, for which demand is impacted by the reference price formed by consumers' shopping experience. We characterize the product introduction timing and pricing strategies explicitly for two successive product generations, and propose a quasi-analytic solution method, based on the structure of the memory-dependent problem, for an arbitrary number of generations.

We also extend our analysis to a duopoly environment. Our results help firms manage development and sales of their multiple product generations. Finally, we also include the summary of our recent results on the application of vehicular traffic theory to blood rheology, a collaborative effort with the

Department of Cardiology The theory of multiproduct pricing is well developed in stylized models, although a unified theory has yet to be developed. As such, empirical analyses are rarely guided by strong theoretical hypotheses and are therefore scarce. This paper analyses the interactions of ticket, parking, and concession prices in Major League Baseball for the period 1991-2003 using a principal components methodology.

The approach allows inferences to be formed about the factors underlying intertemporal price variation in the absence of information about costs and demand. The most important factor influencing prices in baseball is a general increase in the demand for baseball, but general demand shifts explain less than half of all price variation. The second most important factor is pricing interactions between tickets and concessions that are consistent with theories of nonlinear multiproduct pricing.

Secondary empirical analysis confirms these economic interpretations. The results show that the principal components methodology is an effective way to draw inferences about the economic forces underpinning pricing in a multiproduct context using data on prices alone. Utilization of a simple multiproduct price competition model revealed the presence of a complete strategy equilibrium.

The equilibrium becomes efficient when overall social surplus is maximized. Moreover, an equilibrium outcome is obtained when the willingness to pay function of the consumer is convex. This signifies weak competition and the surplus is being taken by the firms. On the other hand, a concave willingness to pay function reveals that the equilibrium price of a product also marginally accounts for the total willingness to pay.

DIFFERENTIAL AND INCREMENTAL COSTING

DIFFERENTIAL COSTING

Decisions involve choosing between alternatives. In business, each alternative will have certain costs and benefits that must be compared to the costs and benefits of the other available alternatives. A difference in cost between any two alternatives is known as differential cost.

A difference in revenue between any two alternatives is known as differential revenues. Differential cost includes both cost increase (incremental cost) and cost decrease (decremental cost). In general the difference (cost and revenue) between alternatives are relevant indecision making. Those items that are the same under all alternatives can be ignored.

The accountant's differential cost concept can be compared to the economist's*marginal cost* concept. In speaking of changes in cost and revenue, the economists employ the term *marginal cost and marginal revenue*. The revenue that can be obtained from selling one more unit of product is called marginal revenue, and the cost involved in producing one more unit of a product is called marginal cost. The economists marginal cost is basically the same as the accountant's differential concept applied to a single unit of out put.

Example: Differential cost can be either variable or fixed. To illustrate assume that a company is thinking about changing its marketing method from distribution through retailers to distribution by door to door direct sale. Present cost and revenues are compared to projected costs and revenues in the following table.

Description	Retailer Distribution (Present)	Direct SaleDistribution (Proposed)	Differential Costs and Revenues
Revenue (variable)	$700,000	$800,000	$100,000
	---------	---------	---------
Cost of goods sold (V)	350,000	400,000	50,000
Advertising (V)	80,000	45,000	(35000)
Commissions (F)	-0-	40,000	40,000
Warehouse depreciation (V)	50,000	80,000	30,000
Other Expenses (F)	60,000	60,000	-0-
	----------	----------	----------
Total	540,000	625,000	85,000
	----------	----------	----------
Net Operating Income	$160,000	$175,000	$15,000
	=======	=======	=======
F = Fixed V = Variable			

According to the above analysis, the differential revenue is $100,000 and the differential cost is $85,000,leaving a positive differential net operating income of $15,000 under the proposed marketing plan. The net operating income under the present distribution is $160,000, whereas the net operating income under door to door direct selling is estimated to be $175,000. Therefore the door to door direct distribution method is preferred, since it would result in $15,000 higher net operating income.

Note that we would have arrive at exactly the same conclusion by simply focusing on the differential revenue, differential cost, and differential net operating income, which also shows a net operating advantage of $15,000 for the direct selling method. The company can ignore other expenses of $60,000. Because it has no effect on the decision. If it were removed from the calculation, the door to door selling method would still be preferred by $15,000. This is an extremely important principle in management accounting.

Using Those Empty Seats

Many corporate jets fly with only one or two executives on board. Priscilla Blumwondered why some of the empty seats could not be used to fly cancer patients who specialized treatment outside their home area. Flying on a regular commercial airline can be an expensive and grueling experience for cancer patients. Taking the initiative, she helped found the Corporate Angle Network, an organization that arranges free flights on some 1,500 jets from over 500 companies. Since the jets fly anyway, filling a seat with cancer patient does not involve any significant incremental cost for the companies that donate the service. Since its founding in 1981, the Corporate Angel Network has arranged over 14,000 free flights.

OPPORTUNITY COST

Definition

Opportunity cost is the potential benefit that is given up when one alternative is selected over another. To illustrate this important concept, consider the following examples:

- *Example* 1: Vicki has a part-time job that pays her $200 per week while attending college. She would like to spend a week at the beach during spring break, and her employer has agreed to give her the time off, but without pay. The $200 in lost wages would be an opportunity cost of taking week off to be at the beach.
- *Example* 2: Suppose that Neiman Marcus is considering investing a large sum of money in land that may be a site for future store. Rather than invest the funds in land, the company could invest the funds in high-grade securities. If the land is acquired, the opportunity cost will be the investment income that could have been realized if the securities had been purchased instead.
- *Example* 3: You are employed in a company that pays you $30,000 per year. You are thinking about leaving the company and returning to school. Since returning to school would require that you give up $30,000 salary. The forgone salary would be anopportunity cost of seeking further education.

Opportunity cost is not usually entered in the accounting records of an organization, but it is a cost that must be explicitly considered in every decision a manager makes. Virtually every alternative has some opportunity cost attached to it.

SUNK COST

Definition

A sunk cost is a cost that has already been incurred and that cannot be changed by any decision made now or in future.

Example: Sunk costs cannot be changed by any decision. These are not differential costsand should be ignored in decision making. To illustrate a *sunk cost*, assume that a company paid $50,000 several years ago for a special purpose machine. The machine was used to make a product that is now obsolete and is no longer being sold. Even though in hindsight the purchase of the machine may have been unwise, no amount of regret can undo that decision. And it would be folly to continue making the obsolete product to recover the original cost of the machine. In short, the $50,000 originally paid for the machine has already been incurred and cannot be differential cost in any future decision. For this reason, such costs are said to be sunk costs and should be ignored in decision making.

INCREMENTAL COSTING

What is Incremental Costing

Incremental cost is the cost associated with increasing production by one unit. Because some costs are fixed and other variable, the incremental cost will not be the same as the overall average cost per unit. The cost figure can be used for a variety of economic calculations, most notably the point at which increasing production ceases to be efficient.

A very simple example would be a factory making widgets where it takes one employee an hour to make a widget. As a simple figure, the incremental cost of a widget would be the wages for the employee for an hour plus the cost of the materials needed to produce a widget. A more accurate figure could include added costs, such as shipping the additional widget to a customer, or the electricity used if the factory has to stay open longer.

The incremental cost total is always made up of purely variable costs. It represents the added costs that would not exist if the extra unit was not made. That means that many fixed costs such as rent on a factory or buying a machine are not usually represented. However, if an economist wanted to be extremely precise, they might include some element of these fixed costs where they could specifically link them to the production of the extra unit. For example, producing even one extra widget would cause a tiny bit extra wear and tear on the machine.

In many cases, the average cost of a unit will be higher than the incremental cost. This is because the average cost takes account of fixed costs. For example, if a company spends a set sum on machines each year, this cost will be represented in the average cost of each unit produced on those machines. It will not be included in the incremental cost because producing one extra unit does not require any more spending on buying machines. Where this happens, the incremental cost is lower than the existing average cost and thus increasing production by one unit slightly lowers the average cost: this is known as economy of scale.

This is not always the situation, however. In most situations there will eventually come a point where increasing production gives an incremental cost which is higher than existing average cost. Perhaps the most common example would be where a factory's workforce is working to full capacity.

Adding just one more unit to output would either require paying overtime or spending money on recruiting new staff. In this situation, the incremental cost is higher than the existing average cost and thus drives the

INCREMENTAL COST CONCEPTS

Incremental costing methods measure the economic consequences of decision alternatives. Incremental costs are typically used to answer the generic question: "How will the total costs of the organization change if I make a decision to do X — as opposed to continuing with the *status quo* (or some other baseline alternative)?" The decision in question may involve a major financial impact to the organization, or may involve a relatively small potential impact.

How much more (or less) will it cost for the organization to employ its own sales force as opposed to continuing to employ a network of exclusive resellers? How much additional cost will be incurred by the organization to provide one more hour of childcare this coming Thursday — or provide a large corporate customer with childcare for one thousand employees over the next eighteen months?

For this reason, incremental methods are naturally appropriate to provide cost information relevant to making decisions. This strict focus on identifying relevant information for a decision is a hallmark of incremental analysis — and distinguishes incremental cost methods from most other cost accounting methods.

By contrast, the cost information used in financial accounting and public financial reporting is based on standard "cookbook" formulas. Use of such formulas allows an organization to quickly apportion its total costs to different sub-units or activities — and to declare, for example, that the cost of producing its "WhisperSensitive" line of baby monitors last quarter was $453,281 and an average of $15.25 per unit. The uniformity of the cookbook (promulgated by bodies such as the Financial Accounting Standards Board) is intended to ensure arms-length objectivity, allow for the comparison of the financial health of different organizations, and offer relative simplicity of application and audit.

Outside of the niceties of financial accounting, however, the conditions rarely exist for an organization to identify a single, definitive cost per unit or total cost of its products or services. In recognition of this reality, the measure of an incremental cost depends on the particular decision whose cost is being evaluated.

5

Strategic Cost Management

KNOWING CUSTOMERS' EXPECTATIONS

Providing a product or service that customers perceive as excellent requires a company to know what its customers expect. This is the most critical component of delivering excellent customer service. Virtually every company thinks it knows what its customers want. However, if a company is only slightly inaccurate about its assumptions, it could lose its customers' business to another company that has more accurately filled their needs. Being only "slightly" inaccurate can lead an organization to spend money, time, and effort on things that are not important to customers. And in a worst-case scenario, it can mean not surviving in an intensely competitive environment.

EXPECTATION GAP

At times a gap occurs between what customers expect and what management presumes they expect. This often happens because companies overlook or do not fully understand customers' perceptions and expectations. In spite of a strong commitment and sincere desire to provide quality service, many companies fall dramatically short of the mark, usually because they have an internally directed rather than externally directed focus. An internally directed focus assumes that the company knows what customers should want and delivers or produces that. This orientation often leads to providing products and services that do not match customers' expectations- important features and benefits may be left out and levels of performance may be inadequate. In looking at several different types of organizations, common elements contribute to the gap between customer expectations and the product or service offered.

The common elements are:

- Inadequate "bilateral" communication between front-line personnel and management.
- An absence of regular interaction between management and customers.
- An absence of a strong market research programme.
- An absence of customer service accountability.

COMMUNICATING WITH FRONT-LINE EMPLOYEES

Front-line employees are in regular contact with customers. As a result, they know a great deal about customers' perceptions and expectations. This information must be regularly passed on to management. When channels of communication are closed or inadequate, managers cannot know about problems occurring in product and service delivery as well as critical information about changing customer expectations.

Communication between front-line employees and management can be enhanced in a number of ways:

- Formal types of communication (*e.g.*, memos, suggestion cards, and open meetings).
- Informal communication (*e.g.*, discussions over coffee, walking around the facility, going out into the field).

It is essential to assess customers' perceptions and expectations regularly, but it is also very important to assess whether managers understand the needs and expectations of front-line employees. Managers who communicate with front-line people not only build morale but also learn a tremendous amount about their customers, thereby reducing the expectation gap.

Some questions to ask concerning the communication between management and front-line employees in an organization are:

- How often do managers have direct contact with front-line employees?
- Do managers encourage suggestions from front-line employees concerning the quality of products or services?
- Are there too many levels of management, causing managers to be cut off from direct contact with and feedback from front-line employees?
- Are there formal or informal opportunities for front-line employees to communicate with management on a regular basis?
- Has management adequately determined and monitored the expectations of front-line employees?
- Do front-line employees feel strongly supported?

INTERACTION BETWEEN MANAGEMENT AND CUSTOMERS

The larger a company is, the more difficult it is for managers to deal directly with customers. Consequently, managers have less information about customers' perceptions and expectations. However, in smaller companies, managers can receive more direct information concerning their customers.

Even when they are regularly given reports, managers readily lose the customer perspective if they do not have the opportunity for direct customer contact. Theoretical knowledge is a poor substitute for a face-to-face encounter. To truly understand and appreciate customers' needs and expectations, managers should experience firsthand what really happens in the field—in stores or on the customer- service line—by answering the service line themselves or dealing with customers face to face. Managers can better empathize with employees if they have experienced some of what employees deal with on a regular basis.

Here are some questions to consider concerning regular interaction between management and customers:

- Does the company have a programme in which managers rotate to different service positions within the organization?
- Does top management make it a priority to get out in the field and see customers?
- Do managers randomly interact with customers (*e.g.*, those waiting in line, browsing in the store, or calling the service desk)?

NEED FOR A STRONG MARKET RESEARCH PROGRAMME

Because marketing research is an important tool in assessing customers' perceptions and expectations, a company that fails to regularly collect such information may be more likely to have a significant customer expectation gap. To effectively deal with expectation versus performance issues, marketing research measurements should focus on product or service quality issues.

These might include:

- Which features and benefits are most important to customers?
- How much do customers expect, at what price and in what time frame?
- What do customers think the company should do if problems occur in product or service delivery?

  Determining what customers expect is essential to providing superior quality. Regardless of a company's size and resources, there are ways to obtain this kind of information.

Questions to consider concerning a company's marketing research efforts include:

- Are research findings shared throughout the company when appropriate?
- Are the research findings integral to the company's strategic planning?
- Can research findings be readily understood and used by managers?
- Does research focus on quality of service provided?
- Is research conducted on a regular basis to generate high-quality, reliable information about what customers want and expect?

CUSTOMER-SERVICE ACCOUNT ABILITY

Policies and procedures are important, but when they impede a firm's ability to meet customer needs, they are counterproductive.With many companies experiencing an increase in policies and procedures over the last several years, initiative has been stifled and employees are less willing to get involved.

For companies to compete effectively in an increasingly competitive marketplace, employees must be enabled to identify problems, resolve them, and share suggestions with management. They should not be allowed to withdraw into a bureaucratic environment and assume that someone else will take care of problems. All the while, customers may be migrating elsewhere.

The following list provides questions to ask regarding customer service accountability:

- Are employees encouraged to "take ownership" of a problem, and are they supported in their efforts?
- Is the business unduly bureaucratic, and does it encourage an attitude of "someone else will take care of it"?
- Does the business empower its employees to find ways in which customers can be better served?

Any organization, regardless of size, can reduce customer expectation gaps if it improves communication between managers and front-line employees, increases interaction between management and customers, develops a strong market research programme, and insists on accountability for customer service.

KEEPING CUSTOMERS

Customer retention is one of the most important strategic issues companies have faced in recent years. Retention is critical for increasing profits and remaining competitive. Studies show that a 5 per cent change in the rate of customer retention can shift profits from 25 per cent to 100 per cent in either direction. In manufacturing, measuring the number of defects is an important index of quality. In measuring service, the number of defections (customers going elsewhere) is important.

Many companies underestimate the cost of customer defections. Few companies track defections (otherwise known as migration) or invest in reducing them. Companies should measure customer migration, and their goal should be customer retention. They must regularly evaluate and modify training programmes, information systems, organizational structure, complaint handling procedures, hiring objectives, incentives, and even the company culture. Providing superior customer service is an effective strategy for increasing customer retention, which can lead to an increase in profits, because customers will beat a path to the company that provides superior customer service.

HIGH COST OF MIGRATION

Failure to realise the high cost of losing customers stems in part from aggressive selling and marketing. In many companies, the work involved in keeping customers is seen as dull and tedious. Selling is what is truly exciting. Many companies view unhappy customers as chronic complainers who are not worth the effort required to satisfy them. It is true that some customers are habitual complainers, but too often companies apply this label to every customer who complains. If this attitude permeates a company, dissatisfied customers will probably receive poor treatment and their problems will remain unaddressed. Prospective and first-time customers usually are treated well during the selling courtship. Many companies aggressively pursue new customers, but these customers go right out the door if service is poor. They come in with great expectations but leave with disappointment, frustration, and possibly resentment.

MARKETING: A TWO-PART PROCESS

The marketing function should be viewed as a two part process:

1. Getting customers.
2. Retaining customers.

The first part of the marketing process rarely has inadequate resources and seldom suffers from a lack of attention. Sales budgets, advertising campaigns, and promotional efforts usually take a significant percentage of a company's operating budget. However, retention marketing often has little or no budget at all.Research shows that, depending on the specific industry, it costs between five and seven times as much to get a new customer as it does to keep an existing one. Most companies have little difficulty defending the significant costs of acquiring new customers. But what if the new customers are only replacements for dissatisfied customers?

Such companies find themselves barely holding on to customers, or worse, they experience a net loss of customers. Companies that do strive to retain customers have return policies, customer complaint departments, and occasional customer mailings. But few companies engage in aggressive, well-constructed strategies of retentionoriented marketing that keep customers happy and mend relations with dissatisfied customers.

MOMENT OF TRUTH

Every point of contact a customer has with a company (whether by phone, in person, or by mail) is a point at which service is delivered—or not delivered. It is a point at which the customer forms one more impression and makes one more judgment about the company. Some call it the "moment of truth." Nordstrom's, a department store, operates by the following maxim: "Listen to the customer; the customer is always right. Do anything to satisfy the customer." Every time a company fails to live up to a promise to its customers, it loses some credibility.

Advertising, public relations, architectural design, and other high-profile efforts may create favourable impressions. But the critical difference in customer retention usually occurs in less glamorous areas. For example, customers may be impressed by the behaviour and appearance of employees, the way phones are answered, the clarity and accuracy of billings, or the overall promptness and reliability in handling complaints. "Little things" are important, and companies must be vigilant and consistent in their attention to detail. Such vigilance may require redefining the role of marketing, rearranging priorities, and reallocating budgets.

OBSTACLES TO SUPERIOR CUSTOMER SERVICE

There are several obstacles to customer service that at one time or another affect most businesses.

Attitude that Custmor are Replaceable

The days of monopolistic enterprises and taking customers for granted have long since passed away. Customers should be considered valuable assets that are obtained only through hard work and at considerable expense. Although employees are often relieved when disgruntled customers leave, this is an unfortunate attitude for any employee or business to have.

Insensitive Managers

The old expression that "no two people are alike" applies to both employees and customers. Problems develop when managers become insensitive to the characteristics or behaviour of their employees and customers. Managing the human element is a considerable challenge in providing superior customer service. Managers must continuously respond to changing situations.

They must be able to make instantaneous decisions in an environment in which education, experience, skills, perceptions, values, and prejudices have a direct impact on transactions with employees and customers. Other concerns-such as divorce, financial trouble, or sick children- also affect employee-customer transactions. Given these human idiosyncrasies, companies must monitor, train, motivate, evaluate, and periodically retrain employees so that they are empowered to be of assistance to customers.

Budgetary Problems

Some companies do not properly fund efforts to improve customer service. As a result, they end up with inconsistent customer-service strategies and poor implementation of programmes to improve customer service. In a highly competitive economy, budgetary constraints can drive away frustrated customers who may be told, for example, that there are not enough qualified people, or that there simply are not enough people to catch up on back orders. In many companies, the financial resources required to meet customer needs exist, but they are allocated elsewhere. Insufficient funding inherently devalues the importance of customer service in the minds of frontline employees.

Lake of Strong Commitment

In many cases, management lacks a strong commitment to superior customer service. Managers may claim to have a strong commitment, but in reality they pay only lip service to customer service. Unless management undertakes a full-scale effort and requires an intense commitment to superior customer service throughout the organization, the prospects of achieving superior customer service are seriously diminished.

Inconsistecy

Customers usually measure a product or service by the satisfaction they expect and subsequently receive. If a customer is sold a product or service that fails to live up to its promises, dissatisfaction is the result. Customers who are oversold or promised undeliverable levels of satisfaction usually forget the salesperson and concentrate instead on the product or service involved and the company behind it. Thus, companies must strive for consistency in the delivery of products and services, in representations made about product and service characteristics, and in the professionalism of all employees who deal with customers.

Lack of Listening

Managers are typically concerned with the big picture, so they seldom have the time to get out and really listen to what customers need and think. Many managers are comfortable believing that if customers are not complaining, things must be going all right. But this can be a dangerous assumption. Managers must be available to both employees and customers. They must observe and listen purposefully and systematically. Most important, they must be open to discussion: They should not be defensive, closed-minded, or apprehensive about being proved incorrect.

Inertia

Computer systems, policy guides, and procedures often take on a life of their own in many companies. Customers usually feel frustrated when they are told, "I'm sorry, but our policy is... ," or "There is nothing I can do about it." In some companies, the computer systems are often handy excuses for mistakes. Although computer systems, policies, and procedures are important, they can stifle a company's primary mission—to sell and serve customers—if they are not kept in check. Companies that excel in providing superior customer service focus on the customer and strive diligently not to allow "the system" to interfere with what is best for the customer.

Different Frames of Reference

Words frequently used to describe customer service include "prompt," "reliable," "satisfaction," "courtesy," "professional," "timely," and "quality," along with such phrases as "quick response to customer complaints," "accuracy in billing,""prompt repairs,"and "satisfaction guaranteed."For these words and phrases to have relevance, specific definitions, measurements, or other explicitly stated standards have to exist. For example, "quick response to customer complaints" might be defined to mean "within 24 hours,"whereas "accuracy in billing" might mean that if errors are identified within seven days of receipt, a correction will be made.When definitions are clearly understood from the start, a company and its customers will have a common denominator for measuring the quality of service.

Lack of Perspective

Providing high-quality customer service is not a programme that can be bought and paid for in a short time. High-quality customer service cannot be effectively implemented and sustained through memos, short-lived promotional efforts, or advertising campaigns designed to boost sales. Management must view high-quality customer service as an ongoing process. The "tyranny of the urgent" often prevents managers from taking steps that will keep customers the company worked so hard to get.

HOW TO INCREASE CUSTOMER RETENTION

Just as there are frequently encountered obstacles to superior customer service, there are also several suggested ways to help a company successfully retain as many of your customers as possible.

Reliability

Customers want consistent performance most of all.

To be reliable, a company should strive for the following:

- Do what you say you are going to do.
- Do it when you say you will.
- Do it right the first time.

Credibility

Customers will go back to businesses that want to help them and have their best interests in mind. Customers do not want hidden agendas, fine print, hardsell tactics, or extra charges. They want the products or services they buy to be free of danger, risk, and doubt.

Responsiveness

We live in a time of instant gratification. When customers want service, they usually want it immediately. Being responsive requires being available, accessible, and willing to help customers whenever they have a problem.

Empathy

Being empathetic means putting oneself in the position of a customer.

Management must ask itself whether it would do business with the company. Every customer is unique and wants to be treated uniquely. To accomplish this, companies must ask the right questions, listen intently, and then design products or services to meet stated needs.

Select Front-Line Employees Carefully

Companies oriented towards customer service should have customer-friendly people in front-line positions. Such positions are not for everybody. Great care should be exercised in selecting prospective employees based on their personality traits and other skills.

A psychological consulting firm has singled out the following attributes as especially helpful for employees in front-line positions:

- An ability to make sound judgments in a stressful setting.
- A problem-solving orientation.
- A desire to be liked.
- A naturally optimistic outlook.

Provide Sufficient Employee Training

Customers want to be served by knowledgeable employees. Thus, employees should be well trained before interacting with customers. Employee training should not be viewed as a one-time entrance requirement. Regular training sessions are needed to keep employees updated on new policies and procedures, new product features and benefits, competition, customer needs, new programmes, developments in other parts of the company, and core corporate goals.

Create a Sense of Belonging

Employees also need a sense of their company's mission and their role within the company. They need to receive encouragement to enhance their roles while also receiving recognition for contributions made. Regardless of the methods used by different companies, employee recognition is an important motivator and a fundamental tool for nurturing an environment committed to customer service.

Avoid Premature Release of Products, Concepts, or Policies

Taking a new product or service to market before it is ready, changing policies rapidly, or introducing a new computer system before all the bugs are worked out erode customer satisfaction levels. Companies must take great care not to sacrifice customers while trying to achieve progress. Customers want consistency and stability.

Make Things Easy for the Customer

Making things easy for the customer requires careful planning, coordination, and diligence. When companies do not work at these fundamentals, customer service *can* suffer.

Following are ways to make things easier for customers:

- Install a toll-free number.
- Provide adequate incoming phone lines.
- Hire enough employees to answer phones quickly.
- Use business-reply mail (postage-paid).
- Implement easy refund and exchange procedures.
- Provide prompt and accurate information.
- Do not assume that the customers have extensive knowledge about a product or service.
- Speak and write in plain English. Do not use highly technical terms or company jargon.
- Debrief customers who leave the company for competitors.

If a Customer Leaves, Ask Why

Whenever the company loses a customer, find out why. Few customers are more honest or candid than a dissatisfied customer.

INVESTING RESOURCES IN THE RIGHT PLACES

It is important that companies regularly assess their competitive positions. Such an assessment can help identify strengths and weaknesses vis-a-vis the competition, thereby enabling companies to focus on their strengths and eliminate weaknesses. Few companies can effectively compete against all competitors on all fronts simultaneously. It is important, therefore, to identify key strategic points of difference so that a company can allocate its finite resources optimally.

The key areas to evaluate include:

- Markets
- Customers and the products or services offered to them
- Personnel
- Operations, facilities, and technology
- Finances

To be valuable in the marketplace, companies must maximize the return on available and invested capital. They must regularly evaluate their allocation of resources to different areas.

MARKETS

Many companies make decisions about critical components of their operations as if they were in a vacuum: They show little sensitivity to, or awareness of, what other companies are doing in the market.

To be effective, they should be asking questions such as:

- What are the trends in the market?
- In which direction is the market headed?
- What do the customers want (versus what they need)?
- Is the company aware of the difference?
- What is the size of other competitors in the market?

To have strategic significance, terms or units of measure should be used that enable companies to compare themselves to competitors. Statistics regarding the number of employees or customers a competitor has may have a marketing impact. Other information- such as the amount of capital invested, asset base, profits, inventory levels, the number of inventory turns, the number of support personnel, and the number of sales representatives-can help a company determine the investment required to compete effectively and identify areas that may not be well served.

CUSTOMERS AND PRODUCTS OR SERVICES OFFERED

Why does a company offer the products or services it offers? Is there a rational process in place by which new products or services are added or deleted from a company's portfolio? Is there a threshold of revenue generation below which a product or service will no longer be carried or offered?

Too often companies offer products or services that management feels should be offered, or they continue to offer the products or services that they have historically offered, as opposed to what the market dictates.however, companies should periodically assess their offerings and determine whether customers and potential customers are aware of all the products or services in their portfolios. Not long ago, a large, well-known law firm disclosed in a meeting that it had budgeted a significant sum towards practice development. Before launching the development campaign, the firm performed an assessment on existing clients to determine their awareness of the services offered.

Much to the chagrin of the firm's partners, almost two-thirds of the clients used more than one law firm for their legal work. Further analysis revealed that none of those clients used other law firms because of dissatisfaction but, rather, because they did not realise all the other services available from the firm. Thus, the law firm realised that one of its biggest challenges was to increase the awareness of existing clients before spending significant funds on pursuing new clients.

In another case, a company offered 12 different kinds of services to its customers. Upon careful objective analysis of customer input, the company determined that the customers really had a viable interest in only 7 of the 12 services. At that point, the company had a choice to make: to pursue additional customers that may have an interest in the other services or drop the other services and the costs associated with offering them.

The key point in these examples is that by getting objective information from customers, both organizations could make decisions that enabled them to allocate re- sources where they could generate the greatest return.without this information, both organizations would have continued operating in a manner that presumed business as usual and thus consumed resources inefficiently. A well-designed customer questionnaire can prove helpful in determining the awareness, utilization, and interest levels of customers.

OPERATIONS, FACILITIES, AND TECHNOLOGY

Companies should periodically assess competitive

OPERATIONS, FACILITIES, AND TECHNOLOGY

Companies should periodically assess competitive strategies utilized in terms of operations, facilities, and technology. Information concerning competitors in these key areas can provide important insight regarding their strategic direction.

It is particularly helpful to consider how competitors compare in the following areas:

- Locations of branch offices, field offices, and the types of buildings used.
- Creative channels of distribution used.
- Databases, communication networks, and computers employed.
- Technology used downstream with customers, branch offices, field offices, and sales representatives.
- Facility management, overall appearance, and the integration of other offices or facilities.

Because many companies must increasingly compete based on how they allocate scarce capital, a company's ability to profitably compete will increasingly depend on the proper deployment and utilization of operational capabilities, facilities management, and technology. Customer input is a critically important tool in assessing these areas.

FINANCIAL ALLOCATION DECISIONS

Customer satisfaction information is helpful in allocating the financing and operating responsibilities needed to manage a company. Financing responsibilities pertain to how a company obtains the capital needed to provide for assets. Operating responsibilities relate to how a company uses those assets once they have been obtained.

Return on Total Assets

One tool that is helpful in making financial allocation decisions is a calculation of the return on total assets. The formula for return on total assets can be used in assessing a product or service, overall financial performance, or the re- turn on an individual customer. It is a measure of how well assets are utilized—that is, a measure of operating performance.

Cost-Benefit Analysis

Another financial measurement, cost-benefit analysis, can prove helpful in allocating a company's financial resources. By carefully measuring specific levels of customer satisfaction on a product-by-product or service-by-service basis, a company can analyse how each element is faring from a customer's perspective.

Break-Even Analysis

Break-even analysis is a tool that helps a company assess whether it should continue providing a particular product or service. Simply defined, the break-even point occurs when total sales revenue equals total expenses .Break-even analysis helps a company determine whether to go forward in launching a new product or service or to continue offering an existing product or service.

The calculated break-even point, determines how many units (*e.g.*, Products, services, engagements, memberships, patients, or clients) must be successfully engaged for a company at least to cover its costs.while reviewing the numbers derived from a break-even analysis to assess the reasonableness or probability of attaining a particular profit level, a company can factor in valuable customer-based information gleaned from an assessment of awareness, utilization, and interest to aid in the process of determining whether such levels are also realistic in light of customer satisfaction.

PLANNING FOR THE FUTURE

Planning for the future requires a thorough and realistic understanding of existing products, services, markets, margins, profits, return on allocated capital, and availability and skills of employees. When contemplating a company's specific mission, management must have a clear understanding of how well the company is doing today. As has been demonstrated, customer input and assessment of satisfaction can play an enormously important role in setting objectives.

PRUDENT PLANNING

Prudent planning helps a company, regardless of its size, focus on where it wants to be three to five years in the future. Too often, managers are focused only on short-term needs and prospects, largely because of their immediacy. As a result, long-term problems and opportunities are deferred or given only slight attention. Management must distinguish between current operating challenges and longer-term goals and plans. Some executives search for ways to increase the size, efficiency, and profitability of their company's operations. But if the forecasted performance of existing operations fails to produce expectations of profitable growth, many of them build on the operations that presently exist and accept the status quo.

STRATEGIC PLANNING

Some executives are not satisfied with nominal growth rates into the future. Empowered with well-founded, customer-based information (*e.g.*, measures of customer satisfaction; information about awareness and utilization of products and services; customer wants, needs, expectations; perceived strengths and weaknesses; and suggestions for improvement), they stretch the forecasts and establish new and challenging standards of performance for the future. Increasingly, companies realise the importance of strategic planning. Several large companies go to the extreme of considering a range of plans that cover simultaneous possibilities across a wide set of assumptions.

However, this involved approach usually requires a highly structured strategic planning process and a large planning staff. Although this type of intensive approach has considerable benefits, few companies can afford such a commitment. Smaller companies or larger companies without extensive strategic planning resources can use a simplified approach more effectively. The underlying assumption with this approach is that a person or group can only commit parttime efforts to the strategic planning process.

CALL TO ACTION

A management consultant recently wrote, "Future historians may well describe the 1980s and possibly the 1990s as the era of customer sovereignty. Perhaps 'customer rebellion' is more accurate."1 To a large extent, which organizations will prosper in today's economy will depend on which organizations recognize the "customer rebellion" and make the preparations necessary to provide superior customer service. Every organization must vigorously assess the status and quality of its relationships with both external customers (existing, potential, and past) and internal customers (employees).Where do we stand? What do we need to improve? How can we improve?

In doing so, remember the following points:

- Customers, potential customers, and former customers perceive value in their own terms. If an organization wants to meet their needs, it must always look at products and services from their perspective.
- Customers, potential customers, and former customers think that an organization's reason for being in business is to meet their needs.
- If an organization sincerely desires to deal successfully with dissatisfied customers, employees must be empowered to focus on saving the customer, not the sale.
- An organization must strive to provide dissatisfied customers with a positive reason for dealing with the organization again.
- In all likelihood, an organization's employees will not treat customers or potential customers any better than they themselves are treated by the organization.
- Input from customers, potential customers, or past customers is invaluable. An organization should actively seek, appreciate, and review this input.
- The entire process by which an organization creates and delivers its products and services should exhibit superior customer service and support the creation of high levels of customer satisfaction.

Regardless of the size of an organization, it is increasingly difficult to compete primarily on the basis of price or product. In many cases, product differentiation is imperceptible. Thus, in the burgeoning battle for the customer, the key is usually not product superiority (or at least not for long) but service. The quality of service provided has rapidly become the standard by which organizations are judged. Thus, customer satisfaction— and continual improvement in customer satisfaction—has become a primary indication of sustainability.

In a world of increasing complexity and automation, the successful organization must find the means by which it can operate efficiently and profitably while maintaining a commitment to manage with integrity, compassion, intelligence, competitiveness, and an unwavering commitment to providing superior customer service and generating high levels of customer satisfaction. Although not on the balance sheet, customers are the greatest asset that any organization has. They need to be treated as treasured, longterm investments that, if properly nurtured and cultivated, will provide significant dividends.

How does a company know how it is doing with its customers, its prospective customers, and its employees? Are they satisfied? Do they perceive that the company has a strong commitment to providing superior service? The only way to know for certain is to ask—candidly, objectively, and following a good methodology. As Yogi Berra said so well, "The only way to begin is to begin." Regardless of the type or size of an organization, management can seize the competitive advantage, provide superior customer service, and build high levels of customer satisfaction.

6

Total Cost Management

INTRODUCTION

To sustain long-term profitability, corporate managers must consider environmental policy as an essential component of corporate strategy for achieving and maintaining competitive superiority. In response to increasing public concern for environmental issues, recent court decisions and more aggressive legislation and regulatory policies have greatly expanded corporations' potential liability.

Thus, corporations need to reconsider their environmental efforts and to proactively manage, rather than react to, environmental problems. Total cost management (TCM) is a business paradigm for managing all company resources and the activities that consume those resources with a focus on stimulating and managing changes. Under the TCM paradigm, companies can consider the entire environmental impact of their products by looking for substitutes for inputs that are hazardous and for processes that can reduce the generation of waste.

TCM offers a systematic approach to continuously improve operations and reduce waste generation throughout the product life cycle. Firms will find such integration desirable to reduce costs, reduce liability, and minimize adverse community concerns over their operations.

BACKGROUND

The extant literature indicates that cost management systems of world-class manufacturers play a unique role. The focal point of such systems is to provide needed support for company-wide strategic planning and revitalization. Advanced manufacturers must adopt an integrated cost planning approach with their market-based strategic product development. World-class manufacturers perform extensive cost planning to manage costs through cost reduction at the product design and development stage.

The fact that most cost decisions are made prior to production in the engineering design, prototype and vendor sourcing stages is the basis for this emphasis. This is the stage where many decisions are made that will eventually determine environmental costs. Cost planning activities generally involve value engineering and target costing analyses. Value engineering examines the functions that products are to perform and then evaluates those functions with respect to customer demands and function costs. Value engineering goes beyond the analysis of production costs and includes the analysis of a product's entire life-cycle to determine the cost implications of design and product development decisions in a particular product.

In addition, target cost analysis is often used to gather information and to foster commitment from all departments involved. Each new product, or major revision of an existing product, will be developed based on cross-functional input from sales and marketing, engineering design, engineering production, and cost management. The formal target cost is jointly determined by all functions involved which is set between the allowable cost based on customers' expectation and the potential cost based on the current technology and production methods.

As a result, the purposes of designating target costs are to encourage cost reduction and control and to achieve the corporation's strategic goals. In addition, target costing supports activity-based costing to develop the cost of quality data that promote quality being designed into products. To meet the challenge of environmental conservation and waste management, world class manufacturers must include environment policies into their strategically oriented, integrated systems. Studies of technologically intensive companies have shown that the key to achieving a sustainable competitive advantage is sound management of technological innovation. Technological innovation programmes should be an element of a company's overall business strategy and unite activities in all functional areas including R&D, product design, process design, manufacturing, marketing and environmental preservation.

TCM creates the environment for cross-disciplinary cooperation and manages the process towards innovation and environmental preservation. In addition, TCM provides tools to incorporate changes in the views of business ethics and social responsibility.

TOTAL COST MANAGEMENT APPROACH TO SUSTAINABILITY

TCM does not accept costs as "given" but instead as a point of reference upon which to constantly improve. The tools of environmental economics continue to remain useful, but they must be viewed as guides for improvement. Environmental economics is justifiably concerned with the externalities created by the divergence in private costs and social costs. TCM is more normative in viewing more of these costs as part of private costs.

At the firm level, economic analysis focuses on the adjustment towards equality between the marginal private cost of control and the marginal cost (damage) to the firm. TCM is focused on learning to become more efficient in preventing pollution instead of correcting pollution, thereby shifting the marginal cost of control downward. TCM is also focused on recognizing that more cost "should" and will be borne by the firm, thus shifting the marginal damage upward.

Combining these two directional shifts will continually move the firm towards (but not necessary to) zero pollution. Based on the target costing process outlined by Cooper and Slagmulder (1997), TCM offers the following features that promote the development of innovative environmentally friendly products. Establish.

MARKET-BASED PRICING

It has always been a risky and challenging task to develop profitable new products as companies face ever-increasing competition. The development of innovative, environmentally friendly products would pose even more uncertainties because their market prospects are largely unknown. Target costing is driven by market price and desired profits and thus, creates the critical alignment between the innovative products with the marketplace.

TCM demands a highly disciplined process based on thorough market analysis of what customers want and what price they are willing to pay. In support of launching an innovative product its target price cannot be established in a vacuum but needs to be determined by external market factors, in particular, the strength of the new product compared to competitive offerings and market prices for comparable products. For the innovative environmentally friendly products, customers can be expected to pay more for them because these products offer more perceived value than their existing peers do.

Research has shown that thirty per cent of customers will pay up to 20 per cent extra for the environmentally friendly products and many products (*e.g.*, Green Vista, Eco-sport, Green Tag, green electricity) have commanded such price premiums. TCM helps firms to better understand the availability of competitive products and their perceived values and to ensure the most realistic possible selling prices of the environmentally friendly products.

B2B E-COMMERCE

The recent development of Internet and e-commerce open up many new opportunities for more free flow of information between suppliers of innovative products and their potential customers. The Internet enables the seamless flow of information through a web-based platform that links customers, suppliers, and contents for the benefits of all the partners participate in the supply chain. It provides the registered users the opportunities of conducting market analysis by interacting with those operators, technicians, engineers, and business executives who are active or have an interest in improving operations involving solid-waste handling and disposal.

The Solid Waste site also offers B2B features such as "Request for Quote" (RFQ) that allow a firm to create responses online, track and manage responses and requests (invitations to quote, submit quotes, acceptances, rejections, etc.), and correspond online with potential buyers. Industry-based independent web sites offer competitive products' market price information. Online business-to-business e-commerce platforms and makes it easier for a firm to determine the customer perceived value and, thus, help them to determine the new product's target price.

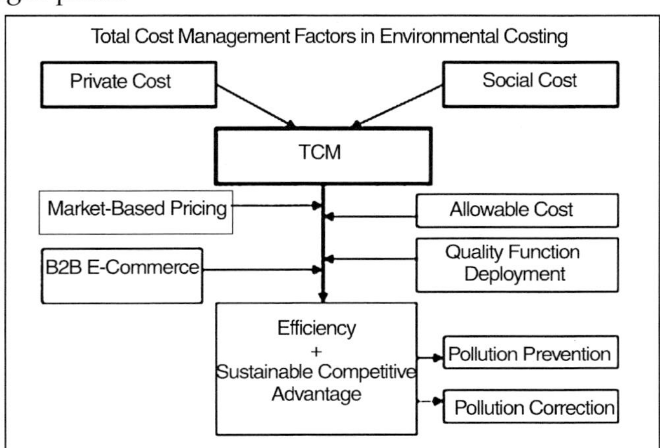

Fig. Total cost Management Factor in Envvironment Costing

DETERMINE THE ALLOWABLE COSTS

The market-based target prices of the new products determined above become the driving force of new product design because:

Allowable cost = Target price – Target profit margin

The target margin is established to ensure achievement of the company's long-term profitability. Since the allowable cost is derived from external conditions, the risk is that the allowable cost will not be achievable with the existing product design and production facilities.

In order to achieve allowable cost, an interactive process using the cost tables and quality function deployment (QFD) will be used and continuously updated to reflect the current and alternative materials and engineering methods. The cost tables contain detailed estimates of the costs of various parts or activities depending on the materials, manufacturing methods and functions involved.

Quality function deployment is typically used for systematically analyzing the product features, component functions and customer preferences in a matrix format. Both cost tables and QFD are used to formulate a value index to direct the new product's value engineering activities to achieve the target costs. An example of constructing high-density textile particle boards for furniture application from recycled textile waste is used to demonstrate how QFD can direct value engineering activities to reduce the total product costs. In the example the QFD matrix also is used to aid in the evaluation of the original target market.

QFD OF HIGH-DENSITY TEXTILE PARTICLE BOARD FOR FURNITURE APPLICATION FROM RECYCLED TEXTILE WASTE

The idea of evaluating the possibility of manufacturing high-density particleboard from recycled textile waste had two drivers. On the one side the manufacture of particleboard from wood chips requires the use of adhesives that contain toxins. On the other side the textile industry has long tried to recycle its waste material. In most cases it makes economic sense, but in some cases it is not possible and alternative uses have to be found. When alternative uses are not found, the waste material typically ends up on landfills, and synthetic materials do not decompose for a very long time.

Within the scope of TCM, the waste cost to the textile industry includes the cost of the wasted raw material including all processing cost up to the manufacturing step where the waste is generated and the disposal cost of landfilling the waste materials. The potential costs to wooden particleboard manufacturers for health hazards due to the release of formaldehyde is harder to determine. The case study concentrates on target costing concepts that are used in the product development steps for synthetic particleboard.

While a marketable product has not yet been produced, the results of the target costing analysis lead to implications in the manufacturing process as well as the marketing of the boards. Following the process of target costing as described by the Consortium for Advanced Manufacturing International, a target price was established through market research and competitive analysis of wooden particleboard. The specific market niche was determined as outdoor construction panels because of the superior water resistance of synthetic materials. Tests had shown that the synthetic samples absorbed extremely low amounts of water, and therefore no deterioration of the product was to be expected.

Customer requirements were determined through testing standards and discussions with building contractors. The price range for the particleboard in the market at the time of the study ranged from $11.59 to $16.05 for a 4 by 8 feet panel (5/8-inch thickness). 4-Layer plywood (stronger and better aesthetics, just as to the contractors) sold for $17.47 to $18.74. The Quality Function Deployment matrix (QFD matrix) links the customer requirements systematically with product components or functions. At the same time the customer requirements are ranked by relevance or importance, and the own product can be compared with competitor rankings as to how well the requirements are being fulfilled.

The customer requirement rankings for the requirements that were discussed with the potential users of the synthetic particleboard. The Relative

Rankings show how much each of the requirements contributes to the overall requirements a potential customer has for the product. These rankings serve as a guide in product development, showing which needs ought to be addressed with how much effort. The competitive ranking is based on some discussions with building contractors and to a large extent on the testing results that were performed on manufactured synthetic samples and on purchased wooden samples. The results are somewhat theoretical because the man ufactured samples were small lab samples rather than full size 4 by 8 feet sheets. As they would be revealed through market research, and how important these requirements are to the customer on a 1 to 5 scale.

These rankings are then set in proportion under relative rankings and can be compared with actual ratings of the products in the customers' minds. In this case one can see some distinct problems of the synthetic particleboard at this stage of the development. The comparison with the wooden competitor clearly shows areas of the product that require further improvement or at the very least they show the necessity to make new tools to replace nailing and screwing more appealing. From a marketing point of view the table also shows that the areas with competitive advantage are not ranked as very important in the contractor market. As a result of this analysis, the target market should be redefined with a focus on areas that require water resistance, shaping, and less dependence on traditional nailing or screwing.

- *Compatitive Ranking*: Wood Practiceboard refers to how wooden practiceboard ranks for this requirment.
- *Competitive Ranking*: Synthetic Practiceboard refers to how synthetic practiceboard ranks for this.

The QFD matrix for the synthetic particleboard. It shows a correlation matrix that links customer needs with manufacturing steps in the production of synthetic particleboard. Typically this matrix shows a correlation of requirements with product components, but in this case manufacturing steps influence the features of the product. The degree of correlation between each customer requirement and each manufacturing step is determined by engineers in product development and manufacturing. For this example the researchers determined the correlations based on various testing results.

Table QFD Matrix for Synthetic Particalboard- Correlation Matrix for the Influence of Manufacturing Steps on Customer Requirment

Manufacturing Step Requirment	Web Formation	Temperature	Pressure	Surface Treatment
Strength	■■■	■■■	■■■	
Screw Withdrawel Resistance	■■	■■■	■■■	■
Nail WithdrawalResistance	■■	■■■	■■■	
Ease of Nailing		■■	■	■■■
Ease of Screwing		■■	■	■■■
Weight/Ease of Handling	■	■	■■■	
Water Resistance		■■	■■	■
Ability to Shape		■■■	■	■
Ability to Tool		■	■■	■■■

■■■ = Strong Correlation
■■ = Moderate Correlation
■ = Weak Correlation

When linking the relative ranking of the customer requirements from table with the degree of correlation of the requirement with the different manufacturing steps in table, it is possible to deduct how important specific manufacturing steps are to satisfying customer requirements overall. This step constitutes a functional cost analysis of the manufacturing steps, and the results are shown in the summary table. The higher values indicate a higher importance in achieving customer satisfaction, and these steps should then be allowed a higher portion of the manufacturing cost.

Table. Result of the Functional Cost Analysis of Manufactureing Steps

Manufacturing Steps	Web Formation	Temperature	Pressure	Surface Treatment	Relative Ranking
Componant Value	13.1%	33.2%	32.9%	20.8%	100%

In this case the table shows the significance of temperature and pressure during the manufacture of synthetic particleboard from an engineering perspective and the impact they will have on customer requirements. A subsequent step compares the perceived value the components (or manufacturing steps) contribute to the product with the actual cost of these steps. The relative value of each manufacturing step and the actual cost of this step. The cost is expressed as a percentage of the total cost (respectively the total value).

The actual cost is based on a subjective estimation, as some of the equipment needed for full-scale production of the synthetic particleboard does not exist yet. By dividing the relative value by the actual cost one finds a value index. Close to 1, the value index shows that the cost reflects the value of this step to the customer. If the value index is below 1 (cost higher than component's value), the cost of this manufacturing step needs to be reduced.

If the value index is higher than 1 (cost less than component's value), the component or manufacturing step needs to be enhanced. The purpose of the value index is not to reduce overall cost but to distribute the cost portions just as to the perceived value for the customer.

Table: Value Index for Synthetic Practiceboard

Manufacturing Step	Actual Cost(%)	Relative Value	Value Index
Web Formation	35.0%	13.1%	0.37
Temperature	25.0%	33.1%	1.32
Pressure	28.0%	32.8%	1.17
Surface Treatment	12.0%	20.0%	1.73

In this case the value index shows that the cost of the manufacturing step "Web Formation" clearly exceeds the value the customers obtain from it, while the surface treatment could be enhanced. It also indicates that the temperature step could be enhanced in order to meet the customer requirements better.

The case study shows how target-costing concepts can be used not only for traditional product components, but also to analyse different manufacturing steps. The results of the QFD matrix also aid in assessing the original target market. In the illustrated case it will be necessary to focus on a different segment where traditional tools are less important, and water resistance and the ability to shape the material are more important.

CONCLUSION

Total cost management is a feasible approach of integrating environmental preservation activities over the entire product life cycle into corporate long-term strategies. Environmental conscious manufacturing is made possible through TCM because it seeks to reduce overall product life cycle costs and conserve resources. The case presented in the study explores the possibility of transforming a specific textile waste product into a useful product.

Although the evaluated example has not been commercialized, this research shows how target cost management can be used to promote the development of commercially viable and environmentally friendly products in an effort to recycle textile wastes. This case demonstrates that TCM offers a dynamic modeling approach that will adjust to technological innovation. TCM helps build a corporate culture that stimulates creativity and proactively manages technological innovations that are beneficial to the environment.

Total cost management is a feasible approach of integrating environmental preservation activities over the entire product life cycle into corporate long-term strategies. Environmental conscious manufacturing is made possible through TCM because it seeks to reduce overall product life cycle costs and conserve resources. The case presented in the study explores the possibility of transforming a specific textile waste product into a useful product.

Although the evaluated example has not been commercialized, this research shows how target cost management can be used to promote the development of commercially viable and environmentally friendly products in an effort to recycle textile wastes. This case demonstrates that TCM offers a dynamic modeling approach that will adjust to technological innovation. TCM helps build a corporate culture that stimulates creativity and proactively manages technological innovations that are beneficial to the environment.

7

Cost Control Techniques

INTRODUCTION

The cost control definition suggests that a company should investigate good procedures for finding out the reason why the costs of the company are not as per the pre-decided or budgeted costs. Thus, cost control can help a company determine, if it is really spending more than it should actually spend. Though it is not essential to be a finance expert to understand the definition of cost control, planning and actually implementing the cost control techniques can be quite a big challenge.

It is essential for the senior level managers to have a good understanding of the cost control software which is a part of effective cost control techniques. The next few paragraphs will give you more information about the cost control management and the cost control techniques.

TECHNIQUES AND WAYS FOR CONTROLLING COSTS

The first step in the cost control management is to find out the cost centers and arrive at a conclusion in how much percentage they differ or vary from the standards of the industry. It is also important to study how the close competitors of your company manage to control their costs and in turn, maximize their profits. Before discussing about the cost control methods or the cost control techniques, it is very important to carry out a very proper cost analysis. The costs incurred by all the departments of the company should be considered so that, you can chalk out some smart cost control strategies to overcome these financial problems.

It is very important to find out the exact and relevant reasons for why the costs of the company are more than the standards adhered to by the industry. The most important of all the cost control techniques is to appoint a small team of highly qualified and experienced people well versed in the financial management team to manage the daily finances of the company in a very professional and systematic manner. The finance team should take correct decisions in favour of the company and opt for less expensive materials and resources for the company without compromising on their quality. You should be very clear about the number of employees you require for a particular project. There are many companies who find it difficult to earn decent profits as their employee count is way beyond the necessity. You can also consider the idea of recruiting employees on contract basis to cut down your costs. While deciding how much salary to pay to a particular employee, you need to be very careful. You should decide the salary strictly on the basis of overall performance. Instead of giving awards to the employees in the form of frequent salary hikes, you should give out bonuses to eligible employees. Following practices recommended in cost method of accounting may benefit your company.

The cost control software can be helpful in doing the work in comparatively less time and with more accuracy. In the times of recession, many firms resort to cost control techniques such as reducing the extra facilities to the employees such as the recreational facilities. The cost control techniques might also include cutting down the expenditure incurred on traveling by air and luxury hotel accommodations in order to harness the cash flow. As a part of the cost cutting measure, few firms may postpone or cancel their plans of acquiring new companies, investing in new businesses and buying new machinery or systems. The cost control techniques should be utilized to save cash and bring back the financial strength of the company.

The cost control techniques used by different organizations are different and are largely dependent on their business model and strength of their balance sheet. The better the implementation of these techniques, the better would be the future of the concerned organizations.

BUDGET

- A budget is generally a list of all planned expenses and revenues. It is a plan for saving and spending. A budget is an important concept in microeconomics, which uses a budget line to illustrate the trade-offs between two or more goods. In other terms, a budget is an organizational plan stated in monetary terms.
- *Business start-up budget:* The process of calculating the costs of starting a small business begins with a list of all necessary purchases including tangible assets and services, working capital, sources and collateral. The budget should contain a narrative explaining how you decided on the amount of this reserve and a description of the expected financial results of business activities. The assets should be valued with each and every cost. All other expenses are like labour factory overhead all freshmen expenses are also included into business budgeting
- *Corporate budget:* The budget of a company is often compiled annually, but may not be. A finished budget, usually requiring considerable effort, is a plan for the short-term future, typically one year. While traditionally the Finance department compiles the company's budget, modern software allows hundreds or even thousands of people in various departments to list their expected

revenues and expenses in the final budget. If the actual figures delivered through the budget period come close to the budget, this suggests that the managers understand their business and have been successfully driving it in the intended direction. On the other hand, if the figures diverge wildly from the budget, this sends an 'out of control' signal, and the share price could suffer as a result.

- *Event management budget:* A budget is a fundamental tool for an event director to predict with reasonable accuracy whether the event will result in a profit, a loss or will break-even. A budget can also be used as a pricing tool.
- *Budget types:*
  - *Sales budget:* The sales budget is an estimate of future sales, often broken down into both units and dollars. It is used to create company sales goals.
  - *Production budget:* Product oriented companies create a production budget which estimates the number of units that must be manufactured to meet the sales goals. The production budget also estimates the various costs involved with manufacturing those units, including labour and material.
  - *Cash Flow/Cash budget:* The cash flow budget is a prediction of future cash receipts and expenditures for a particular time period. It usually covers a period in the short term future. The cash flow budget helps the business determine when income will be sufficient to cover expenses and when the company will need to seek outside financing.
  - *Marketing budget:* The marketing budget is an estimate of the funds needed for promotion, advertising, and public relations in order to market the product or service.
  - *Project budget:* The project budget is a prediction of the costs associated with a particular company project. These costs include labour, materials, and other related expenses. The project budget is often broken down into specific tasks, with task budgets assigned to each.
  - *Revenue budget:* The Revenue Budget consists of revenue receipts of government and the expenditure met from these revenues. Tax revenues are made up of taxes and other duties that the government levies.
  - *Expenditure budget:* A budget type which include of spending data items..

BUDGET PREPARATION

A critical aspect of intervention planning is preparing a budget of income and expenses. The budget must include funding for materials and supplies for the intervention activities, but also for staff, facilities, and promotion. Keep in mind that each intervention requires different resources, and organizations have unique capacities to conduct interventions with existing resources. The following are typical budget categories.

CATEGORIES FOR AN INTERVENTION BUDGET

- *Personnel and benefits expense:* Personnel includes all individuals who will have responsibilities in the intervention. Others who may be hired to help with the project, such as consultants or contractors, are not budgeted in Personnel, rather are included in the Purchased, Consultant or Contractual Services. Fringe benefits are typically budgeted at a per cent of the personnel salary, and are dependent upon the benefits paid by the employer.
- *Things to consider:* Do you have enough people to implement the intervention? Will you need to hire additional part-time or full-time staff to help you? What benefits will be paid and to whom? Will your staffing needs change over the duration of your intervention from year to year?
- *General Office Expenses:* Includes office supplies needed to support the intervention.
- *Things to consider:* What basic materials or supplies are needed to support the intervention? You should be able to budget more for office supplies the first year of the project and less in subsequent years.
- *Intervention Supplies and Materials:* Intervention materials are the actual materials you will need to implement your intervention.
- *Things to consider:* How many participants you are anticipating? Can you prepare the materials yourself or do you need to hire someone to prepare them for you? Do you need to conduct research or a needs assessment before designing your materials?
- *Meeting and Activity Expenses:* Space outside your organization's office may be needed for meetings or intervention activities. Some places may charge a rental fee as well as for use of audio visual equipment, such as projectors or TVs. Food and drinks provided at the meeting may be included in this category or in Intervention Supplies, depending on the organization's preference.
- *Things to consider:* Does your current office space accommodate everything you will need for the intervention? Do you have room to conduct meetings with other partners or internal staff? Do you have appropriate space to conduct your intervention activities or will you need to use other spaces? Will any of your partners donate space for meetings or intervention activities? Will you need to rent facilities to conduct your intervention? Will you need to travel to your intervention's participants or partners, if so where will you meet with them?

- *Transportation/Travel Expenses:* Transportation can involve providing a means for participants to travel to your intervention activities in order to increase participation or providing transportation for you and your staff to travel to other locations to conduct intervention activities. This may also include fees or stipends to attend professional meetings or perform interviews and surveys out-of-town.
- *Things to consider:* Do your participants have access to public or personal transportation or will you need to provide it? Do your staff members need to travel to participants' homes or communities to conduct intervention activities? Will your staff need to travel to conferences or to make presentations outside of your city?
- *Purchased, Consultant or Contractual Service Expenses:* These expenses are payments to individuals or companies for a specific service, usually occurring temporarily during the project, that are not completed by the regular project staff.
- *Things to consider:* What specific expertise and services will you need in planning, implementing and evaluating your intervention?
- *Indirect Costs:* Indirect costs are the expenses incurred by the organization to keep the organization operating. Indirect cost are typically calculated by multiplying an agreed upon percentage by the total direct costs, or by the total of personnel and benefit costs. These costs are sometimes also referred to as administrative costs.
- *Things to consider:* Will your organization obtain sufficient indirect costs from your intervention income? Are there partners who are willing to cover some indirect costs?
- An "in-kind" donation is a contribution of time, service or goods made by a donor to help support the operations or services provided by your organization. It isn't cash. Therefore the donor does retain a degree of control over the donation that doesn't occur when the donor gives you a cash donation. Because of this "relationship" your organization should keep the donor well informed on how their donation is being used.

As you prepare your budget it is critical you account for anticipated in-kind donations. If you don't track these donations, you aren't truly acknowledging the total capacity of your organization. Also tracking these donations will help you better acknowledge the donors for their contribution.

BUDGET PREPARATION WORKSHEET

When creating your intervention budget, take into consideration that your budget and allocation of funds may vary from year to year. For example, in Year 1, many of your funds may go into buying supplies or investing money in materials for start-up. In Year 2 and beyond, you may be spending most of your budget disseminating your intervention materials or on evaluation efforts. It is important to create your yearly intervention budget to reflect these changes.

PERSONNEL

Personnel refers to all staff members who will be involved in the various intervention activities. Others helping with the intervention, such as consultants or technical assistance, are not considered Personnel, but are rather included in the Purchased Services Total. Remember: When creating Year 2 and beyond budgets, it is important to adjust for Personnel salaries based on increases in cost of living.

When calculating Personnel salaries for Year 2 and beyond, multiply personnel by the expected increase of cost of living for each year.

Calculating Personnel:

- *Base Salary:* For each personnel position, state the base salary for the position.
- *% of Time:* For each personnel position, determine the per cent of that person's total time that will be used to work on the intervention project.
- *Project Salary:* For each personnel position, determine the project salary by multiplying base salary by% of time.
- *Fringe Benefit%:* Fringe benefits include all taxes, as well as health insurance, paid time off, retirement, and other benefits provided. Fringe benefits may or may not be offered to all employees. Fringe benefit%s are at the discretion of the organization based on amount of funding and what it offers its employees in terms of benefits. Fringe benefit for a graduate research assistant may be a little as 3% perhaps providing worker's compensation only, as opposed to 20- 40% for senior full time employee of the project receiving full benefits.
- *Fringe Amount:* To determine fringe amount, multiple the fringe benefit percentage rate by the project salary amount. (Remember: {Base Salary} X {% of Time} = {Project Salary})
- *Total:* To determine the total cost of each personnel position, add the project salary + the fringe amount.
- *Principal Investigator:* Includes project time associated with such positions as project direct, principal investigator, or any co-principal investigators that provide the main leadership to the project.
- *Project Staff:* Includes salary costs of the project staff such as project manager, project coordinator, or senior staff, who directly work on the project. Project staff can also include nurses, statisticians, researchers, graduate assistants, epidemiologist or any other staff with roles directly related to aspects of the project.

- *Administrative Staff:* Includes any staff providing administrative support, such as secretaries, administrative assistant, bookkeeper, data entry staff or any staff used for this type of work.
- *Other Staff:* Any other staff not included in the other personnel categories, such as a stipend or salary for interns
- *Other Direct Costs:* These are direct non-personnel cost of any materials and resources that are necessary for completing the research or intervention.
- *General Office Supplies and materials:* Includes any of the fixed costs of having your organization remain in operation. Office operations and equipment are included in this category. These categories encompass computers, software, office supplies/materials, telephones, copy machines, office furniture, postage, etc. You may spend more on office supplies and materials in your first year of the intervention than in subsequent years.
- *Intervention Materials:* Intervention materials are those that are needed to implement your programme that are not already included general office supplies and materials. Intervention materials include any money spent on incentives or promotions for intervention participants. This can also include the costs for materials such as pre/post surveys and copies, other intervention materials such as brochures, posters, or any other materials created to promote the intervention, including distribution costs of intervention materials. Intervention material costs may vary from year to year.
- *Meeting and Intervention Activity Space:* Includes cost for the use of meeting or intervention activity space. If these types of activities occur outside the office, you may need to rent a meeting room. Some places may also charge a fee for use of audio visual equipment, such as projectors or TVs. Food and drinks provided at the meeting should also be included in this category.
- *Transportation/Travel:* Refers to travel and transportation costs for project staff or consultants to perform intervention duties. This may include fees or stipends to attend professional meetings or perform interviews or surveys out-of-town. Transportation/Travel costs can also include those incurred by providing a means for participants to get to your intervention activities in order to increase participation.
- *Other:* Refers to any other costs not covered in the other direct costs. This might include workshop fees, data purchases, and subscriptions to journals or any other miscellaneous programme costs.

Purchased Services

This refers to fees paid to individuals or companies for a specific service, usually occurring temporarily during the intervention that is not completed by the regular project staff. Purchased services may vary from project year to project year.

- *Consultants:* Includes individuals providing expert or professional advice for an agreed per diem rate. Consultants could provide services such as proposal review, speaking engagements, or services for an advisory board/committee. Consultants are usually hired on an hourly or daily rate. When calculating consultant fees, include the hourly rate and how many hours you expect them to be needed for that project year.
- *Contracts:* Includes agreements entered into with individuals or companies, to provide a specific service to the project. Contracts could include hiring a company to survey participants by phone or to design intervention materials. Contracts are usually negotiated for a set amount for the provided service.
- *Technical Assistance:* Includes any fees for professional technical services, such as; setting up or maintaining computer systems, providing training on software programmes, or providing repairs for office technology. Technical assistance can vary from company to company and by service, some may charge an hourly rate or charge a set amount for maintenance.

Iidirect Costs

This is a percentage that includes costs incurred by the organization as a result of the intervention, but that is not easily identifiable with any specific component of the intervention. Indirect costs are sometimes also referred to as facilities and administrative costs. Indirect costs include building maintenance costs, utilities, property insurance, accounting, or legal expenses. If your intervention is being housed in university space, your indirect cost may be upwards of 30-60%, however if your space is in a community organization's building, it may be much lower, for instance, 10-15%. Remember: Indirect Cost is a percentage that is multiplied by the total direct cost to determine your total project cost

GRAND TOTAL

Project budget total (Personnel Total + Other Direct Cost Total + Indirect Cost Total) for Year 1. Remember that you are calculating your project budget by year or cycle, and that your expenses may fluctuate from year to year. You will need to take into consideration how your budget will change from year to year and what categories may need more or less money during the course of the intervention. It is also important to remember increases in cost of living for personnel salaries.

BUDGET CONTROL SYSTEM

The State University of New York Fiscal and Accounting Procedures for Mandatory Student Activity Fee Programmes require the custodial and disbursing agent to establish and maintain budgetary accounts. The basic structure for recording and monitoring revenues and expenditures is the Annual Operating Budget. As part of its accounting system, Sub-Board I provides a Budgetary Control System modeled after those commonly used by governments and other not-for-profit entities which satisfies the fiscal guidelines, policies and procedures of the Board of Trustees and the State University of New York. All student governments and clients for whom Sub-Board I acts as Fiscal Agent must use the Budgetary Control System.

UNDERSTANDING THE BUDGET

A budget is your management's plan or blueprint, in structured form, which projects or anticipates the desired outcome of financial activity for a specific set of resources, for a fixed period, usually one year. For our purposes, the Annual Operating Budget is divided into two separate components: Estimated Revenues - What are the anticipated sources of revenue and how much can management realistically expect to receive? Estimated Expenditures - How much does management expect to spend, and for what purposes are resources to be spent?

IMPORTANCE OF BUDGET

A budget acts as the formal process that establishes the authority on how funds are to be collected and spent. Management's objective is to provide a logical, detailed and realistic spending plan. Once a plan has been decided upon and is formally adopted by the student government/client governing body, the budget acts as an effective management tool by providing a means of identifying and allocating limited resources and monitoring their use.

The budget also is used to help prevent the student government/client from overspending. Budget reports provide management with information on operations, allowing the organization to monitor and control spending and revenue collection while they are in progress. Hence, budgets alone are meaningless unless they are used to motivate responsible action and to direct operations towards accomplishing objectives that have been established by management as desirable. The budget is the single most important source of financial information. Almost all financial transactions are recorded in the budget. The budget is used to track all cash receipts, encumbrances and cash disbursements, and provides a means of tracking these transactions back to original source documents.

STRUCTURE OF BUDGET

In determining the basic elements of Estimated Revenues and Estimated Expenditures, a logical structure must be developed to codify and arrange the elements into units or sections that reflect the nature and structure of the operations themselves. The basic structural tool is the budgetary account. A budgetary account identifies a specific source of revenue or a particular type of expenditure by using a budgetary account number.

Sub-Board's Budgetary Control System uses the following budgetary account number format:

- *Fund:* The first three digits of the account number identify the student government/client and the overall purpose of the funds accounted for in a particular budget, *e.g.* operating funds, capital funds, etc.
- *Department:* The next four digits of the account number identify the department, division, activity center, etc. within the internal operations of the student government/client.
- *Line Item:* The next four digits of the account number identify the specific source of revenue or the type of expenditure for a particular department, *e.g.* Advertising Revenue, or Telephone Expense.
- *Project:* In certain situations, the account number may be extended by an additional four digits to further identify a particular project.

HOW DOES THE BUDGETARY PROCESS BEGIN?

The first step in the budgetary process is for the student government/client to review its operations. What is working well and what needs to be changed? What are the goals and objectives for the coming budget year? What projects does the student government/client wish to support? Which recognized clubs and organizations has management agreed to fund? What are the primary sources of revenue? Clubs, organizations, project managers and department heads may be required to submit budget requests to whoever is responsible for preparing the initial or "proposed" budget.

These requests can then be reviewed and modified before being incorporated into the proposed budget. It may also be helpful for whoever is preparing the proposed budget to review past budgets – historical information can be very helpful in determining how the student government/client has operated in the past and can help identify areas that management would like to continue, eliminate or change. All student governments/clients must prepare their budgets just as to the fiscal year.

The fiscal year begins on August 1 and ends on July 31 of the following year. Once the proposed budget has been prepared, it must be formally approved or adopted in accordance with the student government/client constitution, by-laws or governing rules. During this process, the budget may be discussed, modified, or challenged before being formally adopted. For student governments/clients that maintain more that one fund in addition to the operating budget, a separate budget for each Fund must be adopted.

AFTER THE BUDGET IS ADOPTED, WHAT IS THE NEXT STEP?

For all student governments/clients subject to administrative review and certification, approved budgets must be submitted using the Required Budget Format to the Administrative Designee no later than June 1 prior to the start of the fiscal year. A copy of the approved budget must also be submitted to the SBI Accounting Office by the same date, June 1. For independent clients whose budgets are not subject to administrative review and certification, approved budgets must be submitted to the SBI Accounting Office no later than June 1 prior to the start of the Fiscal Year.

Budgets must be accompanied by a completed Certification of Budget Form signed by at least two officers or authorized representatives of the student government/client, attesting that adoption and approval procedures were correctly followed. For student governments/clients that maintain more than one budget, a separate Certification of Budget Form must be submitted with each budget. In order to continue operating without an interruption in accounting services, budgets must be submitted by the due date of June 1.

WHAT HAPPENS AFTER THE BUDGET IS SUBMITTED AND CERTIFIED

Upon receiving the adopted budget, Sub-Board I will review the budget for accuracy and conformity to fiscal guidelines. Budgets must be balanced; *i.e.* Total Estimated Revenue must equal or exceed Total Estimated Expenditures. Unbalanced budgets will be returned to the student government/client unprocessed.

Estimated Revenues and Estimated Expenditures must be based on realistic projections. Assuming that budgets have been submitted by the required deadline, in the required format, and with the proper officer certification, and the administrative designee, where applicable, has approved the budgets, Sub- Board I will enter the adopted budgets into the accounting system. On August 1, the adopted budgets will go into effect. All student governments/clients will receive initial budget reports as of August 1, before any activity begins, as verification that Sub-Board I has accurately entered the budgets. The student government/client should closely review these initial budget reports and report any problems or errors immediately to the SBI Accounting Office for correction.

WILL ANY ACTIVITY FROM THE PRIOR YEAR BUDGET HAVE AN EFFECT ON THE CURRENT BUDGET

Since there may be financial activity in process between the end of one fiscal year and the beginning of the next, the budget will be affected in several ways.

- On the revenue side, the Fund's cash balance as of July 31 will be added to Estimated Revenues and Annual Revenue Receipts in the new budget on the first day of the new fiscal year, August 1. This cash balance, if sufficient, can be used as a reserve to accommodate outstanding encumbrances and accrued payroll expenses. Any remaining cash balance not reserved for other purposes may be re-appropriated in the new budget. This adjustment will take place as soon as all cash activity has been recorded and reconciled for July, usually sometime in early August.

- On the expenditure side, any encumbrances outstanding at the end of the fiscal year will be added to budgeted expenditures in the next fiscal year's budget. The date that this adjustment actually takes place depends on the final accounting of year-end activity, preparation of year-end financial statements, the progress of the annual independent audit, etc., and usually takes place sometime after October 15. Until this final accounting for outstanding encumbrances is completed and the prior year budget is "closed", the accounting system will automatically account for encumbrances from the prior fiscal year that are paid in the new fiscal year. This is done so that budgetary expenditures for the new fiscal year are not depleted by payments for which encumbrances existed in the prior fiscal year's budget.
- Accrued payroll expenses, if any, as of July 31 will be added to Estimated Expenditures in the next fiscal year when the new budget goes into effect on August 1. You must provide a sufficient reserve in your budget to accommodate this additional appropriation and to maintain a balanced budget. This adjustment to the budget will take place after all payroll activity has been received and recorded, usually sometime in September.

WHAT IF THE BUDGET NEEDS TO BE MODIFIED OR ADJUSTED DURING THE COURSE OF THE FISCAL YEAR

It is not realistic to prepare a budget at the beginning of the fiscal year and then leave it as a rigid plan of action. Important unforeseen changes in internal or external conditions may require budget revisions during the fiscal year. It is essential that management receive timely information on its actual results in comparison with the plan. A comparison of actual operating results with the original budget plan would show management what the organization did in comparison with what it initially planned to do.

It may not reveal, however, how well the organization did with regard to how it should have performed under the conditions which actually existed. Therefore, Sub-Board I will provide periodic budget reports to assess performance of actual results with the original plan and the adjusted budget plan. Whenever an adjustment or revision to the original budget is necessary, the student government/client must notify Sub-Board I of the adjustment(s) to be made by entering a Budget Adjustment into the on-line KVS Accounting System. Budget Adjustments require the approval of two officers.

In addition, student governments and independent clients who are subject to administrative review must have all budget adjustments or changes to the budget reviewed and certified by the administrative designee. All approvals can be done on-line. Sub-Board I will update the budget adjustments only after all approvals have been obtained.

ZERO-BASED BUDGETING

Zero-based budgeting is a technique of planning and decision-making which reverses the working process of traditional budgeting. In traditional incremental budgeting, departmental managers justify only increases over the previous year budget and what has been already spent is automatically sanctioned. No reference is made to the previous level of expenditure. By contrast, in zero-based budgeting, every department function is reviewed comprehensively and all expenditures must be approved, rather than only increases. Zero-based budgeting requires the budget request be justified in complete detail by each division manager starting from the zero-base. The zero-base is indifferent to whether the total budget is increasing or decreasing. The term "zero-based budgeting" is sometimes used in personal finance to describe the practice of budgeting every dollar of income received, and then adjusting some part of the budget downward for every other part that needs to be adjusted upward.

It is more technically correct to refer to this practice as "zero-sum budgeting". Zero based budgeting also refers to the identification of a task or tasks and then funding resources to complete the task independent of current resourcing.

Advantages:

- Detects inflated budgets.
- Drives managers to find cost effective ways to improve operations.
- Efficient allocation of resources, as it is based on needs and benefits.
- Forces cost centers to identify their mission and their relationship to overall goals.

  Identifies and eliminates wasteful and obsolete operations.
- Identifies opportunities for outsourcing.
- Increases communication and coordination within the organization.
- Increases staff motivation by providing greater initiative and responsibility in decision-making.
- Useful for service departments where the output is difficult to identify.

Disadvantages:

- Difficult to define decision units and decision packages, as it is time-consuming and exhaustive.
- Forced to justify every detail related to expenditure. The R&D department is threatened whereas the production department benefits.
- Honesty of the managers must be reliable and uniform. Any manager that exaggerates skews the results.
- In a large organization, the volume of forms may be so large that no one person could read it all. Compressing the information down to a usable size might remove critically important details.

- Necessary to train managers. Zero-based budgeting must be clearly understood by managers at various levels to be successfully implemented. Difficult to administer and communicate the budgeting because more managers are involved in the process.

INCREMENTAL BUDGETING

Incremental Budgeting uses a budget prepared using a previous period's budget or actual performance as a base, with incremental amounts added for the new budget period. The allocation of resources is based upon allocations from the previous period. This approach is not recommended as it fails to take into account changing circumstances. Moreover, it encourages "spending up to the budget" to ensure a reasonable allocation in the next period. It leads to a "spend it or lose it" mentality.

Advantages:

- Conflicts are avoided when departments appear to be treated similarly.
- Co-ordination between budgets is easier to achieve.
- Managers can operate their departments on a consistent basis.
- The budget is stable and change is gradual.
- The impact of change can be seen quickly.
- The system is relatively simple to operate and easy to understand.

Disadvantages:

- Assumes activities and methods of working will continue in the same way.
- Encourages spending up to the budget so that the budget is maintained next year.
- No incentive for developing new ideas.
- No incentive to reduce costs.
- The budget may become out-of-date and no longer relate to the level of activity or type of work being carried out.
- The priority for resources may have changed since the budgets were originally set.
- There may be budgetary slack built into the budget, which is never reviewed. Managers might have overestimated their requirements in the past in order to obtain a budget which is easier to work within, and which will allow them to achieve favourable results.

STANDARD COSTING

Standard costing is an important subtopic of cost accounting. Standard costs are usually associated with a manufacturing company's costs of direct material, direct labour, and manufacturing overhead. Rather than assigning the actual costs of direct material, direct labour, and manufacturing overhead to a product, many manufacturers assign the expected or standard cost.

This means that a manufacturer's inventories and cost of goods sold will begin with amounts reflecting the standard costs, not the actual costs, of a product. Manufacturers, of course, still have to pay the actual costs. As a result there are almost always differences between the actual costs and the standard costs, and those differences are known as variances. Standard costing and the related variances is a valuable management tool.

If a variance arises, management becomes aware that manufacturing costs have differed from the standard costs. If actual costs are greater than standard costs the variance is unfavourable. An unfavourable variance tells management that if everything else stays constant the company's actual profit will be less than planned. If actual costs are less than standard costs the variance is favourable. A favourable variance tells management that if everything else stays constant the actual profit will likely exceed the planned profit.

The sooner that the accounting system reports a variance, the sooner that management can direct its attention to the difference from the planned amounts. If we assume that a company uses the perpetual inventory system and that it carries all of its inventory accounts at standard cost then the standard cost of a finished product is the sum of the standard costs of the inputs:

- Direct material
- Direct labour
- Manufacturing overhead
  - Variable manufacturing overhead
  - Fixed manufacturing overhead

VARIANCE ANALYSIS

Variance analysis is usually associated with explaining the difference (or variance) between actual costs and the standard costs allowed for the good output. For example, the difference in materials costs can be divided into a materials price variance and a materials usage variance. The difference between the actual direct labour costs and the standard direct labour costs can be divided into a rate variance and an efficiency variance.

The difference in manufacturing overhead can be divided into spending, efficiency, and volume variances. Mix and yield variances can also be calculated. Variance analysis helps management to understand the present costs and then to control future costs. Variance analysis is also used to explain the difference between the actual sales dollars and the budgeted sales dollars. Examples include sales price variance, sales quantity variance, and sales mix variance. A difference in the relative proportion of sales can account for some of the difference in a company's profits.

RESPONSIBILITY ACCOUNTING

Responsibility accounting is an underlying concept of accounting performance measurement systems. The basic idea is that large diversified organizations are difficult, if not impossible to manage as a single segment, thus they must be decentralized or separated into manageable parts.

These parts, or segments are referred to as responsibility centers that include:

- Revenue centers,
- Cost centers,
- Profit centers and
- Investment centers.

This approach allows responsibility to be assigned to the segment managers that have the greatest amount of influence over the key elements to be managed. These elements include revenue for a revenue center costs for a cost center a measure of profitability for a profit center and return on investment for an investment center.

CONTROLLABILITY CONCEPT

An underlying concept of responsibility accounting is referred to as controllability. Conceptually, a manager should only be held responsible for those aspects of performance that he or she can control. In my view, this concept is rarely, if ever, applied successfully in practice because of the system variation present in all systems. Attempts to apply the controllability concept produce responsibility reports where each layer of management is held responsible for all subordinate management layers.

ADVANTAGES AND DISADVANTAGES

Responsibility accounting has been an accepted part of traditional accounting control systems for many years because it provides an organization with a number of advantages. Perhaps the most compelling argument for the responsibility accounting approach is that it provides a way to manage an organization that would otherwise be unmanageable. In addition, assigning responsibility to lower level managers allows higher level managers to pursue other activities such as long term planning and policy making. It also provides a way to motivate lower level managers and workers. Managers and workers in an individualistic system tend to be motivated by measurements that emphasize their individual performances. However, this emphasis on the performance of individuals and individual segments creates what some critics refer to as the "stovepipe organization."

Others have used the term "functional silos" to describe the same idea. Information flows vertically, rather than horizontally. Individuals in the various segments and functional areas are separated and tend to ignore the interdependencies within the organization. Segment managers and individual workers within segments tend to compete to optimize their own performance measurements rather than working together to optimize the performance of the system. An implicit assumption of responsibility accounting is that separating a company into responsibility centers that are controlled in a top down manner is the way to optimize the system. However, this separation inevitably fails to consider many of the interdependencies within the organization. Ignoring the interdependencies prevents teamwork and creates the need for buffers such as additional inventory, workers, managers and capacity. Of course, a system that prevents teamwork and creates excess is inconsistent with the lean enterprise concepts of just-in-time and the theory of constraints.

For this reason, critics of traditional accounting control systems advocate managing the system as a whole to eliminate the need for buffers and excess. They also argue that companies need to develop process oriented learning support systems, not financial results, fear oriented control systems. The information system needs to reveal the company's problems and constraints in a timely manner and at a disaggregated level so that empowered users can identify how to correct problems, remove constraints and improve the process. These critics, accounting control information does not qualify in any of these categories because it is not timely, disaggregated, or user friendly. This harsh criticism of accounting control information leads us to a very important controversial question. Can a company successfully implement just-in-time and other continuous improvement concepts while retaining a traditional responsibility accounting control system?

Although the jury is still out on this question, a number of field research studies indicate that accounting based controls are playing a decreasing role in companies that adopt the lean enterprise concepts. In a recent study involving nine companies, each company answered this controversial question in a different way by using a different mix of process oriented versus results oriented learning and control information. Since each company is different, a generalized answer to this question for all firms in all situations cannot be provided.

8

Project Management

INTRODUCTION

Project management is the discipline of planning, organizing, securing and managing resources to bring about the successful completion of specific project goals and objectives. It is sometimes conflated with programme management, however technically that is actually a higher level construction: a group of related and somehow interdependent engineering projects. A project is a temporary endeavor, having a defined beginning and end (usually constrained by date, but can be by funding or deliverables), undertaken to meet unique goals and objectives, usually to bring about beneficial change or added value. The temporary nature of projects stands in contrast to business as usual (or operations), which are repetitive, permanent or semi-permanent functional work to produce products or services.

In practice, the management of these two systems is often found to be quite different, and as such requires the development of distinct technical skills and the adoption of separate management. The primary challenge of project management is to achieve all of the engineering project goals and objectives while honoring the preconceived project constraints. Typical constraints are scope, time, and budget. The secondary—and more ambitious—challenge is to optimize the allocation and integration of inputs necessary to meet pre-defined objectives.

HISTORY

Project management has been practiced since early civilization. Until 1900 civil engineering projects were generally managed by creative architects and engineers themselves, among those for example Vitruvius (1st century BC), Christopher Wren (1632-1723) , Thomas Telford (1757-1834) and Isambard Kingdom Brunel (1806-1859). It was in the 1950s that organizations started to systematically apply project management tools and techniques to complex engineering projects. As a discipline, Project Management developed from several fields of application including civil construction, engineering, and heavy defence activity. Two forefathers of project management are Henry

Gantt, called the father of planning and control techniques, who is famous for his use of the Gantt chart as a project management tool; and Henri Fayol for his creation of the 5 management functions which form the foundation of the body of knowledge associated with project and programme management. Both Gantt and Fayol were students of Frederick Winslow Taylor's theories of scientific management. His work is the forerunner to modern project management tools including work breakdown structure (WBS) and resource allocation.

The 1950s marked the beginning of the modern Project Management era where core engineering fields come together working as one. Project management became recognized as a distinct discipline arising from the management discipline with engineering model. In the United States, prior to the 1950s, projects were managed on an ad hoc basis using mostly Gantt Charts, and informal techniques and tools. At that time, two mathematical project-scheduling models were developed.

The "Critical Path Method" (CPM) was developed as a joint venture between DuPont Corporation and Remington Rand Corporation for managing plant maintenance projects. And the "Programme Evaluation and Review Technique" or PERT, was developed by Booz Allen Hamilton as part of the United States Navy's (in conjunction with the Lockheed Corporation) Polaris missile submarine programme; These mathematical techniques quickly spread into many private enterprises. At the same time, as project-scheduling models were being developed, technology for project cost estimating, cost management, and engineering economics was evolving, with pioneering work by Hans Lang and others.

In 1956, the American Association of Cost Engineers (now AACE International; the Association for the Advancement of Cost Engineering) was formed by early practitioners of project management and the associated specialties of planning and scheduling, cost estimating, and cost/schedule control (project control). AACE continued its pioneering work and in 2006 released the first integrated process for portfolio, programme and project management (Total Cost Management Framework). The International Project Management Association (IPMA) was founded in Europe in 1967, as a federation of several national project management associations. IPMA maintains its federal structure today and now includes member associations on every continent except Antarctica. IPMA offers a Four Level Certification programme based on the IPMA Competence Baseline (ICB).

The ICB covers technical competences, contextual competences, and behavioural competences. In 1969, the Project Management Institute (PMI) was formed in the USA. PMI publishes A Guide to the Project Management Body of Knowledge, which describes project management practices that are common to "most projects, most of the time." PMI also offers multiple certifications. The American Academy of Project Management (AAPM)

International Board of Standards 1996 was the first to institute post-graduate certifications such as the MPM Master Project Manager, PME Project Management E-Business, CEC Certified-Ecommerce Consultant, and CIPM Certified International Project Manager. The AAPM also issues the post-graduate standards body of knowledge for executives.

APPROACHES

There are a number of approaches to managing project activities including agile, interactive, incremental, and phased approaches. Regardless of the methodology employed, careful consideration must be given to the overall project objectives, timeline, and cost, as well as the roles and responsibilities of all participants and stakeholders.

The Traditional Approach

A traditional phased approach identifies a sequence of steps to be completed. In the "traditional approach", we can distinguish 5 components of a project (4 stages plus control) in the development of a project:

1. Project initiation stage;
2. Project planning and design stage;
3. Project execution and construction stage;
4. Project monitoring and controlling systems;
5. Project completion.

Not all the projects will visit every stage as projects can be terminated before they reach completion. Some projects do not follow a structured planning and/or monitoring stages. Some projects will go through steps 2, 3 and 4 multiple times. Many industries use variations on these project stages. For example, when working on a brick and mortar design and construction, projects will typically progress through stages like Pre-Planning, Conceptual Design, Schematic Design, Design Development, Construction Drawings (or Contract Documents), and Construction Administration.

In software development, this approach is often known as the waterfall model, *i.e.*, one series of tasks after another in linear sequence. In software development many organizations have adapted the Rational Unified Process (RUP) to fit this methodology, although RUP does not require or explicitly recommend this practice. Waterfall development works well for small, well defined projects, but often fails in larger projects of undefined and ambiguous nature.

The Cone of Uncertainty explains some of this as the planning made on the initial phase of the project suffers from a high degree of uncertainty. This becomes especially true as software development is often the realization of a new or novel product. In projects where requirements have not been finalized and can change, requirements management is used to develop an accurate and complete definition of the behaviour of software that can serve as the basis for software development. While the terms may differ from industry to industry, the actual stages typically follow common steps to problem solving — "defining the problem, weighing options, choosing a path, implementation and evaluation."

Critical Chain Project Management

Critical Chain Project Management (CCPM) is a method of planning and managing projects that puts more emphasis on the resources (physical and human) needed in order to execute project tasks. The most complex part involves engineering professionals of different fields (Civil, Electrical, Mechanical etc) working together. It is an application of the Theory of Constraints (TOC) to projects.

The goal is to increase the rate of throughput (or completion rates) of projects in an organization. Applying the first three of the five focusing steps of TOC, the system constraint for all projects is identified as are the resources. To exploit the constraint, tasks on the critical chain are given priority over all other activities. Finally, projects are planned and managed to ensure that the resources are ready when the critical chain tasks must start, subordinating all other resources to the critical chain. Regardless of project type, the project plan should undergo Resource Leveling, and the longest sequence of resource-constrained tasks should be identified as the critical chain.

In multi-project environments, resource leveling should be performed across projects. However, it is often enough to identify (or simply select) a single "drum" resource—a resource that acts as a constraint across projects—and stagger projects based on the availability of that single resource.

EXTREME PROJECT MANAGEMENT

In critical studies of Project Management, it has been noted that several of these fundamentally PERT-based models are not well suited for the multi-project company environment of today. Most of them are aimed at very large-scale, one-time, non-routine projects, and nowadays all kinds of management are expressed in terms of projects. Using complex models for "projects" (or rather "tasks") spanning a few weeks has been proven to cause unnecessary costs and low maneuverability in several cases·

Instead, project management experts try to identify different "lightweight" models, such as Agile Project Management methods including Extreme Programming for software development and Scrum techniques. The generalization of Extreme Programming to other kinds of projects is extreme project management, which may be used in combination with the process modeling and management principles of human interaction management.

Event Chain Methodology

Event chain methodology is another method that complements critical path method and critical chain project management methodologies. Event chain methodology is an uncertainty modeling and schedule network analysis technique that is focused on identifying and managing events and event chains that affect project schedules. Event chain methodology helps to mitigate the negative impact of psychological heuristics and biases, as well as to allow for easy modeling of uncertainties in the project schedules.

Event chain methodology is based on the following principles.

- Probabilistic moment of risk: An activity (task) in most real life processes is not a continuous uniform process. Tasks are affected by external events, which can occur at some point in the middle of the task.
- Event chains: Events can cause other events, which will create event chains. These event chains can significantly affect the course of the project. Quantitative analysis is used to determine a cumulative effect of these event chains on the project schedule.
- Critical events or event chains: The single events or the event chains that have the most potential to affect the projects are the "critical events" or "critical chains of events." They can be determined by the analysis.
- Project tracking with events: Even if a project is partially completed and data about the project duration, cost, and events occurred is available, it is still possible to refine information about future potential events and helps to forecast future project performance.
- Event chain visualization: Events and event chains can be visualized using event chain diagrams on a Gantt chart.

Prince2

PRINCE2 is a structured approach to project management, released in 1996 as a generic project management method. It combined the original PROMPT methodology (which evolved into the PRINCE methodology) with IBM's MITP (managing the implementation of the total project) methodology. PRINCE2 provides a method for managing projects within a clearly defined framework.

PRINCE2 describes procedures to coordinate people and activities in a project, how to design and supervise the project, and what to do if the project has to be adjusted if it does not develop as planned. In the method, each process is specified with its key inputs and outputs and with specific goals and activities to be carried out.

This allows for automatic control of any deviations from the plan. Divided into manageable stages, the method enables an efficient control of resources. On the basis of close monitoring, the project can be carried out in a controlled and organized way. PRINCE2 provides a common language for all participants in the project. The various management roles and responsibilities involved in a project are fully described and are adaptable to suit the complexity of the project and skills of the organization.

PROCESS-BASED MANAGEMENT

Also furthering the concept of project control is the incorporation of process-based management. This area has been driven by the use of Maturity models such as the CMMI (Capability Maturity Model Integration) and ISO/IEC15504 (SPICE - Software Process Improvement and Capability Estimation).

AGILE PROJECT MANAGEMENT

Agile Project Management approaches based on the principles of human interaction management are founded on a process view of human collaboration. This contrasts sharply with the traditional approach. In the agile software development or flexible product development approach, the project is seen as a series of relatively small tasks conceived and executed as the situation demands in an adaptive manner, rather than as a completely pre-planned process.

PROCESSES

Traditionally, project management includes a number of elements: four to five process groups, and a control system. Regardless of the methodology or terminology used, the same basic project management processes will be used.

Major process groups generally include:

- Initiation
- Planning or development
- Production or execution
- Monitoring and controlling
- Closing

In project environments with a significant exploratory element (*e.g.*, Research and development), these stages may be supplemented with decision points (go/no go decisions) at which the project's continuation is debated and decided. An example is the Stage-Gate model.

Initiation

The initiation processes determine the nature and scope of the project· If this stage is not performed well, it is unlikely that the project will be successful in meeting the business' needs. The key project controls needed here are an understanding of the business environment and making sure that all necessary controls are incorporated into the project. Any deficiencies should be reported and a recommendation should be made to fix them.

The initiation stage should include a plan that encompasses the following areas:

- Analyzing the business needs/requirements in measurable goals
- Reviewing of the current operations
- Financial analysis of the costs and benefits including a budget
- Stakeholder analysis, including users, and support personnel for the project
- Project charter including costs, tasks, deliverables, and schedule

PLANNING AND DESIGN

After the initiation stage, the project is planned to an appropriate level of detail. The main purpose is to plan time, cost and resources adequately to estimate the work needed and to effectively manage risk during project execution. As with the Initiation process group, a failure to adequately plan greatly reduces the project's chances of successfully accomplishing its goals.

Project planning generally consists of:

- Determining how to plan (*e.g.* by level of detail or rolling wave);
- Developing the scope statement;
- Selecting the planning team;
- Identifying deliverables and creating the work breakdown structure;
- Identifying the activities needed to complete those deliverables and networking the activities in their logical sequence;
- Estimating the resource requirements for the activities;
- Estimating time and cost for activities;
- Developing the schedule;
- Developing the budget;
- Risk planning;
- gaining formal approval to begin work.

Additional processes, such as planning for communications and for scope management, identifying roles and responsibilities, determining what to purchase for the project and holding a kick-off meeting are also generally advisable. For new product development projects, conceptual design of the operation of the final product may be performed concurrent with the project planning activities, and may help to inform the planning team when identifying deliverables and planning activities.

EXECUTING

Executing consists of the processes used to complete the work defined in the project management plan to accomplish the project's requirements. Execution process involves coordinating people and resources, as well as integrating and performing the activities of the project in accordance with the project management plan. The deliverables are produced as outputs from the processes performed as defined in the project management plan.

MONITORING AND CONTROLLING

Monitoring and controlling consists of those processes performed to observe project execution so that potential problems can be identified in a timely manner and corrective action can be taken, when necessary, to control the execution of the project. The key benefit is that project performance is observed and measured regularly to identify variances from the project management plan.

Monitoring and Controlling includes:

- Measuring the ongoing project activities;
- Monitoring the project variables against the project management plan and the project performance baseline;
- Identify corrective actions to address issues and risks properly;
- Influencing the factors that could circumvent integrated change control so only approved changes are implemented

In multi-phase projects, the monitoring and control process also provides feedback between project phases, in order to implement corrective or preventive actions to bring the project into compliance with the project management plan.

Project Maintenance is an ongoing process, and it includes:

- Continuing support of end users
- Correction of errors
- Updates of the software over time

In this stage, auditors should pay attention to how effectively and quickly user problems are resolved. Over the course of any construction project, the work scope may change. Change is a normal and expected part of the construction process. Changes can be the result of necessary design modifications, differing site conditions, material availability, contractor-requested changes, value engineering and impacts from third parties, to name a few. Beyond executing the change in the field, the change normally needs to be documented to show what was actually constructed.

This is referred to as Change Management. Hence, the owner usually requires a final record to show all changes or, more specifically, any change that modifies the tangible portions of the finished work. The record is made on the contract documents - usually, but not necessarily limited to, the design drawings. The end product of this effort is what the industry terms as-built drawings, or more simply, "as built." The requirement for providing them is a norm in construction contracts. When changes are introduced to the project, the viability of the project has to be re-assessed. It is important not to lose sight of the initial goals and targets of the projects. When the changes accumulate, the forecasted result may not justify the original proposed investment in the project.

Closing

Closing includes the formal acceptance of the project and the ending thereof. Administrative activities include the archiving of the files and documenting sessions learned.

This phase consists of:

- Project close: Finalize all activities across all of the process groups to formally close the project or a project phase
- Contract closure: Complete and settle each contract (including the resolution of any open items) and close each contract applicable to the project or project phase.

Project Control Systems

Project control is that element of a project that keeps it on-track, on-time and within budget. Project control begins early in the project with planning and ends late in the project with post-implementation review, having a thorough involvement of each step in the process. Each project should be assessed for the appropriate level of control needed: too much control is too time consuming, too little control is very risky.

If project control is not implemented correctly, the cost to the business should be clarified in terms of errors, fixes, and additional audit fees. Control systems are needed for cost, risk, quality, communication, time, change, procurement, and human resources. In addition, auditors should consider how important the projects are to the financial statements, how reliant the stakeholders are on controls, and how many controls exist. Auditors should review the development process and procedures for how they are implemented. The process of development and the quality of the final product may also be assessed if needed or requested. A business may want the auditing firm to be involved throughout the process to catch problems earlier on so that they can be fixed more easily. An auditor can serve as a controls consultant as part of the development team or as an independent auditor as part of an audit.

Businesses sometimes use formal systems development processes. These help assure that systems are developed successfully. A formal process is more effective in creating strong controls, and auditors should review this process to confirm that it is well designed and is followed in practice.

A good formal systems development plan outlines:

- A strategy to align development with the organization's broader objectives
- Standards for new systems
- Project management policies for timing and budgeting
  Procedures describing the process
- Evaluation of quality of change

PROJECT MANAGERS

A project manager is a professional in the field of project management. Project managers can have the responsibility of the planning, execution, and closing of any project, typically relating to construction industry, engineering, architecture, computing, or telecommunications. Many other fields in the production engineering and design engineering and heavy industrial also have project managers. A project manager is the person accountable for accomplishing the stated project objectives. Key project management responsibilities include creating clear and attainable project objectives, building the project requirements, and managing the triple constraint for projects, which is cost, time, and scope.

A project manager is often a client representative and has to determine and implement the exact needs of the client, based on knowledge of the firm they are representing. The ability to adapt to the various internal procedures of the contracting party, and to form close links with the nominated representatives, is essential in ensuring that the key issues of cost, time, quality and above all, client satisfaction, can be realised.

PROJECT MANAGEMENT TRIANGLE

Like any human undertaking, projects need to be performed and delivered under certain constraints. Traditionally, these constraints have been listed as "scope," "time," and "cost". These are also referred to as the "Project Management Triangle", where each side represents a constraint. One side of the triangle cannot be changed without affecting the others.

A further refinement of the constraints separates product "quality" or "performance" from scope, and turns quality into a fourth constraint. The time constraint refers to the amount of time available to complete a project. The cost constraint refers to the budgeted amount available for the project. The scope constraint refers to what must be done to produce the project's end result.

These three constraints are often competing constraints: increased scope typically means increased time and increased cost, a tight time constraint could mean increased costs and reduced scope, and a tight budget could mean increased time and reduced scope. The discipline of Project Management is about providing the tools and techniques that enable the project team (not just the project manager) to organize their work to meet these constraints.

WORK BREAKDOWN STRUCTURE

The Work Breakdown Structure (WBS) is a tree structure, which shows a subdivision of effort required to achieve an objective; for example a programme, project, and contract. The WBS may be hardware, product, service, or process oriented. A WBS can be developed by starting with the end objective and successively subdividing it into manageable components in terms of size, duration, and responsibility (*e.g.*, systems, subsystems, components, tasks, subtasks, and work packages), which include all steps necessary to achieve the objective.

The Work Breakdown Structure provides a common framework for the natural development of the overall planning and control of a contract and is the basis for dividing work into definable increments from which the statement of work can be developed and technical, schedule, cost, and labour hour reporting can be established.

PROJECT MANAGEMENT FRAMEWORK

The Programme (Investment) Life Cycle integrates the project management and system development life cycles with the activities directly associated with system deployment and operation. By design, system operation management and related activities occur after the project is complete and are not documented within this guide. In the US United States Department of Veterans Affairs (VA) the programme management life cycle is depicted and describe in the overall VA IT Project Management Framework to address the integration of OMB Exhibit 300 project (investment) management activities and the overall project budgeting process.

The project closing phase activities at the VA continues through system deployment and into system operation for the purpose of illustrating and describing the system activities the VA considers part of the project.

INTERNATIONAL STANDARDS

There have been several attempts to develop Project Management standards, such as:

- Capability Maturity Model from the Software Engineering Institute.
- GAPPS, Global Alliance for Project Performance Standards- an open source standard describing COMPETENCIES for project and programme managers.
- A Guide to the Project Management Body of Knowledge
- HERMES method, Swiss general project management method, selected for use in Luxembourg and international organizations.
- The ISO standards ISO 9000, a family of standards for quality management systems, and the ISO 10006:2003, for Quality management systems and guidelines for quality management in projects.
- PRINCE2, PRojects IN Controlled Environments.
- Team Software Process (TSP) from the Software Engineering Institute.
- Total Cost Management Framework, AACE International's Methodology for Integrated Portfolio, Programme and Project Management)
- V-Model, an original systems development method.
- The Logical framework approach, which is popular in international development organizations.
- IAPPM, The International Association of Project and Programme Management, guide to Project Auditing and Rescuing Troubled Projects.

PROJECT PORTFOLIO MANAGEMENT

An increasing number of organizations are using, what is referred to as, project portfolio management (PPM) as a means of selecting the right projects and then using project management techniques as the means for delivering the outcomes in the form of benefits to the performing private or not-for-profit organization. Project management methods are used 'to do projects right' and the methods used in PPM are used 'to do the right projects'. In effect PPM is becoming the method of choice for selection and prioritising among resource inter-related projects in many industries and sectors.

PROJECT COST MANAGEMENT

Project cost management (PCM) is a method which uses technology to measure cost and productivity through the full life cycle of enterprise level projects. PCM encompasses several specific functions of project management that include estimating, job controls, field data collection, scheduling, accounting and design. Beginning with estimating, a vital tool in PCM, actual historical data is used to accurately plan all aspects of the project. As the project continues, job control uses data from the estimate with the information reported from the field to measure the cost and production in the project. From project initiation to completion, project cost management has an objective to simplify and cheapen the project experience.

SEQUENCE AND TIMING

To begin with, the fifth phase, 'Determine technical specifications', is really a catch-all that involves defining the metadata that the collection will use, determining the search and display functionality, determining the file formats that will be used, and selecting a CMS. As we have seen, all of these tasks are themselves fairly complex, and ideally should be completed before actual production of content begins, given that each has implications for tools, workflows and procedures.

For example, during this phase, desired search and display functionality may influence file formats, which may in turn determine the tools that are used during the creation of the files. Likewise, search and display requirements and the functionality of the CMS will determine what types of structural metadata need to be created. Second, even though it is convenient to view the phases as a sequential list, in practice it is not always possible to complete one and move on to the next sequentially.

Two examples:

1. The original goals for a collection may need to be revised later because of technical or budget issues that arise.
2. Securing the rights to include a large amount of material could take more time than initially anticipated, resulting in delayed digitisation and the need to alter workflows in order to finish the work on time.

In addition, some of the activity that is defined early in our list of phases may continue past the beginning of later phases. The best example of this is the clearance of permission to include material in the collection. Depending on national copyright laws, material should not be digitised before permission to do so has been secured, which means that some material may be 'held back' from the project execution phase. However, this material can remain in the clearance queue while the project moves forward and other material is digitised and made available. One of the most challenging roles of a project manager is balancing the complex relationships between the various phases in a project.

One phase that should happen at a specific point in the planning of a digital collection is the development of the budget. This activity should happen after the workflows and project objectives have been finalised, not before. As suggested, cover 'evidence-based budgeting', which requires that workflows and procedures be sufficiently developed to perform representative samples of the work in order to determine how much time they take. It is important that the creation of a budget follows the development and testing of workflows; otherwise, cost and estimates and production milestones will be highly speculative.

The more information available before the budget is created, the more accurate the budget will be. To summarise, even though we can identify a fairly linear progression between distinct phases in the development of a digital collection, in many cases it will be necessary to adopt a more flexible approach. The exception is developing the budget: accurately projecting the cost of executing a project requires that as many decisions are finalised early in the planning process as possible.

PLANNING THE IMPLEMENTATION

Another area of complexity not reflected in the list of phases provided above is planning the implementation of the project itself.

This activity, broken down into specific tasks, clusters around phases 5, 6 and 7:

- Define project objectives and preliminary milestones
- Determine technical specifications
- Develop workflows
- Determine preliminary procedures based on workflows; begin project
- Documentation
- Determine what resources you need (hardware, software, staff)
- Decide if you will outsource
- Develop budget
- Evaluate and acquire necessary resources
- Finalise milestones
- Finish project documentation
- Hire and train staff, if necessary
- Start production

This series of tasks begins with identifying objectives and milestones and ends with the start of production work. The remainder of this section will cover each of these aspects of planning the implementation.

DEFINING PROJECT OBJECTIVES AND PRELIMINARY MILESTONES

A collection's goals are the starting point for defining the objectives of the project. Objectives should describe the desired outcomes of the project, specifically the deliverables expected at the end of the project (if a specific end point has been defined).

Milestones describe desired outcomes at specific points in time throughout the project and are used to assist in monitoring the progress of the work being completed.

Once we have a clear statement of the project's goals, we can determine how much work needs to be done by compiling an inventory that lists all of the major groups of content that will be included in the collection based on physical format, and within each group, the number of documents that need to be digitised.

It is useful to define these groups by physical format (text, image, audio, video), as the ultimate purpose of this inventory is to help us plan the amount of work that will need to be competed and how long it will probably take. Each format group will require its own workflow (or at least major section of a workflow).

Finally, in addition to the number of documents within each format group, it is necessary to calculate how many components or parts of each document will need to be processed.

For text, the countable unit is pages; for graphic materials, it is usually the entire document (*e.g.* a single photograph); for audio and video, it is each separate document, but as these two formats must be digitised in real time they are generally quantified by their duration. Again, the goal of this inventory is to determine the amount of work that will need to be completed during the project, so the inventory needs to be fairly granular.

It is better to define more format groups than fewer because you can combine similar groups later; by contrast, defining your format groups too narrowly can introduce unnecessary complexities into your cost estimates. To proceed with our example, during the content evaluation and selection phase of collection planning, the following calculations were used to estimate the total number of pages published in the period 1900-1920.

The two newspapers are of the same physical format, but we are putting each newspaper in its own group simply to assist in determining the total number of pages: The number of issues to include in the collection was determined during the evaluation phase.

The staff evaluating the material concluded that in general one issue per month of the Herald and one issue every 2 weeks of the Daily would provide a representative sample of the articles, advertisements and other content in the newspapers. Based on this assessment, approximately 9840 pages need to be digitised.

Table. Sample Calculations for Estimating Extent of Source Material

Newspaper	Average No of Page Per Issue	No. of Issues Per Week	No. of Issues in Collection	Approx. no Pages in Collection
County Herdle	15page/issue	1	240(one per Month	3600
Crighton Daily	12page/issue	5	520(one every 2 weeks)	6240

The project is to be performed over a period of 10 months (that is Zthe period during which the funding is available). Therefore, 984 pages need to be scanned every month (or 246 every week), on average, during this time. Based on the information we have at this point, the preliminary monthly milestones for the project can be represented:

Table. Sample Production Milestones

End of Month	No. of pages to be disitised
1	984
2	1968
3	2952
4	3936
5	4920
6	5904
7	6888
8	7872
9	8856
10	9840

These milestones are preliminary at this point because we have not performed the detailed calculations necessary to determine how many staff as suggested, need (and we do not have enough information to do that at this point). As suggested, almost certainly need to revise these milestones as information about funding and resources becomes available, but it is good to have a general idea of how much content as suggested, be expected to produce at this point so that we can at least start planning for staff, hardware and other resources. In some cases, the project is not intended to complete all of the work required to fulfil the collection's goals, such as when the collection has open-ended goals or when the collection is intended to be completed in specific phases over an extended period of time. In these cases, defining milestones and using them to track project status is still essential, if only to track how much is being spent in staff salaries

THE ROLE OF WORKFLOW

As suggested by its position in the implementation list, workflows need to be developed as early as possible.

From a project management perspective, a clearly defined workflow provides information necessary to:

- Determine the tasks required to achieve a specified set of outcomes and the order in which these tasks must be completed.
- *Determine costs*: The only sound method of determining the resources required to perform a given set of tasks (and the costs of performing those tasks) is to perform a representative set of those tasks and document actual costs carefully. Workflow modelling and evaluation is therefore necessary prior to estimation of costs associated with the production of digital content.
- Clarify duties and responsibilities. Systematic workflow definitions can help clarify who is responsible for what and can serve as the basis for negotiations between partner libraries, vendors, consultants and other participants in the creation of a digital collection.

The deals exclusively with workflow development, will expand on these three functions, but at this point it should be apparent that workflow development is a crucial component of project management.

PROJECT DOCUMENTATION

In the next stage as suggested, cover documentation as it relates to project operations: documentation of detailed procedures, rationales for decisions, administrative metadata and general best practices for creating operational documentation. A number of other kinds of documentation that are not particular to digital collection development must be managed efficiently. These types of documentation are required for any type of project (*e.g.* they apply to retrospective cataloguing of print materials as well as digitising content) but are worth mentioning here nonetheless.

These include:

- *Finances:* Financial aspects of a project need to be documented very carefully. Financial audits are a real possibility, particularly if funds have been received from public agencies, and any funder has the right to ask for documentation on how project managers are spending its money.

  Many institutions rely on centralised financial services (at the library or parent organisation level) to assist in this documentation. Periodic reporting to funders is much easier if sensible documentation procedures are established early in the project.
- *Staffing Documentation:* Job descriptions, docume-ntation regarding position creation, applicants' forms and resumes, and other types of documentation should be handled in accordance with your institution's normal practices.
- *Results of monitoring the project:* As suggested, discuss the importance of documenting the results of monitoring later in this stage.

- *Meeting minutes:* Notes and minutes from project staff meetings should document the status of the project, issues that require attention and action items.

Documentation should be viewed as a regular activity and not one that is performed on an as-needed basis, and it should be built into each of the phases identified earlier as part of large-scale collection planning, from defining the goals and scope of the collection to project and ongoing collection evaluation.

Every phase needs to be documented in some way, but in particular, evaluating and selecting source material, clearing permission to use the source material and determining the technical specifications for the collection all require considerable documentation. Given that creating and maintaining useful documentation is timeconsuming, it can take considerable staff resources, and therefore should be included in the overall staffing and budget for a given collection or project.

STAFFING

The tasks that operational staff perform will be defined in project workflows. Similar tasks should be grouped into roles, which are general types of staff positions that can be used in planning and in developing job descriptions.

Stephen Chapman provides the following list of staff roles typically involved in digitisation projects:

- Project manager
- Selector
- Conservator, curator, or other analyst of the source materials
- Preparations technician (may also be curator, who, in turn, may also be the selector)
- Cataloger to create or enhance bibliographic records and to withdraw materials for conversion
- Scanning technician or photographer
- Quality control technician (may also be the scanning technician)
- Metadata analyst (may also be the cataloger)
- Data entry technician
- Programmer or other database expert who integrates metadata and images into a coherent resource (also known as the digital object)
- Systems administrator or other manager of electronic records and systems
- Network administrator to implement security and other access requirements (may also be the systems administrator)
- Developer or designer of the user interface

These roles may not apply to every project, depending on the nature of the source material and the workflows that you have defined. For example, the staff required to work on a collection of born-digital material will differ from the staff required to work on a digitisation project. Also, some of these roles, such as cataloguers and network administrators, may be assumed by existing staff who perform these functions as part of their regular jobs. Having existing library staff perform work in short-term projects is a good way to save on staff costs, and many funders consider existing staff time to be 'in kind' contributions.

However, if existing library staff are to work on the digitisation projects, they must be allowed to devote the required time and not have the extra work simply added to their existing responsibilities. In some cases this means that the digitisation project takes priority over other activity or that someone else can take on work displaced by the digitisation project without exceeding their own normal workloads. A number of factors should be considered when creating job descriptions for project staff.

First, new positions may be based on existing ones if they exist, particularly for roles such as cataloguers, systems administrators and software developers as the skills required for these positions are in general not specific to the work that is required in digital library development projects. On the other hand, many positions in Chapman's list are quite specialised and project managers may have difficulty finding models for suitable job descriptions. Second, much digitisation work is repetitive and detail-orientated, particularly that of scanning or digitisation technicians. Therefore, it is important to build variety into their job descriptions.

Two strategies for ensuring variety are:

1. Have each staff member fill multiple roles or
2. Have each role perform a variety of tasks.

The disadvantages of setting up positions in this way is that it may be more difficult to fill such positions because of the variety of skills required, and when a person leaves a project, multiple roles are left vacant. Planning for staff training in digitisation projects can be challenging. In short-term projects that have a defined duration, staff filling positions created specifically for the project will need to be trained early in the project period. For training to occur, hardware and software must be operational, and procedural documentation must be ready. Staff taken from other parts of the library will also need to be trained on project operations but this can sometimes be done before the training of new staff happens, provided documentation and tools required for their work are ready.

As stated earlier, an individual project manager should be identified as being responsible for the project. This person is directly involved in the planning of the project, assembling and allocating the required resources, monitoring the progress of the work, managing the budget, and for evaluating the project and often for evaluating the collection after the work is complete. Project staff should report directly or indirectly to the project manager; if there is a separate supervisor of project operations, most project staff will report to this person, who in turn reports to the project manager. In small operations, the project manager and supervisor can be the same person, but in larger operations, the demands of both of these roles can quickly surpass a single person's capacity.

In fact, larger projects will probably need more than one supervisor, especially if the production work is done in shifts that exceed a normal work day or if it is done at more than one physical location. In some cases a committee, instead of a single individual, performs the role of project manager. Committees are common in large-scale or long-term projects, and in multi-institution projects. However, smaller, shorter projects are often best managed by a single individual who can draw on the expertise of others when needed. 'Project operations', I will cover the roles of project supervisor, digitisation technician and quality control technician in detail.

HARDWARE AND SOFTWARE RESOURCES

If your library does not already have the hardware and software resources necessary to create the desired content, you will have to acquire them. Unfortunately, acquiring scanners and other digitisation hardware is not as straightforward as it might sound, so project plans must include suitable lead times if production is to start on a given date. A number of factors will help you determine the requirements for the hardware and software you will need to create your collection's content.

First, information gathered during the source material evaluation phase, such as format (still images, sound, etc.), physical dimensions and physical condition, should be considered when selecting digitisation hardware. Second, fully developed workflows can assist in the selection of hardware and software by helping define the most efficient set of steps in which to create content and metadata.

The desired set of steps can then be used to define criteria for evaluating hardware and software. For example, if you know that you will in general be using TIFF as the format for the master versions of image files you are creating, you can include the ability to create TIFF files in your scanner evaluation criteria. Limitations in hardware and software can often be compensated for in workflows, but usually this compensation involves additional tasks, which add to overall project costs.

'Project operations', will provide additional, detailed information on evaluating suitable hardware and software. It may be tempting to evaluate and acquire hardware and software based on the requirements of a single collection or the workflows of a single project, particularly if these resources will be purchased from funds allocated specifically for that collection or project.

However, if a library intends to develop additional digital collections or participate in collaborative collection development initiatives, acquiring hardware and software that can produce files meeting a variety of criteria is a much sounder strategy. Acquiring a scanner whose maximum output resolution is the exact resolution required in the current project is less preferable to acquiring a scanner that can output images at much higher resolutions. Typically, the better the hardware, the more expensive it is, but all other things being equal, if you can afford hardware that exceeds the requirements of your current project, you should consider acquiring it as future projects may have more demanding technical specifications than the current project.

Realistically, however, you need to work within your budget, and if you can only afford digitisation hardware and software that meets but does not exceed the requirement of your current project, then that is what you should buy. To a large extent, exactly when you evaluate and acquire any new hardware and software does not matter, except that you will need to know the minimum technical specifications that content in your collection will adhere to, and you need to know if you have the funds to buy the required resources. Obviously you will need to have all tools in place in time to document procedures prior to training new staff.

This applies to hardware, software used in the production of the content and metadata, and the CMS you will be using. Project deadlines and staffing levels can have an impact on how much hardware and software you will need. For this reason, many project managers wait until they know the final deadlines and staff budgets before acquiring new hardware.

OUTSOURCING

Producing digital content, even on a small scale, requires a substantial investment in hardware, software, space and staff resources. Many libraries are not in the position to make these investments or are otherwise happy to avoid making them. Instead, they send original material to a vendor, who creates the digital content and then delivers it to the library, ready for loading into the library's CMS. Alternatively, the vendor may be responsible only for digitising the material and the library will perform other required tasks, such as creating derivative versions for presentation on the web. The latter case applies to libraries that wish to avoid investing in digitisation hardware but still want to be involved in the production of their content. Some libraries also outsource the creation of descriptive metadata, whereas others choose to create their own even if they outsource digitisation or conversion. In some cases, the library does not host its own collections, but contracts with a vendor to host them on its servers.

When deciding whether to invest in the infrastructure necessary to develop and maintain a digital collection, a library may choose from a number of options:

- Performing all work internally,
- Hiring a commercial vendor to perform all or parts of the work required to produce the content,

- Hiring a consultant to plan and oversee the project, with the work done either internally or by a vendor,
- Collaborating with other libraries, and

The information Gertz provides is thorough and detailed and will prove to be extremely useful to libraries considering contracting with commercial vendors for the production of their digital content and metadata. Contracting with other libraries that act as 'vendors' is becoming increasingly common. This type of relationship differs from multi-institutional projects: the 'client' library is simply contracting with the 'vendor' library to do specific types of work instead of contracting with a commercial vendor. Many libraries that have invested in digitisation hardware, software and staff have the extra capacity to do external work, particularly during periods of low activity from their own projects.

In these cases, the client and vendor libraries must come to an agreement that is satisfactory to both parties, and the vendor library must be able to perform the work at rates comparable with those charged by vendors. This type of relationship may be preferred when the client libraries feel most comfortable dealing with other libraries, particularly if they cannot find a commercial vendor that meets their needs. Also, it is not uncommon for larger university and public libraries to act as digitisation and metadata production centres for smaller libraries within their geographical region that may have interesting collections but not the resources to digitise them.

On the other hand, some libraries may prefer to deal with commercial vendors because they feel that it is easier to establish business-like relationships with commercial entities or that it is best to collaborate with other libraries on a more equitable basis than the client–vendor relationship often implies. Hiring a consultant to assist in planning and to oversee project operations is yet another option. A good consultant will have experience in digital library content development, will balance the goals of the collection with the resources available for the project, and will demonstrate flexibility in how problems are solved.

Avoid consultants who are tied to a particular set of technologies (unless the library would adopt those same technologies independent of the consultant's recommendations). Keep in mind that a consultant cannot assist a library with a digital collection project (or any other type of project) unless library staff assist the consultant: clearly communicating the expected outcomes of the consultant's work and freely providing the information the consultant needs are essential. The best possible outcome of hiring a consultant for this type of project (other than a successful digital collection, of course) is successful knowledge transfer; in other words, library staff should be able to plan and manage similar projects on their own in the future, if doing so is part of the library's long-term digital collection development programme. In addition to outsourcing the production of digital content and metadata, some libraries choose to make their collections available using CMSs hosted externally.

Options for making the collection available to end users include:

- Host the collection on servers maintained by the library's parent institution,
- Host the collection on a commercial vendor's servers,

The collection on another library's servers. Like selecting an external source for content production, selecting a vendor or other library to host a collection allows libraries with content to create digital collections without investing in the required infrastructure. Many libraries do not run their own servers or do not have the technical staff required to maintain a CMS. On the other hand, many libraries would rather host a CMS than acquire scanners and specialised software, and employ the staff necessary for creating digital content.

PREPARING A BUDGET

Preparing a budget for a digitisation or conversion project can be somewhat complex because of the following factors:

- *Variability in workflows for different projects*: Digitising or converting still images, text, video and audio source material all require different sets of tasks, and even within each type of source material there can exist a wide range of workflows (we have seen, for example, that there are several substantially different approaches to digitising texts). Collection functional requirements can vary widely as well, as can options for creating metadata. This matrix of implementation variables can result in real challenges for project managers who need to estimate how much it will cost to create a given collection. Costs are determined by the nature of the project workflow, and if mangers cannot predict workflows, they cannot predict costs with much accuracy.
- *Inconsistency in source material*: Even though careful project managers will base cost estimates on representative samples of the source material they are working with, many collections of source material contain hidden surprises that complicate production significantly and therefore have a real impact on a project's overall budget. This impact can be considerable given the cumulative effect of high numbers of unexpected exceptions.
- *Limitations of technology:* Whether due to temporary problems or due to systemic limitations, problems with technology can dramatically affect the likelihood that a project will be completed on time and within its budget. As already stated, by far the safest way to estimate the costs involved in producing specific digital content is to develop appropriate workflows and procedures, perform trials, document the cost of the trials, and then using those costs extrapolate the cost of processing the entire collection of source material. Any other method of determining costs is an educated guess.

Even in the unlikely event that your institution will accommodate budgets that are off by 50–200%, it is safe to say that few external funders will. They will typically want to know exactly how much it will cost to accomplish the goals you describe in the grant applications. This type of evidence-based budgeting is not easy.

It is difficult if not impossible to do on short notice, it can require resources (such as hardware) that are not available prior to receiving the funding you are applying for, and it can be inaccurate if staff performing the trial runs are not proficient at using the available workflows and tools, which they may not be without a few weeks' experience. It can also create a misleading sense of confidence in cost estimates, particularly if the workflows and procedures are not fully developed or if the source material being tested is not typical of the entire collection.

Finally, even though evidence-based budgeting provides fairly accurate data for estimating the costs of staff who are performing the tasks, it does not necessarily provide accurate data on how much time supervisors and project managers spend on tasks not directly related to production, such as documentation, supervision and writing reports. Despite these drawbacks, using empirical evidence to estimate costs lends authority to budgeting, and even if these informed estimates prove to be inaccurate, the information derived from trials will allow you to identify the areas that are inflating actual production costs. In some cases it is not necessary to perform trials on representative samples of source material in order to derive an accurate budget if the project you are planning is very similar to ones you have performed in the past.

In these cases, the known costs from the previous projects can act as a reliable indicator of the likely costs in the new project. However, this method is reliable only to the extent that the source material, metadata requirements and workflows of the two projects are the same. Even slight differences between source material and technical specifications can cause estimated costs to be inaccurate, particularly if the number of items in your collection is large.

COST COMPONENTS

The largest costs for a digitisation project are operations staff (staff performing permissions clearance, metadata production and content creation; supervisors; project managers, etc.), hardware, software, copyright clearance fees and a CMS, whether a vendor product or open source. If your library already has suitable hardware or software, or a suitable CMS, those items will not represent additional real costs. The most common type of cost for any project is staff. It is difficult to generalise about the relative proportions of the various types of cost in a project because of the wide variability in hardware, software and CMS prices, and because staff costs are unknown for any project until workflows have been tested.

Using documented costs from a series of largescale digitisation projects, Steven Puglia found that roughly one-third of the cost of the production of those collections accounted for digitisation, one-third for metadata creation, and the final third for administration, quality control and other activities. Although these findings were derived from actual recorded costs, they should be used as a general guide only and not as an accurate planning formula, for reasons stated earlier. After production is complete, ongoing costs include collection maintenance, promotion and evaluation.

ADDITIONAL PLANNING CONSIDERATIONS

Once the amount of staff time required for a project is known, we can estimate the number of staff we need to hire, the amount of hardware and software we need to procure, and the amount of physical space required to do the work. After fully developed workflows, the next issue to resolve is how much time is required to complete the project.

The number of work days available to you will let you determine how many staff to hire, which in turn will determine how much hardware you need and how much physical space you need. These numbers can be determined by various factors, such as the amount of time a funder gives you to spend their money, the end dates of fiscal years, the availability of staff (*e.g.* scheduling work shifts around major holidays is often problematic), or other factors.

Ultimately, you will need to determine when you plan to launch your collection. This date may or may not be flexible, and you may need to launch the collection before all the content and metadata are ready, but in practice you will probably have to juggle all of the timing factors listed here in order to get a fairly accurate idea of how long your project will take.

Given the total amount of time required to complete the tasks defined in our workflow, and the number of days available within the project timeline, we can estimate the number of hours of work per day that need to be completed. Given the total number of hours of work, we can determine the number of staff required, and from that number, the amount of hardware and physical space they will need to complete the work.

This formula is only a guide – adjustments may need to be made in response to contingencies such as unpredictable availability of staff (*e.g.* most students do not want to work at exam time) and delays due to hardware and other problems. However, the total number of hours of work required to complete a project is a useful basis on which to estimate associated resources.

First, for the conversion technician and metadata specialist, we need to calculate the number of work hours per day required to complete our project:

- Number of hours per day required to complete all work = Total number of hours required to complete all work/number of available days

For the sake of this example, we are told by the library administration that we need to spend all of the money allocated to this project within 4 weeks (or 20 working days):

Table. Hour of Work Per Day Required to Complete all Work

Position title	Hours required to complete all work	Days available	Hours per day required to complete all work
Conversion Technician	84	20	4.2
Metabeta Specilist	56	20	2.8

Using this figure of 4 weeks and the number of hours in a standard working day (in this case 7 hours per day for full-time equivalent staff, or FTE), we can determine the number of positions we need for the conversion technician and the metadata specialist in order to complete work within the given timelines:

The right-most column shows that the number of positions required is less than one FTE for each position title. This is useful in determining how many people to hire, and whether their positions will be full time or part time. In our example, because all of the positions are less than one FTE, we may be able to complete the project in fewer than 20 days if we make the positions full time; if the number of positions were more than one FTE, we would need to hire more than one person, or increase the number of days in which we would be able to complete the project (which the library administration says is not an option). At this point we should finalise our project milestones.

In the earlier example in which we devised some preliminary milestones for the digitisation of the local newspapers, we did not have much information – only how much content was intended to go into the collection and an estimate of how long we had to complete the project. In this example, however, we know an additional and important piece of information: how many staff as suggested, need to complete the project. Once we know that, we can finalise our project milestones. If we monitor the project's progress carefully, as suggested, be able to detect any significant deviations from these refined milestones and take corrective measures if necessary.

Also, now that we have determined the number of staff as suggested, need to hire, we can determine the amount of work space and hardware required. In our example, as suggested, need a separate workstation for the Conversion Technician and Metadata Specialist, and a separate workstation for the Supervisor (the Web Developer will work at home).

The Conversion Technician will need to have the tape player arranged near his or her computer workstation in order to capture the audio. If circumstances were such that we needed to hire more than one FTE staff member for each position (if, for example, we had 80 hours of audio to capture and catalogue in the same number of days), we would need to hire more than one person for each position, which would require more work space, more computer workstations (each with the necessary software), and in the case of the Conversion Technician, more than one tape player and audio capture card

EXECUTIVE THE PROJECT

At this point we are ready to finish project documentation, hire and train staff, and begin the actual production of our content and metadata. Any required hardware, software and work space must now be in place as well.

PROPOSAL WRITING

Project managers are usually required to prepare formal proposals for funding. Funders can be internal (to the institution), private (individuals, foundations, corporations or other organisations) or public (government bodies at any level, from municipal to international).

As suggested, introduce some general information about proposal writing. The jurisdiction that a library is part of can have a significant impact on its eligibility for a particular source of funds, so I will not identify specific sources of funding. The process of applying for funding will be defined differently by each funder. In some cases, the funder will provide a standard form that needs to be completed, sometimes with attachments or appendices containing narrative responses to particular questions.

The form and all supporting documentation must then be submitted by a given date. In other cases, particularly where the amount of available funds is high and the time over which they can be spent is long (*e.g.* from a full year to several years), the application process may involve multiple submissions delivered at different deadlines.

In these cases, funders will issue invitations to applicants to submit to the next phase of the process, with each submission containing more detailed information. Finally, some funding organisations rely on a less formal application procedure that does not involve standardised forms, but instead defines criteria (ranging from general to quite specific) that applicants address in their proposals.

PROPOSAL COMPONENTS

Despite this variety of requirements, most funding proposals contain at least some of the following components. However, they do include some of the more common aspects of funding proposals that you may encounter.

- *Letter of intent:* In application procedures where multiple components must be submitted at different times, the first component often takes the form of a 'letter of intent' indicating that the institution intends to pursue the grants in question and that may give very general information about the proposed collection or project. The funder responds to this letter with an invitation to proceed with the remainder of the application or a statement of why the applicant is not being invited to proceed.

- *Executive summary:* A brief summary of an application, typically containing information such as the name of the applying institution, names of major partner institutions, title and nature of the collection, fund(s) being applied for, amount being applied for, and a brief indication of the relevance of the collection or activity to the funder's stated objectives.
- *Description of your organisation:* Brief and selective description of the library applying for the funds. Frequently this information is detailed in a form that may ask basic information such as principal contact person, year founded, charitable organisation status, number of employees, and so on, while in other cases the funder may require detailed information about the library's previous projects, partners and funders.
- *Project objectives:* A clear statement of what the funds will be spent on, using language that the funders will understand. _ Description of how funder's objectives will be met: Not all funders support 'digitisation', but many support job creation for students, building databases of local content or some other activity that you can incorporate into your project. Funders want to know that their money is being spent on things that matter to them, and you should be prepared to explain why your project meets their objectives.
- *Project work plan:* Some funders require a work plan, which is typically an outline or table indicating major milestones in the project.
- *Project budget:* Budget formats vary widely, from simple forms to sophisticated Excel spreadsheets that include formulas to calculate items such as administration charges, salary calculations, and maximum allowable amounts in various categories such as hardware or copyright licensing fees.
- *Appendices:* Some applications may require other documentation, often grouped together as appendices, attachments or schedules. These documents can vary widely depending on the requirements of the application, but can include letters of support from partners (both for the current project and for previous projects), letters or special forms from officials in the library's parent institution, screen captures or printed pages from prototype websites if applicable, and sample job descriptions or job advertisements.

Assembling the information required for most applications can be time consuming and difficult. For large grants it is not uncommon to treat the application process itself as a 'project' that requires hiring consultants or providing temporary replacements for existing staff. Although the amount of effort required to complete most application procedures should not require additional staff, you should assume that any formal, structured application process will take considerable coordination, particularly if you must involve people outside your library for letters of support, financial information or other reasons. Most funders will not accept applications past their stated deadlines.

PROPOSAL TERMINOLOGY

The following terms are used frequently in funding applications. In some cases, application documentation will actually contain definitions of the terms used throughout the application and even some examples of how the terms are intended to be used. Obviously, paying close attention to the instructions for completing applications is extremely important.

Missing components or misinterpreted questions can disqualify an application, and if the funder receives many more applications than they intend to fund, they will be looking for opportunities to make their adjudication easier.

- *Partners:* Many funding agencies favour applications submitted on behalf of multiple institutions – in fact for larger grants this may be a requirement. Typically, one institution must be identified as the 'lead' or 'principal' partner, if for no other reason than to simplify the funder's accounting procedures (the lead partner would be responsible for distributing funds to partners). The term 'partner' will probably be defined within the application documentation, but participants of all types, from individuals to entire organisations such as commercial companies, universities or government departments, may be considered partners.
- *In-kind contribution:* 'In-kind' describes resources that the institution, as opposed to the funder, is expected to supply. As this term is generally used within the context of a project budget, it will usually be defined very specifically; for example, some funders consider staff salaries to be in-kind, whereas others do not. In-kind contributions are also often subject to formulas that qualify the value of the contributions in some way, such as reducing the value of a $5000 scanner to $500 that can be applied to the institution's contribution. In addition to staff resources, other typical in-kind contributions include hardware and physical space for digitisation and related activities.
- *Cash:* In contrast to in-kind contributions, cash is typically money that an institution must contribute to a project that they would not spend if they were not participating in the project (in other words, it must be additional to their normal operational costs). The most common costs that cash contributions apply to are staffing and

hardware. In general, the same resources cannot be considered cash and in-kind contributions, although some funders allow claiming staff time as a 'cash in-kind' contribution.

- *Outcomes:* Funders will frequently ask for a statement of 'outcomes', which are generally equivalent to your project's goals. To be effective, outcomes should be worded such that they are understandable to readers of your application (*i.e.* free of library jargon) and consistent with the funder's objectives. Many funders will use language that is tied very closely to their mandate or organisational objectives. For example, government agencies at various levels may allocate funds to supporting projects that employ youth; some large private foundations have been requiring any software created with their funds to be released under a specific open-source licence. When describing outcomes, it can be advantageous to adopt some of the language used in the proposal documents, particularly when discussing how your project's objectives align with those of the funder.
- *Deliverables:* Deliverables tend to be more concrete and countable than outcomes. Items that might be expected in response to a question about what deliverables a project will produce include a description of the website/CMS, the number of documents, any standards or reports, or other documentation or software developed during the creation of the content.
- *Evaluation:* Many grant applications will ask how you plan to evaluate the success of your project, and may even ask you to write a final report and sign a release so they can use the report for their own purposes.
- *Sustainability:* Finally, some funders are interested in how long their investment will pay off. If they fund early stages of a project, they may ask what its long-term sustainability is and what the library's longterm goals for the project are. Your response to this type of question will depend on your institution's and your partner's commitment to the project. If a collection is open (content will continue to be added), a statement of sustainability should address how the ongoing activity will be funded; if a collection is intended to be closed (for example, the scope of the collection is narrow and the content appropriate to that scope is likely to make it into the collection within the defined life of the project), a statement of sustainability may only need to address issues of preservation and ongoing evaluation.

REPORTING

If your grant application is successful, you will be expected to report to the funders periodically. Many funders will require clear and comprehensive reports of how their money is being spent. This is as true of funds allocated internally from the library as it is of funds awarded from an external organisation. Every funder will define its own reporting requirements, but typically they will include periodic statements of how much money has been spent, statements of periodic quotas or milestones for deliverables, and progress on other work that is being funded.

MONITORING

Monitoring is essential for any type of project, not just projects producing digital collections. Periodic checks on the progress being made and the identification and correction of any problems as they occur will dramatically increase the chances that a project will meet its defined goals and will do so without exceeding the allocated resources. The most important aspects of monitoring digital content creation projects are ensuring that objectives and milestones are being met, ensuring that the available budget is not being overspent, holding regular staff meetings and documenting the outcomes of issues resulting from those meetings. First, it is more efficient to keep production on schedule throughout a project than to try to make up for low production at the end of the project. Available space, hardware and staff resources will probably be insufficient to increase the output required towards the end of the project to meet overall objectives.

Second, production milestones should be linked to ongoing costs, so that at any time during the project you can predict if the funds allocated to the work will be sufficient. Third, communicating with production staff regularly through regular meetings ensures that problems they encounter are dealt with as early as possible. Finally, because one of the goals of monitoring a project is to address potentially serious issues as early as possible, documenting problems as they arise and are resolved will allow even faster resolution of similar problems should they arise again.

EVALUATING THE PRODUCTION PHASE OF THE PROJECT

In a general sense, the content production phase of a digital collection project should be considered successful if it reaches the project's stated goals. However, evaluating projects just as to specific criteria is desirable for a number of reasons: evaluating a project after its completion can demonstrate to funders that their money was spent the way they intended it to be spent, can validate a project and can identify areas for improvement.

The most useful strategy for evaluating a project is to build evaluation into the project's goals. In other words, one of the project's goals should be to undergo a systematic evaluation. Explicitly stating this goal will help keep the project focused and will encourage project managers to maintain accurate and thorough documentation. The exact criteria by which projects will be evaluated should be determined by the desired outcomes of the evaluation, which should be defined by the project manager(s), the library administration and the project funders.

Criteria will fall into the following categories:

- *Production milestones:* Typical criteria include the project's ability to meet defined production milestones and objectives, and what constitute acceptable deviations from defined objectives.
- *Budget:* Obviously, the project's ability to accomplish its goals within the defined budget is important. Using substantially less money than the amount defined in the budget is less likely to happen than overspending, but funders may not look favourably on what they would perceive as an overestimation of the funds required to complete the project. Careful monitoring will help avoid this situation.
- *Quality benchmarks:* Evaluating the ability to meet defined levels of quality over the duration of the production activity is relatively easy (provided standards of acceptable quality have been clearly defined and documented) and should provide no surprises if quality control has been performed throughout the project.
- *Operational Aspects:* Evaluation of the suitability of the hardware, software and workflows is useful as a planning tool for subsequent projects. Staff job descriptions, scheduling and other aspects of staffing should also be reviewed at the end of each project.

To summarise, careful monitoring during the project is a form of formative evaluation, but summative evaluation of the work involved in creating digital content is an important aspect of overall project evaluation.

EVALUATING THE OVERALL PROJECT

Content production is only one aspect of the 'project' associated with a digital collection. Initial and ongoing promotion, the benefits to users, financial sustainability and ongoing maintenance issues should also be evaluated.

The NISO Framework of Guidance for Building Good Digital Collections defines four principles by which projects should be evaluated:

- A good collection-building project has a substantial design and planning component.
- A good project has an evaluation plan.
- A good project produces a project report and broadly disseminates information about the project process and outcomes.
- A good project considers the entire lifecycle of the digital collection and associated services developed through the project.

The second principle may sound tautological, but it actually emphasises the need for systematic evaluation. As the Framework states, 'An evaluation plan demonstrates the commitment of a project to its stated goals and objectives.'

To support development of effective evaluation plans, the Framework cites the Institute of Museum and Library Services' list of resources on Outcome-Based Evaluation (OBE). As the IMLS describes it, OBE determines the impact of digital collections on users' knowledge, attitudes, skills and behaviours. This impact is evaluated by using techniques such as online questionnaires that test users' knowledge.

The IMLS website offers this example:

- In order to know if online availability had a benefit, an institution needs to measure skills, attitudes, or other relevant phenomena among users and establish what portion of users were affected. To capture information about these kinds of results, a library or museum could ask online visitors to complete a brief questionnaire. If a goal is to increase visitor knowledge about a particular institution's resources, a survey might ask questions like, 'Can you name 5 sources for health information? Rate your knowledge from 1 (can't name any) to 5 (can name 5).' If visitors rate their knowledge at an average of 3 at the beginning of their experience, and 4 or 5 (or 2) at the end, the sponsoring institution could conclude that the web site made a difference in responders' confidence about this knowledge. It should be clear that such a strategy also lets you test your effectiveness in communicating the intended message!

Regardless of whether the narrowly defined activity involved in content production is being evaluated or whether the entire set of activities surrounding the development of a digital library collection is being evaluated, a thorough and effective evaluation plan should be part of the overall project goals.

EVALUATING THE COLLECTION

The third type of evaluation that project managers should perform is evaluation of the collection. This evaluation is actually part of ongoing collection management, and will happen after the 'project' has ended, whether defined narrowly by its production phase or more broadly by a larger set of activities. The NISO Framework of Guidance for Building Good Digital Collections provides seven principles of 'good' collections (good meaning generally appropriate for the user groups the collection is aimed at) that are independent from aspects of projects.

These principles can be used both as planning tools and as evaluation criteria:

- A good digital collection is created just as to an explicit collection development policy that has been agreed upon and documented before digitisation begins.
- Collections should be described so that a user can discover characteristics of the collection, including scope, format, restrictions on access, ownership, and any information significant for determining the collection's authenticity, integrity and interpretation. A collection should be sustainable over time. In particular, digital collections built with special internal or external funding should have a plan for their continued usability beyond the funded period.

- A good collection is broadly available and avoids unnecessary impediments to use. Collections should be accessible to persons with disabilities, and usable effectively in conjunction with adaptive technologies.
- A good collection respects intellectual property rights. Collection managers should maintain a consistent record of rights-holders and permissions granted for all applicable materials.
- A good collection has mechanisms to supply usage data and other data that allows standardised measures of usefulness to be recorded.
- A good collection fits into the larger context of significant related national and international digital library initiatives.

Project managers should develop mechanisms during production that will capture the information needed for testing these attributes, such as entrance or exit surveys on the collection website, usage loggers, in-person interviews, focus groups or general feedback forms that users can complete. Part XII of the NINCH Guide to Good Practice in the Digital Representation and Management of Cultural Heritage Materials provides detailed discussion of the types of mechanisms that can be used to collect information from a collection's users. OBE can also be applied to the collection on an ongoing basis if desired.

MULTI-INSTITUTION PROJECTS

Increasingly, libraries are collaborating on digital collection-building activities. This collaboration is different from the client–vendor relationships between libraries described earlier. Partner libraries come together to create digital collections for the same reasons they come together co-operatively to subscribe to commercial databases and electronic journal collections or to share virtual reference services: to form strategic alliances, to pool resources and to please funding agencies, which to a large extent favour multi-institution projects over ones undertaken by a single institution. The advantages of collaborating that are specific to digital collection building are that the costs of specialised hardware and software can be distributed, expertise can be shared, large projects can be delivered in shorter timeframes, and libraries that are not able to invest in hardware and software can participate by performing other types of necessary tasks, such as clearing copyright permissions and creating descriptive metadata.

Collaborative efforts also have the disadvantage of increased administrative overhead, which can manifest itself in a number of ways, including record-keeping requirements that are not compatible with all partners' local institutional practices, scheduling meetings and holding them via teleconference or video conference, etc., and making sure that all partners meet project milestones and deadlines. From a practical perspective, multi-institution projects introduce a number of complications that need to be taken into account. First, development of workflows that are distributed among multiple partners can be challenging simply because having multiple sites provides more ways of getting the work done: in some multi-institution projects, most or all of the work is carried out in parallel at multiple sites, whereas in others, each partner performs different sets of tasks that are then integrated centrally.

In order to maximise efficiencies, the implications of distributed workflow should be explored carefully during the planning phases of multi-institution projects. Second, all participating institutions must conform to the project's technical specifications. Care must be taken that file formats, file densities, colour depths, sampling rates, metadata formats, the application of metadata creation guidelines and file naming conventions are consistent across all partners. Use of the same hardware and software at all contributing institutions promotes consistency, but in reality being able to use identical resources at each site is not common, particularly if each site possessed its own hardware and software prior to the start of the project.

However, regular checks of output from partners will ensure that inconsistencies are minimised. Third, the number of participating institutions can have a considerable impact on the project's ability to meet production milestones. The more partners fall behind, the harder it is to recover; by contrast, the more partners are involved in producing digital content, the more likely it will be that shortfalls can be taken on by other partners if they have the extra capacity. All of these issues can be mitigated with sufficient planning and continuous communication among partners.

9

Inter-organizational Cost Management

INTRODUCTION

Organizations concerned with managing costs must not only consider their internal activities, but also their relationships with business partners in the supply chain in today's global and competitive economic environment. Effective management of costs that cross organizational boundaries has the potential to improve the overall performance of each organization affected. It is therefore important to understand what factors may lead to the management of these inter-organizational costs and if management of these costs is beneficial. Based on previous research, we develop a model to study potential antecedents to inter-organizational cost management (IOCM) as well as the perceived benefits of IOCM. We empirically test our model by surveying IMA members.

We use path analysis and we find support for our antecedent constructs and our model as a whole. The constructs examined in our model are interorganizational cost management (IOCM), internal cost management (ICM), electronic integration (EI), and absorptive capacity (AC). We further find that IMA members whose organizations engage in IOCM techniques perceive IOCM to be beneficial.

Inter-organizational cost management has evolved to become a strategic capability for organizations that are not satisfied with the incremental cost improvements associated with externally integrated information systems or internally focused cost management processes such as activity-based costing. Instead, managers are seeking higher-order goals such as gaining new competencies through joint learning, gaining market power, creating legitimacy, and moving more quickly into new markets and technologies. One result of this new strategic focus has been the "evolution" of IOCM.

IOCM refers to a set of activities, processes, or techniques that managers can use to manage costs that span organizational boundaries. Some of the techniques associated with IOCM would be easily recognized as an interorganizational application of traditional internal cost management practices, while other techniques may not be related to conventional management accounting.

The outcomes associated with IOCM techniques transcend the transactional cost benefits that are generally provided by supply chain integration by adding strategic advantages, which includes identifying ways of reducing costs and increasing revenues through activities such as joint product development and joint interorganizational cost investigations. However, all of the IOCM techniques are similar in that they are cooperative activities that have a common goal to create value for both partner firms through modification of interorganizational cost structures.

Eisenhardt and Schoonhoven, the transition from a purely transactional focus to a more strategic focus is dependent upon cooperation, collaboration, the sharing of proprietary information, and the generation of mutual knowledge. Similarly, Coad and Cullen characterize IOCM as an institution that is built upon knowledge, skill, relationships, and physical assets which define the institution's capabilities and dynamic capabilities , or the ability to learn and change.

Most studies that investigate IOCM have generally identified critical factors leading to IOCM using qualitative investigations. This research uses a sample of managerial accountants to empirically tests the factors previously identified. Our empirical analysis answers the call from Coad and Cullen to address the "dearth" of empirical IOCM studies. The goals of this research are to first identify the institutional and dynamic capabilities that have allowed organizations to engage in IOCM activities and secondly to examine how the organizations have benefited from IOCM.

The research questions in this study are:

- What capabilities precede IOCM?
- Does IOCM lead to strategic and transactional benefits?

We address the research questions by developing an empirical model that links IOCM and its related benefits to constructs that are expected to be key enablers for IOCM. We selected these constructs as IOCM enablers for our model because they capture many of the factors that were observed to influence IOCM in previous qualitative studies.

These enablers include two capabilities:

1. The focal firm's information technology integration (electronic integration among supply chain members)
2. The focal firm's existing internal cost management capabilities and practices.

One additional enabler is a dynamic capability — a firm's interorganizational absorptive capacity (behavioural relationships) for cost management as perceived by the focal firm. The "focal" firm in our study refers to a specific firm of interest within a supply chain, while the "partner" firm refers to a firm within the focal firm's supply chain, either a customer or a supplier or both. The intense focus by firms to integrate the supply chain has resulted in firms achieving a high level of technical integration among their suppliers and customers, resulting in incremental improvements in efficiencies and productivity by reducing the overall cost of supplies and reducing other transaction costs. Research has also shown that technical integration, through the use of information technology (IT), is an enabler of supply chain effectiveness. At a more strategic level, internal and external IT integration has resulted in an increase of sharing of information, which is a central part of IOCM. Therefore, we contend that IOCM is enabled by electronic systems integration, which we define as the degree to which the IT systems employed throughout the organization are integrated and accessible both internally (within-firm) and externally (outside the firm).

While electronic integration through information technology provides the physical infrastructure to enable IOCM, other factors such as individual knowledge and skills will also impact IOCM. We examine the internal cost management capabilities as one measure of a firm's cost management skills and knowledge. Since many IOCM activities are simply interorganizational extensions of internal cost management practices, the internal knowledge reflected by the use of these practices should enable the organization to develop related inter-organizational cost management practices. Our final antecedent construct in the model is inter-organizational absorptive capacity, which is the ability of two partner firms to "recognize the value of new, external information, assimilate it, and apply it to commercial ends".

This concept has been deemed a "dynamic capability" to reflect its capability of building processes for new markets and reconfiguring resources to gain and sustain competitive advantage. Our interorganizational absorptive capacity construct measures the collective knowledge, communication and trust that exists between partners. These relationship characteristics have all been deemed requisite for developing inter-organization capabilities. The remainder of this paper is organized as follows: First, we examine the extant literature on IOCM in a supply chain context where an organization's partner is a supplier or a customer· Second, we develop the theoretical foundations and the associated hypotheses for the antecedents (electronic integration, absorptive capacity, internal cost management) and consequences (IOCM benefits) of IOCM. Next, we test this model empirically through a survey of management accountants working in supply chain environments. Finally, we conclude with a discussion of our findings.

INTERORGANIZATIONAL COST MANAGEMENT (IOCM)

A fundamental concept of supply chain management is that organizations must look beyond their own boundaries to consider relationships with their suppliers and customers along the value chain. For most of the 20th century, the norm for inter-organizational behaviour has been that of autonomous firms engaging in arm's length transactions with other firms. This internal focus by firms has made it difficult for organizations to take advantage of cost management synergies that may be obtained through the cooperation and collaboration of business partners. These synergies require additional coordination mechanisms to extend cost management programmes beyond organizational boundaries, with the overall objective of finding lower cost solutions than would be possible if the firm and its customers and suppliers attempted to reduce costs independently.

These synergies may be obtained through vertical integration; but now many organizations engage in IOCM instead. These organizations can be described as hybrid organizations who achieve the cost management synergy benefits of vertical integration while maintaining the efficiency of arms-length transactions. From this view, the strategic employment of IOCM can be viewed as a hybrid between strategic intra-firm cost management focus and strategic inter-firm cost management focus as presented by Shank.

STRATEGIC COST MANAGEMENT

The origin of IOCM can be traced to the work of Porter (1985) and Shank (1989). Porter (1985) identified strategic cost analysis as a means of better managing the linkages with buyers and suppliers in a value chain in order to reduce costs and enhance differentiation. Shank builds upon Porter's value chain concept and defines the term strategic cost management as "the managerial use of cost information explicitly directed at one or more of the four stages of the strategic management cycle."

The four stages of the strategic management cycle as defined by Shank are:

1. Formulating strategies
2. Communicating those strategies throughout the firm
3. Developing and carrying out tactics to implement the strategies
4. Developing and implementing controls to monitor the strategy implementation

Based on the strategic management cycle, Shank defines strategic cost management in terms of three underlying themes from the strategic management literature

- Value chain analysis;
- Strategic position analysis; and
- Cost driver analysis.

Shank, each of the three themes represents "a stream of research and analysis in which cost information is cast in a much different light than viewed in traditional management accounting." In general, IOCM blends of inter-organizational value chain analysis and intra-organizational cost driver analysis by focusing on the management of costs related to activities that impact the focal firm as well as its business partners. Even before this combination was described as IOCM, researchers as well as practitioners have recognized the value of merging these ideas. LaLonde and Pohlen were critical of ABC's internal focus because they recognized the potential advantages provided by ABC within a supply chain. Traditionally, the only use of ABC in terms of being extra-organizationally focused is in determining how supply chain partners affect the firm's cost and profitability -- an internally-focused orientation. Organizations have ignored an orientation that looks outside of the firm to determine where in the supply chain activities can best be performed in terms of cost, time, or quality. Dekker and Van Goor also recognize the importance of cooperative relationships within the supply chain and through a case study in the pharmaceutical industry, they demonstrate how ABC can be used to support decisions about relocating and changing logistics activities in order to optimize across the entire supply chain.

The implication of this study is that organizations can benefit by engaging in cost analysis throughout the entire supply chain. In general, organizational boundaries are blurring and strategic exploitation of linkages within the firm's value chain and between value chains of business partners are important to an organization's performance.

INTERORGANIZATIONAL COST MANAGEMENT PRACTICES

From its origins with Porter and Shank, IOCM has emerged in the management accounting field as a general-purpose term referring to a portfolio of specific strategic management accounting practices that are specifically targeted at optimizing and integrating cost management systems in order to jointly reduce costs between partners.

Cooper and Slagmulder, IOCM practices facilitate the coordination of cost reduction in 2 ways:

1. Helps identify ways to make the interface between the firms more efficient and
2. Helps the firm and its buyers and suppliers find additional ways to reduce the costs of products.

Among the accounting practices commonly discussed in IOCM literature are:

- Interorganizational Target Costing
- Interorganizational Kaizen costing
- Open Book Accounting
- Information Sharing

INTERORGANIZATIONAL TARGET COSTING

Target costing focuses on managing the product development and design processes of a firm. Target costing is defined by Cooper as a "structured approach for determining the cost at which a proposed product with specified functionality and quality must be produced to generate the desired level of profitability at the product's anticipated selling price."

Specifically, Cooper identifies 3 steps associated with target costing:

1. Estimate the selling price at which a proposed product will sell, utilizing market research techniques

2. Determine the new product's target profit margin
3. Determine the product's target cost by subtracting the target profit from the target selling price.

Next, organizations apply value engineering techniques to determine how they can effectively design a product that can be manufactured at the target cost. During the value engineering process, an analysis is performed to assess ways of increasing functionality without increasing costs, as well as reducing costs without reducing functionality.

The literature regarding target costing suggests that target costing itself is an internal cost management technique in that it does not actively involve the partner firm in the focal firm's cost management programme. Instead, it is the focal firm's cost management system that contains the design information that is applicable to meeting the target price of a product. It is this design information that can be used by the partner firm to identify where cost reductions may be possible. Therefore, the key extension of target costing that brings it into the realm of IOCM is the active involvement by both the focal firm's and the partner firm's design teams in the joint identification, management, and resolution of cost issues.

Cooper and Slagmulder identify three specific IOCM techniques resulting from target costing processes that progressively involve more collaboration between the focal firm and the partner firm. The first IOCM technique is the functionality-price-quality tradeoffs, which Cooper and Slagmulder identify as useful for resolving minor cost overrun problems and requiring limited interaction between the design teams of the focal and partner firms. The second technique is an interorganizational cost investigation, which is used when FPQ tradeoff analysis is not able to achieve the desired level of cost reductions.

The third IOCM technique related to target costing processes is concurrent cost management, which requires significant interaction and collaboration between design teams and can lead to fundamental changes in both firms' product and processes. Cooper and Slagmulder provide a complete discussion of these three techniques via case analysis, demonstrating how these IOCM techniques have been used in three Japanese supply chains to cooperatively identify mutually beneficial low-cost solutions.

INTERORGANIZATIONAL KAIZEN COSTING

Originating from successful cost management practices in Japanese firms, kaizen costing is a system of incremental and continuous cost reduction improvements of the product manufacturing process. Kaizen costing is similar to target costing in that both processes focus on cost reduction activities. However, target costing focuses on the design and development phases of a product, whereas kaizen costing is used to reduce costs in the manufacturing and delivery phases. Kaizen costing has interorganizational implications in that firms can use kaizen costing to identify and set cost-reduction objectives for suppliers. Cooper and Slagmulder identify the real benefit of interorganizational kaizen costing as being "when the firms in the supply chain cooperate to find new low-cost solutions that they cannot identify in isolation." Guilding go as far as to classify kaizen costing as a strategic management accounting practice when it focuses on an external, market-oriented approach "that is forward-looking and closely aligned to a quest for competitive advantage."

OPEN BOOK ACCOUNTING

Open book accounting refers to the practice of partners within a supply chain opening up their internal accounting information to each other in order to support their collaboration on cost management.

Open book accounting increases the transparency of cost information between partner firms, as evidenced by Lamming:

1. Cost transparency means the sharing of costing information between customer and supplier including data which would traditionally be kept secret by each party, for use in negotiations. The purpose of this is to make it possible for customer and supplier to work together to reduce costs.

By increasing information transparency between partners, open book accounting can improve the effectiveness of other IOCM techniques (*i.e.* by enabling more in-depth and strategic target costing and kaizen costing).

Mouritsen identify open book accounting as an effective inteorganizational management control to "create new possibilities for management intervention." These new possibilities extend the reach of a firm's management beyond the boundaries of their own firm and outward towards the control of a partner firm's activities. Mouritsen demonstrate these new possibilities through a case analysis where they document the benefits of one firm's experience with open book accounting. In the case study, open book accounting not only improved efficiencies in the firm's production system, but also impacted its strategic direction by transforming the firm's core competencies and competitive strategy via the insights gained from access to the supplier's production processes.

INFORMATION SHARING

Ramos points out that managerial accounting systems should include a more comprehensive set of organizational and external data, thus facilitating and perhaps even standardizing the information sharing processes in order to support supply chain activities.

Supply chain management emphasizes the benefits that can be achieved by all parties along the chain through cooperation and information sharing. The operations management literature has explored the role of including customer requirements in the new product development process, as well as including supplier integration in the new product development process. In the accounting literature, Coad and Cullen state that information sharing is critical for partners to jointly learn new skills and identify new opportunities.

This is exemplified by Cooper and Slagmulder who explore the processes that enable firms to collaborate effectively, specifically investigating the role of guest engineers in joint development projects and identifying guest engineers as an example of an IOCM practice that facilitates information sharing. Several specific forms of information sharing have been identified as salient in supply chain integration, including the sharing of real-time information about material flow and the sharing of real-time documents that can be used to create collaborative forecasts and plans and the sharing of information related to order entry, shipping, and billing through business process automation.

Furthermore, Malhotra identify the breadth of information exchange as having an impact on leveraging interorganizational partnerships and specifically identify information related to market demand and forecasts, demand shifts and changes in customer preferences, and the sharing of future plans such as long-term production plans and capital investments.

From the managerial accounting literature, we have identified several practices / techniques associated with interorganizational cost management in a supply chain context. Additionally, we used studies from the operations management field to more fully explore the role of information sharing in managing costs throughout the supply chain. Our synthesis of the primary practices and techniques associated with interorganizational cost management.

ANTECEDENTS AND BENEFITS OF IOCM

Most of the studies on IOCM have been qualitative case studies, with little quantitative analysis addressing IOCM. One exception is the study by Guilding *et al.* Who surveyed 1,292 firms in New Zealand, United Kingdom, and the United States and presented statistical evidence on the extent of strategic management accounting practices. However, Guilding *et al.* did not investigate the antecedents to the strategic accounting practices, of which IOCM is a subset. Given the extent of qualitative work that has been conducted on the topic of IOCM behaviour, this research attempts to bring together some of the findings of the previous research through the development of a theoretical model that succinctly reflects the conclusions of many of the qualitative studies.

Despite the lack of quantitative studies addressing antecedents of IOCM, several of the qualitative case studies have suggested possible antecedents. Mouritsen *et al.* Identify two important prerequisites for open book accounting to be effectively implemented between partners:

- A highly developed sense of trust between partners and
- A system by which information is actively shared.

Cullen *et al.* (1999), in a case study of three firms, identify the quest for continuous improvements as the driving force for adopting IOCM practices. Evans and Ashworth (1996) recognize several factors influencing the success of activity-based costing projects, including the effectiveness of leadership, the adequacy of the resources, the receptiveness of the culture to organizational change, and the effectiveness of the communication strategy.

Mentzer et.al. also suggest several antecedents such as trust, interdependence, technology utilization, cooperation, joint programmes, and information sharing to supply chain performance (*i.e.,* IOCM). Most recently, Coad and Cullen (2006) suggest that behavioural relationship factors (*i.e.* trust and communication) along with skill, knowledge, and physical assets (*i.e.* integrated information systems) are critical in order to engage in IOCM. Based on the qualitative work in the literature, our research categorizes the potential antecedents of IOCM into three areas

- Internal cost management capabilities of the focal firm,
- Electronic integration among supply chain partners (information sharing capability) and
- The absorptive capacity for interorganizational cost management partnership by the focal firm.

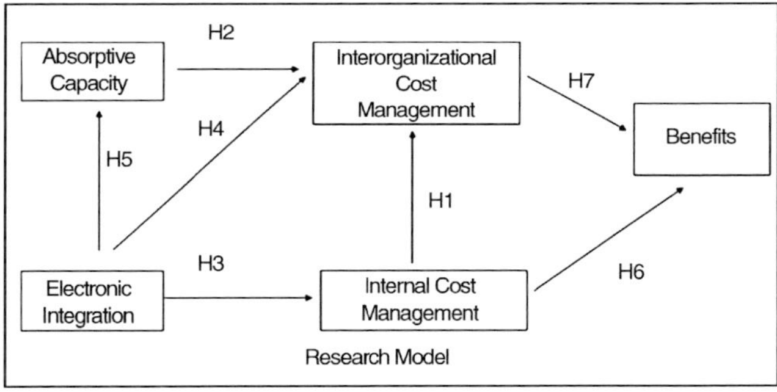

Fig. Research Model

INTERNAL COST MANAGEMENT (ICM)

Cost management uses the information from cost accounting systems in order to understand the nature and behaviour of costs associated with managing firm resources. From the Coad and Cullen (2006) perspective, ICM is a capability that captures an organization's cost management skills and knowledge and supports the evolution of IOCM. Kaplan and Cooper (1998) also view cost management from an evolutionary or maturity perspective in their four-stage model of cost system development that is based on the level of integration of product, service, and customer costing information.

The Kaplan and Cooper model focuses on integration from an internal firm perspective. We view IOCM as an extension of cost management from an internal focus to the external focus, which positions IOCM beyond Kaplan and Cooper's stage 4 of an integrated, internal cost management system. As firms gain more internal expertise within an area, the next step in the maturation process is to move beyond the internal boundaries of the firm and take an external perspective.

ABSORPTIVE CAPACITY (AC)

Originating in the field of macroeconomics, the concept of absorptive capacity refers to the ability of an economy to absorb and utilize external information and resources. Cohen and Levinthal adapted this macroeconomic concept to the organizational level and defined absorptive capacity as the "ability of a firm to recognize the value of new, external information, assimilate it, and apply it to commercial ends". In Cohen and Levinthal's view, the absorptive capacity of an organization is primarily a function of the level of prior related knowledge, as well as a function of the structure of communication between the external environment and the firm.

Following the conceptualization by Cohen and Levinthal (1990), Brown (1997) proposed that a firm's absorptive capacity consists of 3 major components – prior relevant knowledge, the communications network, and the communications climate. Prior relevant knowledge provides the foundation that allows individuals to recognize the potential importance of new information.

The communications network refers to the flow of information across and within organizational boundaries. The communications climate is defined as the organizational atmosphere regarding communications behaviour and it is the absorptive capacity factor that measures trust. Tu *et al.* use Brown's basic 3-component conceptualization of absorptive capacity and add a fourth component — knowledge scanning , which is defined as an organizational mechanism enabling firms to identify and capture relevant knowledge.

Our study positions inter-organizational absorptive capacity as a dynamic capability that enables the interorganizational cost management capabilities of a firm. We operationalize AC using modified items from Tu *et al.* and focus on the 4 dimensions that lead to higher IOCM,

1. Prior relevant knowledge,
2. Communications network,
3. Communications climate, and
4. Knowledge scanning.

ELECTRONIC INTEGRATION (EI)

In our study, electronic integration refers to the capability of an organization's information technology (IT) systems to provide visibility of information to employees both within the focal firm (internal integration) and to the employees of partner firms (external integration). In other words, it is the degree to which the IT systems employed are integrated and accessible both internally (intra-firm) and externally (inter-firm). Our definition is based on Barua *et al* who define systems integration as "the extent to which a firm integrates its various IT systems to provide visibility to customer and supplier data and to allow online information sharing and transaction execution across the value chain."

An organization's level of internal cost management is dependent on the firm's level of IT integration to the extent that integrated systems allow for more accurate tracking of costs and enable the tracking of specific costs to specific activities. Accounting information systems are commonly deployed to support the collecting, processing, and communicating of cost management information to enhance decision-making. In addition to playing a role internally, information technology has also been identified as an important enabler of supply chain integration, allowing multiple organizations to coordinate activities. The presence of IT applications has been shown to be a necessary but not sufficient condition to achieve supply chain integration. Craighead and LaForge developed a taxonomy of IT adoption / integration patterns based on the type of IT applications adopted by firms for use internally and externally and the extent of the adoption downstream and upstream.

Ellram and Zsidisin one of the most important activities of purchasing and supply chain management is cost analysis, (such as examining supplier cost structures and encouraging suppliers to share cost data) requiring the extensive use of IT. Electronic integration has also been studied as a direct antecedent to a firm's absorptive capacity. Malhotra *et al.* explore how firms in supply chain partnerships configure their IT infrastructure and processes to build absorptive capacity to "acquire, assimilate, transform, and exploit information resources." Specifically, Malhotra *et al.* identify two distinct groups of constructs that enhance a firm's absorptive capacity for engaging in supply chain relationships,

1. Integrative interorganizational process mechanisms
2. Partner interface-directed information systems.

In our study, external electronic integration focuses on partner interface-directed information systems that provide the infrastructure support for much of the interorganizational communications that occur between partners. This includes systems that integrate and process data from suppliers and/or customers and systems that allow data to be shared between firms. Tomkins suggests that business relationships are developed and cultivated through stages of experience and trust intensities. Because communications are facilitated due to infrastructure support and can therefore occur more frequently, trust and the overall communications climate can improve as a result of electronic integration.

BENEFITS

Organizational cost management benefits may follow from both internal cost management and inter-organizational cost management (IOCM) practices.

These benefits include:

1. Those that are operational in nature, such as reducing costs associated with daily purchasing or sales transactions and reducing costs through the streamlining of inter-organizational processes and
2. Those that are more strategic-oriented benefits, such as decreasing the response time to market changes and identifying new business opportunities.

In addition to the benefits that are directly related to cost management, a firm should also receive benefits that are more macro-level in nature. These general benefits include measures like perceptions of a firm's financial performance, market share growth, and level of product and service innovation. It is our expectation that benefits related to the capability to manage costs both within and across organizational boundaries will increase as organizations engage in more cost management processes.

RESEARCH METHODOLOGY

This part presents the details about the operationalization of our empirical constructs, the procedures used to develop the survey items, the context of our pilot study, and the procedures used for data collection.

OPERATIONALIZATION OF CONSTRUCTS

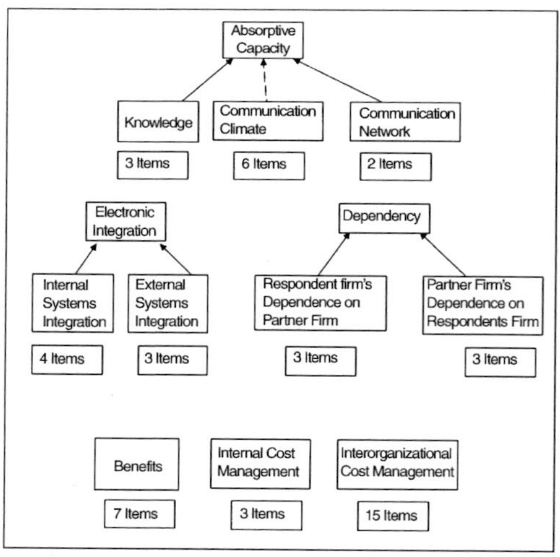

In order to operationalize the empirical constructs with survey items, we examined literature from a variety of business disciplines, including accounting, information systems, and operations and supply chain management. Many of the items used to operationalize the constructs in this study were adopted from previously validated instruments. However, in some cases, when the exact wording of original survey items did not capture the aspect of the construct that we desired, we made minor modifications to the item. When a review of the literature revealed that there were no previous instruments designed to operationalize our construct, we used the literature related to that construct to help us define and develop items that could be used measure the construct. Figure shows the hierarchical structure of the constructs and depicts the number of items related to and used for each first order construct. The remainder of this part provides details regarding how the items for each construct were selected.

ELECTRONIC INTEGRATION

We developed our empirical electronic integration construct by adopting and modifying measures that were previously validated in Barua *et al.* (2004). The original Barua *et al.* (2004) measures had a strong internal systems integration focus, with only one question addressing external systems integration. Because our study focuses on the relationship between two firms, we added two additional items that are expected to capture the external or interorganizational aspect of systems integration.

ABSORPTIVE CAPACITY

We developed our absorptive capacity constructs primarily by adopting and modifying measures that were previous used in Tu *et al.* (2005). Modifications to the original items were made in order to capture the interorganizational absorptive capacity that exists between two partner firms as opposed to a single firm. For items that were intended to assess knowledge, we made additional modifications that would allow us to assess knowledge regarding cost management. In addition to the items modified from Tu *et al.* (2005), two additional survey items were also obtained from instruments used by Stuart and McCutecheon (2000) and Dyer (1997) related to trust and the communications climate between firms.

COST MANAGEMENT

Since there were no previous survey instruments designed to assess the extent to which firm engage in cost management practices, we used the academic literature related to internal and interorganizational cost management to develop the survey items related to our empirical cost management constructs -- internal cost management (ICM) and interorganizational cost management (IOCM). These cost management constructs simply assess whether the respondents' firm engages in multiple cost management practice. ICM describes the degree to which respondents firms engage in internal cost management practices, and IOCM describes the degree to which respondents firms engage in interorganizational cost management practices with a supply chain partner.

BENEFITS

We again turn to the academic literature related to interorganizational cost management processes to develop our benefits construct. Several of the items used in our survey were items used in previous research to assess general firm benefits. These items were adapted for our research. In addition to the established items, we also included several items designed to specifically capture the benefits that should be associated with engaging in interorganizational cost management practices. These items were developed based on benefits directly attributable to cost management practices.

Dependency

Although dependency is not an empirical construct we investigate, we recognize that it is a control variable that must be measured. Dependency is a measure that refers to the level of dependence each firm has on its partner and vice versa. Dependence has been defined in the literature as the extent to which a target firm needs the source firm to achieve its goals.

Andaleeb identifies two important factors that create perceptions of dependence:

1. "The importance or criticality of the resources provided by the source firm" and
2. "The number of alternate sources available to the target firm for the needed resources."

Our construct of dependency is based on those 2 factors.

Q-SORT

Prior to administering our survey, we first evaluated the survey items for reliability as prescribed by Rust and Cooil (1994), which presents guidelines for measuring the reliability of qualitative data through a "q-sort". This is particularly important given the fact that several of our constructs were new and several of items that were based on previous constructs were reworded in order to meet our research requirement. In our initial q-sort, we asked 8 judges to read our preliminary list of 65 items and to categorize each item into 1 of 5 groups (constructs). Two of the eight judges were accounting professors who teach financial and managerial accounting. The remaining 6 judges were Ph.D. students in the accounting (2), management information systems (2), and operations management programmes (2).

The first step of the q-sort analysis is to determine the "proportional agreement." This is the total number of pair-wise agreements between judges across all 65 items divided by the total number of pair-wise comparisons. Next, we used the tables provided by Rust and Cooil (1994) in order to determine the proportional reduction in loss and obtained a value of 1.00, suggesting that the instrument items were reliable.

While this methodology does provide for an overall reliability of the measures based on inter-judge agreement, this methodology does not address any deviation of judgments from the predicted groupings. Therefore, we also examined each item in which there were more than 3 judges who did not place the item into the predicted category (12 out of 65). These 12 items were then examined and reworded to address the likely cause(s) for misclassification.

INITIAL PILOT STUDY

Initially our survey was administered electronically to one stage of the Institute of Management Accountants (IMA) using the same sample frame and methodology used in the study presented here. An e-mail with a link to the survey was sent to each of the 185 members. Out of the 185 members, 20 (10.8%) participated in the survey. Of the 20 respondents, 8 worked in an organization that is part of a supply chain· We used the results of this initial pilot study to revise our survey items.

SURVEY ADMINISTRATION

The revised survey was administered to members of a regional IMA stage. The survey items were presented to respondents via an online survey in which respondents were asked to rate their responses on a Likert-type scale ranging from 1 (strongly disagree) to 7 (strongly agree). The survey was administered via e-mail to 1833 individuals who are registered IMA members of North and South Carolina.

Of the 1833 IMA members surveyed, 333 (18%) of the e-mails were returned as undeliverable, rejected as spam, or were not immediately received because the e-mail recipient was out of the office. A total of 144 IMA members participated in the survey for an overall response rate of 8%. Of those that responded, 95 indicated that they did not fit our target respondent group of managerial accountants working within a supply chain , which left 73 responses from our desired audience. Of the 73, we had 49 individuals complete the entire survey, giving us a final sample size of 49 for our analysis This low response rate may have been due to several factors.

- First, the survey recipients were not targeted to those who were part of a supply chain; it was sent to all IMA members in the regional stage.
- Second, previous studies have found that response rates for Internet-based surveys are usually lower than for equivalent mail surveys.
- Third, we only made 3 contacts to the respondents requesting participation in the survey. Dillman (2000) suggests that for surveys to receive a good response rate, five contacts should be made.

The average age of the 49 respondents was 46, and the gender breakdown is approximately 27% female and 73% male (9 respondents did not disclose their gender). Ninety per cent of the respondents reported 4+ years of college. The firm types represented by the survey respondents include manufacturer (73%), distributor (13%), retailer (4%), and wholesaler (7%). Eighty per cent of the respondents reported their firm had annual revenue > $10 million.

DATA ANALYSIS

To test the research hypotheses, path analysis was used. The path analysis was conducted using the SAS Calis procedure, which is a maximum likelihood method of parameter estimation. The variables used in the path analysis were obtained by deriving principal component scores for each of the empirical constructs in our model using principal components analysis. In the cases where the empirical construct is a second order construct (*i.e.* absorptive capacity, electronic integration, and dependency), we obtain a second order component scores using principal components analysis where the inputs into the analysis are the previously derived first order principal component scores.

Path analysis using component scores is the most appropriate methodology due to the formative nature of our constructs. Because our constructs are formative, there is no expectation that the items should have high internal reliability or consistency. Therefore, the calculation of Cronbach's alpha for our constructs is not applicable in this study and we focused the evaluation of our constructs on their content validity.

By adopting and adjusting constructs and items that have already been successfully implemented in previous research, many of our construct begin with content validity. Additional construct validity is provided though the q-sort process. Finally, our method of obtaining principle component scores for each of the constructs provides further support for construct validity because in general all of the items for each construct grouped together as predicted.

MEASUREMENT VALIDATION

The first phase of our data analysis focused on the measurement properties of the constructs. We performed a principal components analysis on the second order constructs, with all of the first-order items as input. The loadings of the principal components analysis for each of the six empirical constructs. In all cases, we used the principal components axis method and set the prior communality estimates to one, which are the options required in a principal components analysis. When appropriate, we used oblique rotation. We selected oblique rotation over varimax because it was our expectation, based on the literature from which our items were adapted, that the components would be correlated.

The number of components retained was based on the eigenvalue-greater-than-one criterion, where any components with an eignevalue greater than 1.00 are retained. In interpreting the factor loadings, items were said to load on a component if the loading was greater than or equal to.50. The loading of item components ranged from.55 to.97. Components were then named based on the items that loaded on it. In the cases where constructs and items were adopted from previous research, our items loaded as expected based on the loading observed in the previous research. This result provides additional support for the validity of those constructs.

For our second order constructs of absorptive capacity, electronic integration, and dependency, we used SAS's Proc Factor programme to first obtain a component score for each of the first order constructs. These component scores are each a linear combination of only the items that were found to load on that component. Next, we conducted principal component analysis where the first order construct components scores were used as the measure of the first order construct in the formation of the second order construct.

Table. Correlation Between Constructs

	EI	AC	DEP	IOCM	ICM	BEN
EI	1					
AC	0.484	1				
DEP	0.236	0.487	1			
IOCM	0.42	0.535	0.416	1		
ICM	0.392	0.157	-0.179	0.115	1	
BEN	0.45	0.324	0.158	0.536	0.405	1

KEY:
EI Electronic Integration
AC Absorptive Capacity
DEP Dependency
IOCM Interorganizational Cost Management
ICM Inter Cost Management
BEN Benifits

STRUCTURAL MODEL

Path analysis with SAS's Proc Calis was used to assess the structural portion of the model. Goodness-of-fit measures were used to indicate an acceptable fit between the model and the data. Our model has a Goodness of Fit Index of.945, a normed fit index (NFI) of.900, and a comparative fit index (CFI) of.958. Model fit is also assessed by a Chi-square test. Our model has a Chi-square value of 11.16 with 8 degrees of freedom and a p-value of.169. This value does not allow us to reject the null hypothesis that the proposed model is a good fit to the data. Taken together with each of our fit indices meeting or exceeding the desired level of.90, we conclude that our model provides a good fit to the data.

RESULTS

TAble. The Results of the Path Analysis

Dependent Variable: IOCM		
Intercept	Coefficient	–.0177
	andard error	.1415
	t-stat	–.13
	p-value	.9007
ICM	Coefficient	–.0038
	standard error	.1708

	t-stat	–.02
	p-value	.9823
EI	Coefficient	.313*
	standard error	.146
	t-stat	2.14
	p-value	.0382
Dependency	Coefficient	.2008
	standard error	.1480
	t-stat	1.36
	p-value	.1823
ICM* EI	Coefficient	.1287
	standard error	.1186
	t-stat	1.09
	p-value	.2841
ICM * Dependency	Coefficient	.3230
	standard error	.2377
	t-stat	1.36
	p-value	.1817
EI * Dependency	Coefficient	–.2211
	standard error	.1363
	t-stat	–1.62
	p-value	.1125
ICM * EI * Dependency	Coefficient	.359*
	standard error	.161
	t-stat	2.23
	p-value	.0316

This presents standardized path coefficients for the model, the accompanying t-statistics, and a summary of the results of our hypotheses.

- *Hypothesis* 1: In evaluating our initial hypothesis, we find that the use of cost management practices internally does not appear to be a precursor to the use of IOCM. This finding fails to support Hypothesis 1 using path analysis.
- *Hypothesis* 2: Our second hypothesis, which predicts a positive relationship between absorptive capacity and IOCM, is supported with a standardized coefficient of.3006 and a t-statistic of 2.16. This supports our belief that firms with a strong external cost focus as exhibited by knowledge, communications, and trust engage in IOCM practices.
- *Hypothesis* 3: Next, we find support for Hypothesis 3, which predicts a positive relationship between systems integration and internal cost management. This path has a standardized coefficient of.4604 and a t-stat of 3.54. This supports our expectation that a firm's level of internal cost management is dependent on the hesis 4: We did not find a significant relationship between electronic integration and IOCM. H4 is not supported by the path analysis.

- *Hypothesis* 5: We did find support that the degree a firm's IT is integrated impacts the absorptive capacity of the firm. Thus hypothesis 5 is supported with a path coefficient of.3907 and a t-stat of 3.34. While EI consist of both internal and external integration, support for the hypothesis suggests that the external integration between the partners leads to greater trust and a more effective communication environment.
- *Hypothesis* 6 *and Hypothesis* 7: Our final test of the hypotheses focuses on the impact of cost management practices on perceived firm benefits. Hypothesis 6, which predicts that high levels of ICM will lead to perceived benefits, is supported by a path coefficient of.2933 with a t-statistic of 2.34. Hypothesis 7, which predicts that high levels of IOCM will lead to perceived firm benefits, is also supported with a path coefficient of.4428 and a t-statistic of 3.40. Taken together, firms clearly perceive that they are benefiting from both intra-organizational and inter-organizational cost management.

SUPPLEMENTAL ANALYSIS

With H1 and H4 not supported just as to the path analysis results, we were interested in determining if the insignificance of the results could be due to a mediation effect or a moderation (interaction) effect.

ICM and IOCM

We hypothesized in H1 that IOCM is more likely in firms that emphasize internal cost management techniques. However, the results from the path analysis does not support this hypothesis (H1). To further explore the relationship between internal and IOCM, we first investigated a possible mediation effect. For mediation to occur, a series of steps must be met (Baron and Kenny (1986).

The first step is that the independent variable must have a significant regression coefficient when the independent variable is regressed on the dependent variable. When the independent variable ICM is regressed on the dependent variable IOCM, the result is not significant, implying that there is not another variable mediating the relationship between ICM and IOCM. Next, we explored the possibility of an interaction among variables that could explain the lack of a relationship between IOCM and ICM.

Several anomalous characteristics of the data suggested that an interaction effect may be present. First, the correlation between IOCM and ICM is positive, while the path model relationship is negative. Second, although the relationship between ICM and IOCM was found to be insignificant, both of these constructs significantly covary directly and positively with the EI construct, suggesting the IOCM and ICM should also covary. Both ICM and IOCM are also found to significantly covary with the dependency construct, although ICM is found to covary negatively with dependency while IOCM covaries positively. This suggests that IOCM and ICM should negatively covary. Based on these observations, we conducted regression analysis to determine if an interaction existed among these variables (electronic integration, dependency, and ICM)·

The results show a three-way interaction effect between dependency, ICM, and electronic integration that the interaction is positively associated with IOCM. The results also show that electronic integration has a main effect on IOCM. All other interactions were insignificant. The main effect of EI was predicted in H4 and is not surprising because we expect that electronic integration would positively impact the use of IOCM. Similarly, it is expected that within the three-way interaction, EI still serves an enabler of IOCM.

Under this presumption, our three-way interaction can be simply assessed by examining the remaining variables of the interaction, dependency and ICM. In general, the results of this survey appear to capture an environmental relationship where firms that score high on the dependency construct tend to score low on the ICM construct. This is the only inverse relationship that was observed among any of the variables. However, when the dependency construct is high and firms contrarily also have high ICM, the presence of electronic integration appears to lead to higher IOCM values. This assessment is also supported by the ICM *Dependency interaction value which has a high coefficient, but which may not be significant due to the sample size.

In summary, this result can be interpreted to suggest that when partners have the capability to transfer information via relatively highly integrated electronic systems (*i.e.* high EI), firms are more likely to engage in IOCM practices when they unexpectedly are both highly dependent on their partners and engaging in ICM practices. Thus our data does provide some limited evidence supporting H1, where ICM leads to IOCM (in the presence of high EI and high dependency).

ELECTRONIC INTEGRATION AND IOCM

Because our path analysis failed to support our fourth hypothesis, we also performed exploratory analysis on the relationship between electronic integration and IOCM.

There are two possible constructs which could mediate the EI to IOCM relationship:

1. ICM or
2. AC.

Since we already established that ICM does not have a direct relationship with IOCM, it cannot mediate the relationship between EI and IOCM. Therefore, we investigate AC as a potential mediating variable between the EI to IOCM constructs using the Baron and Kenny (1986) steps. The results of the regression analyses that were conducted. In the first step, AC is regressed on EI and the coefficient on EI (.4839) is significant p=.0004. In the second step, IOCM is regressed on EI and the coefficient on EI (.4200) is significant at p=.027. In the final step, IOCM is regressed on both EI and the potential mediator, AC. In the presence of AC, the coefficient on EI (.2104) becomes insignificant at p=.1368 while the coefficient on AC (.5349) is significant at p<.001. The insignificant coefficient of EI in step 3 supports the proposition that AC fully mediates the relationship between EI and IOCM, which can explain the lack of support for H4 in the path analysis.

DISCUSSION

Overall, our results suggest that electronic systems integration, absorptive capacity, and internal cost management all play a role in determining interorganizational cost management practices in a firm, which in turn results in firm benefits.

INTERNAL COST MANAGEMENT (H1)

Although it seems intuitive that a firm emphasizing internal cost management practices could easily mature to engage in inter-firm cost management, the non-support of H1 demonstrates there are perhaps other factors that affect the relationship between ICM and IOCM. As demonstrated by our supplementary analysis, we found that the level of ICM may impact an organization's involvement in IOCM as moderated by the level of dependency between a firm and its partner firm and the extent of the electronic integration between the firms.

There are also alternative reasons that may explain the path analysis results. First, our measure of ICM only contains three items and may not fully capture the degree to which firms use cost management internally. Another potential cause for our findings is that in the partner relationship, it could be the partner whose use of ICM is driving the IOCM activities. If so, Coad and Cullen (2006) suggest that when firms have relative low ICM, using IOCM may result in the firm increasing its own ICM.

ABSORPTIVE CAPACITY (H2)

One result of our study which may be particularly of interest to practitioners is the role of a firm's absorptive capacity in influencing IOCM. Our study provides empirical support that absorptive capacity does indeed enable the interorganizational cost management capabilities of a firm. This suggests that the somewhat intangible factors of absorptive capacity such as employee knowledge, trust, and the communications climate between firms are important enablers of extending cost management practices beyond the walls of a single firm. By focusing on these intangible factors, managers can set the stage for IOCM.

ELECTRONIC INTEGRATION (H3, H4, H5)

The role of information technology infrastructure has long been recognized as an enabler of business capabilities. Our study provides further support of IT enabling even more business capabilities. We find that EI directly enables AC and ICM. Although H4 was not supported in our main analysis, the supplemental analysis shows that EI indirectly enables interorganizational cost management via its impact on absorptive capacity and its role in moderating the relationship between ICM and internal cost management. We conclude that the presence of external electronic integration influences absorptive capacity by acting as an enabler of communication and knowledge sharing.

BENEFITS (H6 AND H7)

The results of this research provide additional support for the importance of employing cost management practices both within the organization and beyond the boundaries of the organization. The benefits of interorganizational cost management range from operational cost-saving strategies to strategic benefits like new business opportunities and increased levels of product and service innovation.

LIMITATIONS AND FUTURE RESEARCH

A primary limitation of this research is the size of our sample. However, despite, the small sample size, we were able to find significant results and support the validity of our constructs through the use of principal components analysis. We plan on extending this research by collecting additional data from a national study of IMA members in order to continue testing our model. This extension will likely use a refined instrument, especially ICM, based on the findings of this study.

Another related limitation to this research is a low response rate. We have several strategies planned to increase the response rate of future survey respondents. First, with the potential assistance of IMA, the next survey will only be sent to those IMA members that represent our target sample. Second, as suggested, also follow the methodology prescribed by Dillman to maximize response rate. Finally, with the potential support of IMA, we feel that we can improve the overall response rate of future surveys.

While we fully expect to improve the sample size and response rate of our survey instrument, we recognize that one weakness of the survey methodology is that the nature of a cross-sectional survey makes interpreting the temporal nature of the constructs difficult. Nevertheless, our use of path analysis provides support for the direction of the predicted relationship.

A final limitation to our research is that data is collected about a supply chain partnership from only one of the partners. Future studies might measure responses from both partners which would allow the researcher to assess the partnership more accurately. This might be especially important when considering the impact of ICM on IOCM because the survey respondent in our study can likely only assess the ICM of his/her own firm.

The absorptive capacity aspect of cost management is a ripe area for future research in collaborative supply chains. The underlying constructs of absorptive capacity (communications climate (including trust), communications network, and knowledge) can be further explored in an interorganizational cost management context.

A final area for future research is to further explore the specific types of IT that support ICM and IOCM. Our research demonstrates that electronic integration in general is an indirect antecedent (through absorptive capacity and internal cost management) to IOCM. Future research might explore the repertoire of interorganizational systems that best facilitate IOCM.

10

Cost Estimating and Forecasting

INTRODUCTION

The private commercial sector is adopting new approaches to the management of design, development and production. These have led to new product and process technologies. These use and produce value within a new revolutionary framework. This crucially impacts on cost. Can it be applied to defence? If so, how will this impact on defence costs and so cost estimating? This paper sets out to answer these questions. In commerce one does not have to contend with defence's endemic and extensive systems integration problems. One also does not have its peculiarity of politically driven monopsonistic demand. A key issue for defence today is thus the extent to which it can adopt best commercial practice and cut costs despite these barriers to its use. The benefits achievable in the wider industrial context are already evident.

They are considerable as a consequence of faster development and more capability deliverable per dollar. However can one expect these benefits to be fully achievable in defence given its technical and socio-political context? The present administration is the US's DoD clearly believes they can. The approach used is prevalent throughout the Atlantic community. It has acquired the name "Smart Procurement". This exploits what in commerce has become the philosophy of "lean production". This seeks to lean out production costs by auditing productive activity against the criteria set by the value it adds for the final customer. The argument is that if an activity does not add such value then it should cease. In defence the value added is the state's wish to maximize its potential to use lethal force per dollar spent to legitimate political ends. Philosophically and practically "lean production" requires customers' demands to pull production down through a well specified energy minimizing flow of activities.

Each should add customer value. There should be no local accumulation of energy absorbing stock. This is distinct from supply driven systems. These achieve economies of scale by pushing production up through a sequence of costly energy batch processes designed to maximize the rate of flow through each So as to minimize unit processing costs. This is only achievable at the expense of large pools of stock waiting for processing at the rate are required to minimize processing costs within each stage.

To achieve its ends SP must therefore ensure it:

- Creates a steady flow of demand not infrequent, stock creating, batches of it.
- Adds value to politically useful military operational capability in each procurement stage: research, development, manufacture, use and disposal

To achieve these SP has to be integrated with the operational context in which the materiel of war will ultimately be consumed. It therefore needs to synchronize procurement with the needs of military operations across the envisaged spectrum of possible conflict. In effect this means that SP, like the "battle space" it is now envisioned supporting by the "Revolution in Military Affairs", needs to be based on the integration of systems across. This is what we might call the "battle-sphere": the weapons systems and their users, the battle-space in which they are used in conjunction with other systems and the industrial, research and social systems that enable all this to occur.

In the defence industrial context supporting the RMA it is thus essential that the design, production, storage and disposing of weapons systems optimizes political-military value across their whole life cycle. This paper sets out to categorize the changes catalyzing SP and highlight their potential impact on cost. It will consider also their likely rate of propagation given current constraints and defence's capacity to ease them. Our focus is the agenda thus implied for cost estimating professionals.

The evidence used is all in the public domain. This seems to indicate that the historical cost base on which current estimates are constructed is fast being eroded. This means the profession has to develop new approaches, it is, but are they coming on fast enough? The whole basis of SP is that costs can be cut using commercial sources and methods particularly if defence accepts commercial not military specifications. Then "Commercial Off The Shelf" "Dual Use" technology can be exploited.

Then it is argued the commercial sectors, for its own benefit will absorb a significant proportion of development costs. We shall explore whether this is a reasonable expectation? Lean manufacturing and distribution networks encapsulate the philosophy of “lean thinking” commerce uses to achieve the described ends. This incorporates Just in Time logistics, low inventories, zero delivery defects, flexible small batch production and so co-operation throughout a supply chain where products are designed not only for use but for limiting the consumption of non-renewable raw materials, manufacture, reliability, ease of servicing and ultimately disposal.

This requires the chain from raw material extraction to re-use or disposal as a single system over which all costs should be minimized no matter by whom born. A key issue for this to be achievable is incentive. The pay-off may be in one part of the network but additional costs in another. These network components are likely to be under different ownership and so control. The distributed processing and flexible military fighting procedures on which the RMA is based are fundamental to this paper.

The digitized battle-space brings changes doctrinally and technically. These challenge the cost estimator even before we look into the process of manufacture and supply. Integrated "Command and Control" C2 makes it possible to economize on one platform's capability by using the capacity of another. To this can be added stealth and total battlefield visibility. Together these create a huge increase in military productivity allowing the use of massive destructive power from a safe platform of action, *e.g.* Apache Longbow. This complicates cost and operational effectiveness analysis not least by hugely increasing the logistic burdens required to sustain the fighting power now capable of deployment.

This new battle-space is more sparsely populated with human beings. This has deep implications for the nature of warfare and so costs. We can now take people away from many of the hazards of war. These lower costs by eliminating the need for the protection currently built into each platform involved in combat. This is already reality for reconnaissance with the increased use of drones. It is now possible to make a choice as to whether target acquisition, or even attack, should be managed on or off a weapons platform. It is envisaged that an army unit could lay of an attack instantaneously to an, artillery battery, a helicopter, a fixed wing aircraft, a ship's guns a few miles of the coast or a submarine based cruise missile 500 or 600 miles way. This has significant implications for the wider international marketability and so cost sharing possible for a weapon system. A weapon system that relies on expensive centrally provided off-platform command, control, guidance and computation or acquisition technology will not be widely affordable.

For example on the joint US UK JASF a US design decision that increased its weapons load at the expense of onboard command and control would leave JASF's other customer, the UK, with a problem. Have a platform only useable in a combined US/UK operation or accept a bill, financial or military, to integrate UK STA technology onto a consequently less lethal platform. These operational implications of new technology should be seen in conjunction with the problems for the SP concepts of evolutionary development based on incremental technological insertion. The idea is that this would allow military technology to stay in step with the now faster advancing civil, COTS, technology. SP seems to believes that technology insertion and so the incrementally procurement of capability can be achieved at the same time as one lengthen the time a platform concept remains in use. This lessens technological risk. It also spreads development and set up costs out over time and more extended, but individually smaller, production runs. This attenuates estimating errors. Error bounds grow exponentially on extrapolation.

In IT product life-cycles are as little as eighteen months. Technological and therefore cost extrapolations can then be limited to a similar period. In the described circumstances it is clear that costing by analogy must be problematic. First if defence has not yet used a commercial practice no direct historical basis exists in defence from which to construct an estimate. Second if commercial data were used directly the very different market structures from which it springs must throw doubts on its defence relevance. With no "actual" costs to measure estimates must use analogy.

There are four bases for this. Each has virtues. Each has problems.

They are:

1. The past,
2. Experience elsewhere,
3. A plan extrapolating from the former two,
4. Creative vision not evidently rooted in experience.

Our argument suggests that future cost estimates can be based only on the last. This requires the simulation of the processes of production, distribution and war fighting, *i.e.* "synthetic environments." However these are rarely created from imagination they are generally embedded in a substantive matrix of practice. These model what might be possible as opposed to what is demonstrable so.

Research exists on this in the USA. In thinking about cost in the holistic imaginative way we have described acquisition costs clearly can not be separated from other costs up and down stream. However even when taking this very broad brush view of a project envisaged one would still have failed to take account of significant costs. One could wrongly consider acquisition in isolation from other costs. Many of the changes we have outlined are not found at the level of project costs nor even in the historically evident overhead of the organizations in which it is embedded. Significant socio-economic changes, effecting costs, are also occurring at the industrial and infra structural level. We thus have to consider the effects of the change described on the cost environment at three levels: societal, the enterprise and the project. As suggested, deal with each in turn.

- First there exists an increasingly sophisticated global network of industrial support activity providing finance, research and development, design, production, distribution and marketing for all types of products and enterprises. We need to consider the impact on defence project costs of this increasingly sophisticated low cost global commercial support infrastructure.
- Second defence production is increasingly a process where the key inputs are produced by many distinct entities. The final result is merely integrated together by one, in the defence case, the "prime contractor". The delivered result is thus produced by a secondary, "virtual", organization for which the prime contractor is merely the impresario.

- Thirdly we need to take cognizance of the impact of new materials and production and development methods on directly attributable project cost. This paper considers the impact on cost of change at each of the above levels. After considering these it takes cognizance of the extent they can penetrate defence. We then consider what barriers exist to their implementation in defence and how these can be lowered before exploring their significance for estimating. Japanese companies led by Toyota have demonstrated that all this can work.

In the defence context we have to ask:

- Are there defence examples that can form the basis of estimates?
- Will the new destroy the estimating utility of existing knowledge?
- Will "smart procurement" lead to a seamless join between commercial and defence practice making analogies from commerce sufficient to defence need?

Even the strongest advocate of SP could not expect affirmative answers to all of these. A monopsonistic buyer, such as a defence department, dealing with a few large prime contractors, can not put itself in a position analogous to that pertaining in a commercial competitive market. If it could, cost estimating would be an irrelevance. The best estimate would be market price. We are thus left with the question of how one might adjust analogues from the commercial world, based on lean manufacturing and JITs experience, to the monopsonistic reality of defence

BANG OF INFRASTRUCTURE CHANGE ON COST

COMMON NATURE OF INFRASTRUCTURE CHANGES

The impact of infrastructure change on the costs of commodities such as food, clothing, cars and IT has been large. The INTERNET and associated e-commerce are fundamentally changing infrastructure costs forever. The word processing system and computer on which this paper is written is indicative of such business process changes. This electronic communication is cheaper and incomparably faster than the mail it replaces. The technical limitations to the universality of its use are slight. Inexpensive truly mobile phones do not yet exist but soon they will.

However even now an oilman working a field in Siberia, two hundred miles from a phone line, can have a daily satellite video conference with his partners on Wall Street regarding their customers demands that day. This determines how much oil he pumps. Oil need only flow from the well head when such demand "metaphorically" pulls it from the ground. This obviates the need for extensive tank farms at wellheads, ports, oil refineries and delivery centers.

The global co-ordination of production and distribution now possible eliminates the need for significant stock. This includes that in the process of distribution, *i.e.* in large expensive high-risk oil tankers. Such infrastructure change has a dramatic impact on cost and choice. The competitive pricing it ensures lowers costs further. This creates an even greater demand for variety of types, means, sources, and quality of supply. The commercial distribution and electronic data interchange systems making such value added possible is too expensive for states to replicate.

United Parcel Service's aircraft fleet is the biggest in the world. They are major truck and warehouse owners. Their volume of business ensures unit costs lower than anything achievable even by government Good in-house orchestration of logistics can produce world beating competitive advantage. One case is that of Caterpillar's success in its fight for market dominance against Komatsu of Japan. Komatsu set out to beat Caterpillar in the supply of large construction machines; comparable in their chassis and power trains to the heavy armor used by the military. Arguably Komatsu's equipment became as good, or even better than Caterpillar's.

However they did not displace Caterpillar from its lead position. Caterpillar had and has a highly effective distribution chain. This intends that spare's be deliverable anywhere on the surface of the globe occurs within 48 hours. Civil engineering contractors faced with hefty penalty clauses or oil companies not pumping oil can not afford unavailable equipment. Komatsu has failed to match this service and so has failed to displace Caterpillar from its lead. Caterpillar's success has not escaped the attention of others: for example the UK company Land Rover. Their commercial market place overlaps Caterpillar's.

They now use Caterpillar's distribution system. In commercial games of war, errors may not lead to death but they can cause bankruptcy. Commercial survival now depends on design trading-off and the cost of after-sales support. Komatsu's failure to overtake Caterpillar underlines this. Modern supply and distribution allows one to operate wherever in the world it is best to do so. In the limit with stabilized demand one need carry no stock outside that in the delivery pipeline and only manufacture products in response to specific demand. This requires a new approach to manufacturing, "lean manufacturing".

However for such technological advance to be sustained at the rate now evident requires process control concentrated in a few suppliers, e. g. UPS, INTEL and Microsoft. They achieve scale economies (volume over time) and scope (volume over space) leveraging low unit costs sustained by a steady pull of demand. This supports the huge initial investments in IPR, people, plant and equipment corporations like INTEL, Microsoft, UPS and Caterpillar need.

To minimize risks such companies take an incremental approach to product development. The aim is a payback period of not more than 2-3 years. A developmental revolution is not possible on such a life cycle. Intel's 84X86 series of microprocessors and Microsoft's MS-DOS/ Windows series are both examples of the benefits of such evolutionary development.

IMPACT OF INFRASTRUCTURE INDUCED CHANGE ON DEFENCE COSTS

The infrastructure changes described impact on costs in many ways, including the cost of costing. Software production is now geographical dispersed. The DOD's "Defence Reform Initiative" insists the US government use UPS and Federal Express' systems in preference to its own. Part of the recent administrative reforms of the US DoD has encouraged the materiel commands of all three services to base much of their procurement systems on "electronic commerce". This allows orders to be sent direct to suppliers. They then deliver direct to military units. This saves on DoD owned storage and distribution systems.

A recent paper indicated cost savings on retail stock of $40 for every $1 spent on UPS or FedEx. For defence to access these advantages it needs to use Commercial Off The Shelf (COTS) items. On economies of scale grounds alone these can be so much cheaper than tailor made defence items that the argument for COTS is compelling. It is already accepted as the source of many electronic components.

COST AND SECURITY LIMITATIONS TO THE USE OF INFRASTRUCTURE CHANGE IN DEFENCE

However, adapting COTS to defence can be more expensive than working to a defence specification. COTS also raise security issues on two counts, security of information and security of supply. On the latter consider the case of DOD's use of UPS or FedEx. This does not compromise the US's national security. These suppliers sustain most of their substantial assets and staff on US territory. In the event of war these can be requisitioned and conscripted. A small country wishing to ensure it can control its distribution and supply system in war may wish to deny defence access to such an approach. The result is then likely to be lower quality and higher costs. On the former information security is costly, *e.g.* vetting, firewall construction, etc. Even without this defence might wish to deny itself access to cost effective practices used by commercial software firms, *e.g.* outsourcing to India. In addition the technical challenges in the commercial sector are now significant so increasingly high quality staff now often choose commercial over defence work.

POSSIBLE ACTIONS TO EXPLOIT

In total war, reliance on traditional systems must be in doubt. Arguably they trap defence into using expensive outmoded systems that may now be penetrated, or out performed, by cheaper commercial ones. As indicated in the absence of direct action to the contrary, generic commercial components are now so much cheaper that it is hard to avoid incorporating them in military systems. This generally puts defence costs on the same downward trend observable for production generally. In operations less than war the practical advantages of such systems may outweigh their security disadvantages. In the Gulf War PCs were bought off the shelf. In Bosnia commercial trucking is used regularly and the American's have used commercial communication systems.

VIRTUAL ORGANISATION AND COSTS

Systemic thinking also impacts on the organization of production, the key idea being the "virtual organization". This is manifest in the role now seen for prime contractors. The globalising business process linking distinct production capacities together, as already described, underpins the "virtual organization". Cheap physical distribution coupled with highly efficient communication makes a widely distributed stockless network of manufacturers possible.

A SIMPLE EXAMPLE OF VIRTUAL ORGANIZATION

Illustrative of this is the portable computer this paper is produced on. This was "made available" by a Taiwanese company, Twinhead. It was assembled and distributed in the UK. The screen was produced by Cirrus Logic in the USA, the hard-drive by Toshiba in Japan. The floppy was made in Taiwan and the modem in the USA by Apex Data. The microprocessor is an INTEL Pentium manufactured who knows where. The mouse is made in Mexico.

The software comes from all over the world but is integrated by Microsoft of Seattle USA. Twinhead may or may not conceive of this package. However, they are the impresarios delivering it. The machine was ordered to an idiosyncratic individual specification on a Monday morning. The machine did not exist then nor were all the parts available to manufacture it. That evening the UK assembly and distribution center ordered the parts needed by FAX. Their suppliers then dispatched these parts by UPS, DHL, FedEx, etc. The next day they began to arrive. Assembly was started. As more parts arrived the machine grew closer to completion. Late Wednesday pre-delivery testing began.

This was completed on the Thursday. UPS were then contacted to pick up the fully tested machine. It was delivered lunchtime Friday. This is "lean enterprise". It is entirely demand-pull. The final product nor the parts to make it did not exist together until the customer demanded it. By changing to demand pull for parts in the US, Toyota has reduced the time from manufacture to delivery from 11 to 2.5 months. For Toyota in the USA, 98% of car servicing and repair is completed within 1 day. In Japan itself, 98% of repair and maintenance actions are completed within 2hrs of demand using only 60% of the stock held in the US.

FEATURES OF THE SUCCESSFUL VIRTUAL ORGANIZATION

Two key features that seem to lead to commercial success within the framework of the virtual organization are partnership sourcing (PS) and a commitment to outsource non-core business. All activity within an organization's boundary uses up senior management time. Optimality requires that this be focused on a business's core skill areas. Management attention directed away from such core areas of activity defocuses on organization clarity of purpose and ultimately results.

Markets, it is argued, produce very high-powered incentives to performance. A competitive market can ensure the cheap high quality supply of many non-core products and services. Arguably market incentives police achievement better than managerial effort, misdirected from what should be its main effort, the organizations core area of competence.

A set of skills core to an organization's ethos can always be identified, (for an organization), eg. buying and retailing, everything else can be outsourced to advantage specialists, each with their own core skills. Each member of a production and distribution network hones its core skills to a level of perfection not achievable in a vertically integrated organization. This ensures the right high quality products get to customers economically. In such a network each player is a high performer in his own right and uses his management to maintain focus on core activities only.

To ensure effectiveness in this process partnership sourcing (PS) is often used. This is designed to ensure that value is added continuously throughout in a supply chain. This requires trust between all those involved. This vitally includes the final customer. Post purchase customer utility is seen to be as important as a sale. If one were to competitively auction each link in a supply chain, one would destroy rather than create trust and so adds to cost.

On the other hand in a vertically organized system, less able people tend to be recruited to non-core activities. Logically one would then expect their skills to be lower and managerial acuity in dealing with them less evident and so costs higher than might otherwise be the case. Evidence on this is limited. The converse has been the principal focus of research, *i.e.* what is the configuration of successful companies.

In private sector virtual organizations professional purchasing management is a core skill. Effective partnership sourcing is a key part of that. Professional buyers choose a supplier on professional grounds based on critical performance criteria and endeavor to stay loyal to him no matter what. If a supplier is bad he is helped to improve before serious consideration is given to replacing him. This approach has proved cheaper than trust destroying compulsory competitive tendering (CCT).

LIMITATIONS: VIRTUAL ORGANIZATIONS APPROACH IN DEFENCE

In the CCT case the buyer has to pay the losers' as well as the winners' bidding costs. The cost of bidding on losing contracts has to be recovered. If one wins one out of five bids then four losing bids are costed into the winning one. With partnership sourcing not only are these costs saved but mutual interest can drive further gains in value and cost. Long term commitment allows the parties to invest mutually to eliminate costs. This is not viable with project by project contracting.

For probity reasons Western style administrations ban PS. Procurement agencies retain the trustdestroying, costly, but politically defensible, system of CCT. CCT ensures arms length relationship between the ultimate user and the supplier. The latter are dealt with through the legalistic, unfriendly and so costly process set up by contract's branches. Their principal and proper function is to ensure auditably fair, non-corrupt dealings with potential suppliers. Their focus is on fairness and equity between suppliers. It is not on efficiency and effectiveness. In contrast PS establishes close but tough relationships based on mutual interest. Anglo-Saxon style governance makes this approach almost impossible for government despite its cheapness in the absence of corruption.

EFFORTS MADE IN DEFENCE TO OVERCOME

In defence many have seen recent reforms as advocating adversarial competition and CCT not PS. This view stems from its insistence on a tough professional relationship between buyer and seller. This, however, can be consistent with PS. The nature of the product procured by defence can be transformed so that CCT could be avoided and PS made effective indirectly. The trick is for the procurement process to change from that of a demander of specific tightly defined final products to the procurer of the services of, "prime contractors".

These orchestrate the activities of others to satisfy the demands of defence. Primes have to be capable of integrating the best offerings in the market to provide the end desired not a pre-defined means of achieving it. Primes are not required to have the ability to manufacture a product only to effectively orchestrate its delivery of the service it is to provide. To illustrate this argument as suggested, use a model of microeconomic reality attributable to Michael Porter of Harvard Business School. This uses what Porter calls the five forces driving business strategy. These forces have arguably been made moribund over much defence purchasing due to the use of cost plus contracting. Under this the choice of a weapons system is on the basis of a technical competition not price. As suggested, now chart our interpretation of recent change in defence procurement practice using Porter's five-force model. In effect we show that what has been done is to create a system of virtual organisations serving defence.

Porter sees the relationship between firms and their environment as subject to 5 key forces. He argues these necessarily drive business strategy: customer demands, distributor buying power, competitor actions, supplier's value for money and new technology. The customer is the politically directed military. The distributor is the defence procurement agency. Each supplier tries to differentiate his product to monopolize his position. This guarantees a return over and above minimal possible cost. Often the only organization capable of delivering what has been specified the supplier will be in a very strong bargaining position. The defence's procurement agency is caught between this unique supplier and the military customer with a specification limiting the agency to one possible supplier. Suppliers will always seek to be in this position and so try to deal directly with the military to ensure a specification ensuring their success in this eg. for a fixed wing US manufactured aircraft capable of VTOL. If this is the requirement then there is only one supplier the procurement agency can go to.

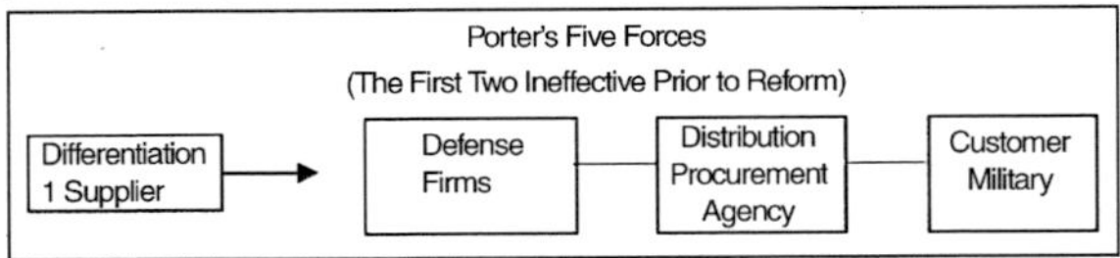

The most important counter to monopolization by differentiation is the "cardinal points" specification. This specifies what is to be achieved not the means. This opens up credible competition to different technological solutions. A prime does not have to have all the skills required to deliver only the ability to orchestrate the activities of those who have. The defence procurement process then purchases an entirely new product, "prime contractorship". This is a generic not a product specific skill. Defence thus outsources the orchestration of procurement. This product is such that a number of organizations have the capacity to deliver it. This undermines differentiated, and so monopolized, supply. The consequence is that the procurement agency now faces a number of potential suppliers. This increases the credible competition faced. This effect is amplified by the existence of alternative technological solution to cardinal points specifications.

This introduces potential credible competition from new technology. The defence procurement process thus specifies what is required rather than how and by whom it is produced. This changes the whole structure of the relationship between a defence department and industry. It inevitably alters contractor conduct and behaviour. In so doing the performance obtainable for a given price/cost is improved. By these means multiple competitive sources of supply can be created even for development work or new systems:

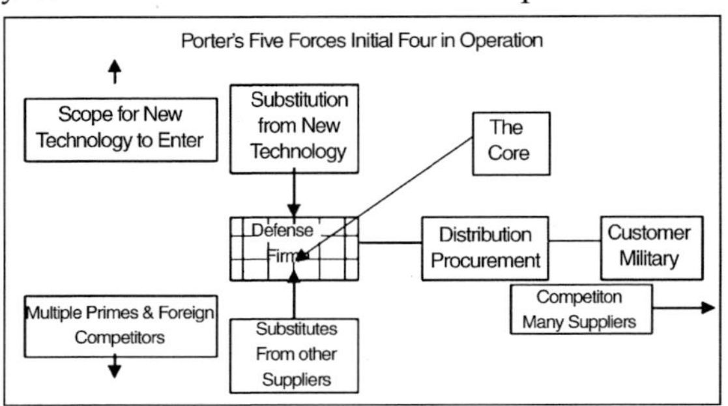

This allows cost plus contracting to be ended. With competitive tendering, fixed prices can be the norm. This has a virtuous incentive effect. Non competitive bidding leads to cost plus contracts, *i.e.* the supplier, audited by defence, calculates the cost of what is produced and gets a "fair" percentage return on that level of cost. This provides an incentive for activities to be brought in house that increase costs.

With no fixed percentage return on cost there is no incentive to maximize them, by retaining high cost in-house production. The incentive is reversed, *i.e.* to limit expensive in-house manufacture. This reinforces the managerial argument against employing non-core specialist. For equity financed firms pursuing shareholders value, outsourcing is then a necessity. The prime retains the lucrative and militarily significant "core" competence of systems integrator; all else is subcontracted.

TRUST

This completes our analysis of the impact of procurement reform in the recent past. It does not include PS. As described competition is a zero sum game between the firm and defence agency procurement and between the firm and its suppliers. If one party in this chain gains the other is seen to lose. True partnerships require trust. This requires win-win games.

PS results from a genuine risk sharing partnership across the spectrum from raw material supplier to prime contractor. It is now said to be part of DoD policy. It is based on non zero sum win-win games. In a “bull”, growing, or stable market everyone can win, supplier, prime contractor and consumer.

In the private sector this results in the production and supply of the high quality reliable very marketable low cost products supplied by the Japanese car and electronics industry. To achieve this requires the “prime” to act like the central firm in a Japanese “Keiretsu” network.

Firms like Toyota, Toshiba, Nissan, and Kawasaki build partnerships based on mutual commitment. They do this with cross investment of resources, physical and intellectual. Particularly Japanese “Primes” post staff at all levels to work with suppliers and in reciprocation suppliers post staff to them.

The idea is to create an operational ethos based on genuine partnership rooted in a deep knowledge of each other’s culture. This in turn is rooted in shared experiences of overcoming the unforeseen and unexpected in the tough minded but mutually advantageous manner indicative of good marriage.

This kind of relationship can not exist with CCT and Western style outsourcing reliant on confrontational litigation. Lean manufacturing or JITs can not flourish in these latter contentious, often litigious, environments. The essence of JIT is trust.

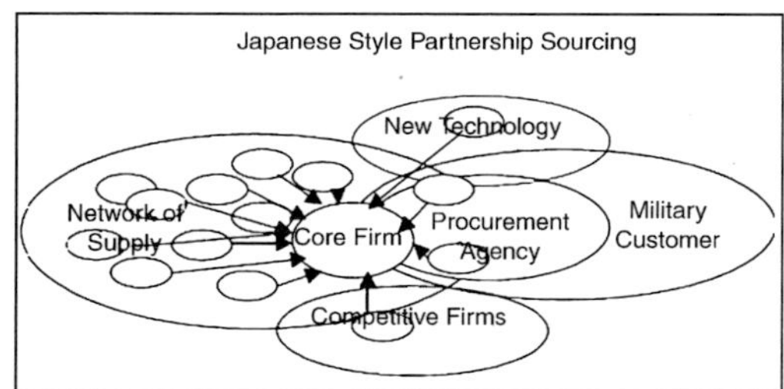

Arguably, implementing such reforms in defence could produce weapons systems very efficiently; conditional on yielding win-win, politically defensible higher returns for all stakeholders. The shareholders in defence companies would get higher returns on the smaller investments that are then required to finance the individual parts of the virtual organization supplying a defence requirement. Thus the financing of the defence supply chain would be easier especially with one partner the final customer the state as a guaranteed power.

The defence customer could even limit the political risks inherent in such partnerships by selling "put options", based on a "cardinal points specification", competitively to potential suppliers. This would eliminate the political risk to the supplier of cancellation. This would allow suppliers to get private finance for development and early production on the basis of commercial risk alone as they would have purchased an irrefutable contract if they can deliver to the cardinal points specification.

This insures them against political induced changes of view on a project's worth. Shareholders and lenders are then left with risks they understand *i.e.* a possible inability to deliver the product to the technical specification at the price contracted for. They can then act to balance market, managerial and technical risk against financial exposure. The political risks are taken out of the equation. They are left with the polity issuing the option. With such clarity in the distribution of risk sharper risk assessments are then possible and so each can then be more efficiently financed.

Workers as stakeholders are also in this win-win game. They get securer employment. Their employment is based on the functional service they supply not the requirements of a particular customer. If one user of the service or function disappears, there will be others requiring their function in other industries. In the vertically integrated organizations, eg typical of the past UK and French defence market, all functions, typing, stores management, etc., were locked into one customer their defence ministry. In a virtual organization, all employees have jobs ultimately dependent on their functional role in the production process not the continued existence of one particular customer for one particular product.

Risks in this system are attenuated and clarified creating room for win-win games. Technical progress is incremental, design is evolutionary and the commitment of any one group to a particular end result, while significant, will not be catastrophic if it fails. Well done, this process produces greater VFM to the final customer. This is not achieved using a hard edged network of individuals and organizations playing zero sum market games but the co-operative fuzzy set of overlapping mutually advantageous relationships. This produces benefits for all.

These are deliverable by getting a proper balance between alternate approaches to organizing production. One uses the superior power of market incentives wherever possible. To be able to do this one needs to make an explicit specification of what is to be delivered preferably in cardinal point terms. This is not possible where the requirement is tacit and so not measurable. Then one has to use a hierarchical delivery system. This has to generate internal incentives for each function based on loyalty to the organization not a specific well defined result delivered. This is costly.

It has to be expensively based on the development of teams rooted in mutual trust and tacit understanding. If this is disturbed in any way performance will be damaged in a non directly observable manner. The virtual organization is a hybrid of market and hierarchical supply. Hybrids are arguably more robust than what spawns them. However, they cannot propagate. They need the systemic separateness of their constituent partners to exist at all.

BRINGING DEFENCE NEARER TO THE VIRTUAL ORGANIZATION

Further steps in this process of reform have been put in place and just beginning to be put in place in the UK under their Strategic Defence Review in the US under the Defence Reform Initiative. Two strategies exist for the achievement of this final step. The first attempts to de-politicize the financing of development and commercial risk. The second sets out to de-bureaucratize the financing of state activity using what is called "Public Private Partnership" (PPP) in the UK This aims to allow the private sector to use its incentive systems to provide capital to satisfy military requirements in partnership with the polity.

Carefully designed, such systems enable government to contract out the risks the state is not well equipped to handle eg. those of ownership, technical or commercial, while retaining those it is equipped to deal with, *e.g.* the political. In the limit such partnerships lead to the private sector retaining ownership of systems and so leases rather than sell them. In peace these would be directed in use by the military and maintained in a fit state by the lessor. In war the public sector would command and direct their use as well as assume the risk of loss with maintenance still perhaps in private "sponsored reserve" hands.

This has the advantage of military C2 unencumbered with non-fighting non-core consideration of the supportability and maintainability of deployed equipment. The logisticians job, whether full time professional military or outsourced sponsored reserves, is to deliver what is practicable as invisibly as possible to the fighting commander whose main effort is fighting within the constraints set by time and available material. The second goes further. It attempts to underpin the above by introducing private sector accounting and budgeting practice into the state. The DoD originally called its approach to this Defence Business Operating Funds in 1997 renamed and expanded as Working Capital Funds for which the SofS for Defence awarded his Hammer price for smashing costs in 1998.

This is an internal DoD regulated market set up between the front line and support functions. Military or state owned suppliers of training and maintenance compete with private sector suppliers. In the UK MoD finance staff calls this "playing shops". It makes those exercising military judgment directly accountable for the full cost of their decisions by simulating high-powered market incentives.

In the UK a more all embracing concept is proposed "Resource Accounting and Budgeting". This makes accountable individuals aware of the full costs or their decisions by communicating it to them. By doing this it is hoped those exercising military judgment will use support functions more economically as they will have a better understanding of the impact of their decisions on the full cost of their actions. At present a commander has no incentive other than expensively generated bureaucratic direction to limit his use, or abuse, of the equipment under his command. With cost communication it is hoped behaviour will change for the better. In illustration currently spares are supplied free at the point of use. A tank engine may cost $500,000. To a commander it is free. To train a driver to use this power train less abusively has a real opportunity cost to a commander, the loss of the driver on a course. Without cost information and outside bureaucratic regulation the commander is "better" to use tank spares at $500,000 than to train drivers at a smaller cost.

The question to be addressed here is whether communicating this cost through the hierarchy, as in the UK, or making commanders, as in the US system, directly accountable for it in a budget produces the most efficient result. Accounting alone, what the UK MoD calls the "Initial Capability" of their accounting and budgeting project only informs commanders of these full cost. Little evidence exists to show that knowing how much something costs is sufficient to alter behaviour.

Experience, and a priori analysis, suggests it will not do so without a considerable investment down through the hierarchy in staff motivation and associated organizational development. This is needed to engender the attitudes and culture required to ensure resources are used in the communal rather than individual interest. In the absence of such an incentive system or an alternate market one behaviour is unlikely to change. If these two approaches de politicization and commercialization of defence accounting engender a significant cost differential between efficient and inefficient predicts ultimately they may be made effective. If this occurs they will have a profound effect on future costs and so add to the cost estimator's problems.

It is precisely because relationships between decision and cost can be vague that industry increasingly uses Activity-Based Costing. This creates a basis for optimizing incentive by developing a clear understanding of the relationship between decisions and resulting costs. Traditional absorption costing only measures the direct costs of activity, it then pro rates overheads. This is now seen as insufficient. When traditional absorption costing was conceived directly attributable costs could be as much as 80% of all costs. Nowadays many direct costs are outsourced and much remaining cost is the overhead of using communal resources, *e.g.* computing power, rather than cost attributable to a specific product. ABC arguably provides one with a more comprehensive understanding of cost and what drives it throughout the value chain. This enables one to highlight far better than previously accretions of cost driven by wasteful supply, production and distribution systems.

A problem then exists in managing resources internally. If the bulk of the cost of a small item produced for a particular customer is in the IT department that processes the order, organizes delivery and invoices for the service then those costs need to be allocated to the activity causing their occurrence. This is servicing the customer and not manufacturing the product. It is customer activity that drives cost, not production management.

It is a lot cheaper in terms of order processing to provide a large number of parts infrequently to a customer than it is to supply a small numbers regularly. There comes a point when the cost of doing this exceeds manufacturing costs. It is this that should influence decision making not the cost of manufacture. Thus, both the PPP and RAB have built into them incentives to contain or lower support costs.

LEAN ENTERPRISE: BASIS FOR COST SAVINGS AT ENTERPRISE AND PROJECT LEVELS

COMMERCIAL BEST PRACTICE IN LEAN PRODUCTION

The modern industrial world spurred by the lowering of infrastructure costs and the possibilities of the virtual organization is moving to the "lean enterprise". This is already occurring in defence companies independent of government encouragement. This approach derives from 40 years of success in Toyota, arguably the most productive high quality car producer in the world.

Table. International Auto Assembly and Parts Manufacture

	Toyota (in Japan)	Japan (Average)	USA (Average)	Europe (Average)
Productivity				
(Toyota = 100)				
Assembly	100	83	65	54
1st Tier suppliers	100	83	71	62
Quality (delivered	30	55	61	61

defects) Assembly	5+	193	263	1373
(per 100 cars) 1st	400+	900	6100	4723
tier suppliers (ppm)				
2nd tier suppliers				
Deliveries (per cent	.04+	.2	.6	1.9
late) 1sttier suppliers	.5+	2.6	13.4	5.4
2nd tier suppliers				
Stocks (1st tier-	Na	37	135	138
suppliers) Hours	248+	81	69	45
Stock turns (per year)				

"The Machine that Changed the World" describes the basis for this success:

- *Value*: Establish one's value proposition as seen by the final customer
- *Value Stream*: Identify the value stream maximizing value delivered to the customer
- *Flow*: Eliminate all batches, queues and re-work to establish a smooth flow from material extraction to final product
- *Pull*: Nothing is produced until customer demand pulls production forward.
- *Perfection*: Improved flow is always possible, as is increased responsiveness.

The dramatic results described have been replicated throughout the industrial world.

DEFENCE ENVIRONMENT: APPLICABILITY AND IMPLEMENTATION

The most interesting application of lean production reported upon in defence is that at the Pratt and Witney Division of United Technologies. Pratt was faced with massive cutbacks in engine orders on the ending of the cold war. It was also faced with a simultaneous downturn in demand for civil aircraft engines. The results achieved in their main engine manufacturing plant are reported on in Womack and Jones as producing savings of over 50% in the cost of a turbine blade. There are 66% of tooling costs with utilized space, inventory and speed of throughput all considerably improved on the basis of a batch size that dropped from 250 to 1.

Aerospace generally provides a number of good illustration of the effects of monumental vs. lean production. The big aerospace firms separate military from civil production. They tend to have monumental production facilities financed by the state operating in a lean style for defence and lean production facilities financed by shareholders operating in a lean way for civil production. The former is designed to minimize the costs of defence department's imposed batch production. They use specialist but expensive tools. Civil plants achieve optimality by using flow production so as to minimize tooling costs.

In defence the prior commitment of the customer, to purchasing aircraft in large batches allows the aerospace firms to calculate set-up tooling and production costs on a known production run. They then minimize production costs for the ordered batch size.

They also get the government to finance any tooling costs. Their viability is conditional on this state finance of batch production. In the civil case the number of aircraft to be built is problematic. Any estimate that can be made of a recovery rate on tooling must therefore also be problematic. Production then has to be flexible. As tooling has to be financed at the expense and risk of the shareholders civil aircraft plants are designed to minimize set-up and tooling costs.

The consequences of the are:

- Military plants have low unit cost recovery rates on tooling relative to labour rates.
- Civil plants have high unit cost recovery rates on tooling relative to low labour rates.

Each type of plant thus has its own distinct comparative advantage. However, civil plants due to the commercial imperative of their market place tend to have an absolute advantage in both. "Dual-use" production, in the same plant, of military and civil aircraft is thus only possible at the margin. The very different capitalization rates required would otherwise results in excessive cross subsidization.

In the past it has been possible to de-merge civil from military production to the absolute cost disadvantage of the latter and so the taxpayer. In doing so one has been able to add shareholder value. Cost plus defence contracts produce good low risk returns and the civil business does not have to carry any of the overheads.

However much of the enabling technologies now used in defence are "dual-use" and driven by civil commercial imperatives not defence military or political ones. These are driving industry to global outsourcing. The economies possible using commercial infrastructure aimed at supporting everyone's product are huge.

This is the basis of the current revolution in communications, transportation and information technology. These are all "decreasing cost " industries. What the economic textbooks call natural monopolies *i.e.* the organization with the largest demand and most fully utilized capacity can outcompete all others.

The result is lower and lower unit cost and faster and faster delivery. This makes it possible for everyone to confidently operate with lower inventories and outsourced supply as described earlier and facilitates the ease of creating the virtual organizations we have described and sets everything up for the lean enterprise structure of production described here. In the new global world economy inventory can be speedily acquired reliably and at low cost just in time to fit production schedules.

LIMITATIONS

This approach does have its limitations even in commerce. In defence security considerations may lead to more costly solution. The advantages of lean systems can be swallowed up in costly contingent inventory or reversionary capabilities if confidence does exist in speedy re-supply in case of need as is the case in defence.

In commerce firms limit the impact of such uncertainty by limiting development and production cycles to be as little as 18 months. These of course limits one to pretty modest improvements in technology from cycle to cycle but these do accumulate in a compound manner pretty quickly over a decade or so. Defence currently has a 10 to 20 year cycle. This is likely to get longer consequent to the post Cold War decline in defence industrial demand.

With traditional thinking, this leads to slower, longer procurement cycles and in the absence of any obvious direct threat, contingent stocks and in-service support are cut and or outsourced. While this is presented as consistent with "lean thinking" it is not embedded, as it is in the commercial sector, in a system ensuring responsive resupply when required. It is to how that might be achieved in defence that we now turn.

APPROACHES

The preceding arguments make it clear that in the new age the environment for the arms industry has changed significantly.

- There are ever-shorter product life cycles for the "dual-use" technology that defence has come to rely, on both technological and cost grounds, especially in the electronics industry
- There are ever-longer procurement cycles for high technology weapons that increasingly incorporate commercial off the shelf products that then need to be expensively integrated into the high technology weapons systems now in vogue.

One suggested solution to this is to evolve systems with incremental technology insertion. This is a partial move from batch to flow and so lean production. However, modular insertion in a highly integrated system can be very expensive given the massive reconfiguration that may be required. Modern production techniques make it possible to consider substituting small batch more frequently purchased equipment, *i.e.* more flow like manufacture as a direct substitute for in-service support and maintenance.

The key to "Lean Production" is constant production rates throughout the system fuelled by increasing or at least unvarying demand. "Lean production" identifies the "takt" time, *i.e.* the rate at which one has to produce to satisfy demand it does not focus on minimizing the unit costs of tooling and machine time for a given batch. To use it defence has to find a way to generate steadier demand. The a priori cost advantages are already clear from our previous arguments.

Post Cold War warning times for military deployment are longer and arguable more controllable than in the past. In the Cold War a huge army was pre-positioned in Germany ready to fight ideally at a few weeks notice but ready to act on a shorter time scale, days or even hours. With the scenarios now being considered production rates can in theory be slowed right down when conflict is not in the offing and speeded up when a distant prospect of a deployment arises. If at the same time the equipment replacement cycle could be shortened one could then make a strong moves towards lean production. The idea would be to sustain productive capacity over time. This coupled with a shorter procurement period would enable the defence technology cycle to be brought more closely into line with developing commercial ones. Spares would then be available from production. The need to hold large stocks would go.

However, this creates logistical support problems. It would entail initially replacing older equipment at a slower but probably more affordable rate. This means having weapons of different marks in service at the same time. However this configuration problem is already reality for many weapons systems currently in service. Much of this has been retrofitted with enhancements as and when it has proved possible.

In addition modern military equipment is already becoming ever more reliant on COT's IT. This has very fast development and production timescale. When a COTS components fails it generally cannot be replaced with its like but by the latest similar COTS item designed independently of the wider system into which it needs to be integrated. Costly re-design and integration is then an inevitable cost anyway. It therefore seems sensible to build the process of doing this systematically into the structure of ones through life procurement process in a lean manner. To achieve this one would require a cardinal points specification covering development, acquisition, utilization and disposal as the basis of all defence contracts.

This would leave the commercial supplier, ideally seen as in partnership with defence, to trade-off reliability, with in-service support with sustainability, *i.e.* design costs, with more frequent more costly support with costly stocks of materiel. With such a contract on offer, contractors might find it cheaper to keep production lines open working at slower rates rather than produce everything including a lifetime supply of spares and ammunition in one huge batch at the beginning of a weapons systems working life. Defence currently orders equipment and materiel in large volume over a short span of years. Spares and munitions for support and sustainment are bought up front and stored for the life of a project. Such costs are significant. So is the waste that occurs because estimates of usage prior to in-service experience are inevitably wrong.

This leads to large eventually redundant stock holdings or alternatively very extensive re-contractors to replace out of stock items. A further downside is that given that the costs of running out of sustainment in combat are so high contingent over-provision is almost inevitable. Prior to the US's introduction of revolving funds and the recent capitalization of the UK MOD's accounts there was no proper means for accounting for these inventory carrying costs. The material bought, although often never used, was, under cash accounting, effectively written off on purchase and its costs as inventory never subsequently accounted for.

However the concern today is not that we may have too much but that faced with a war we may have insufficient stock to sustain a campaign. However even now using the traditional batch system one faces this prospect. Any production line will probably have been closed many years before a conflict occurs. It may then be impractical, never mind expensive, to open it up again on any useful timescale. By the time it was possible the war might be over with lives, sovereignty or crucial interests lost.

Serious problems thus exist for both technology updating and sustainment. If manufacturing capacity is not kept in being, a problem exists for defence that needs to be addressed urgently. This cannot be solved cheaply, as seems to be currently thought by un-integrated technology insertion, reconstitution of production facility or technology demonstrators. If industry could contract to supply the availability of a military capability, this pessimistic outlook might be changeable. To achieve this we need to avoid contracting for a pre-specified platform to a specific design supplied with a huge stock of spares.

Modern warfare requires rapid deployment and high mobility with a sustainable high tempo of operations. This requires the very latest in technology. To support such a capability one might find the most cost effective way to achieve it was to sustain manufacturing capacity with smaller orders over a longer period of time. This would eliminate much of the support infrastructure now needed to sustain defence. Lean production might then seem a sensible and practical basis on which to establish defence production.

To gain the full benefits of the commercial best practice we have described defence restructuring needs to be considered systemically. Part of this is to see the defence industry as organized to provide a manufacturing capacity as a direct substitute for support. It would first have to establish demand pulled flows of value for defence products not batch pushed supply. This requires major changes in procurement, financing and military practice. If equipment management and war-fighting doctrine does not change significantly defence will not be able to access the potential cost savings we have described. If defence manufacturing could work on a shorter cycle of flow based procurement say over 5 to 10 years rather than the current 15-20 year of batch procurement things could change dramatically.

The current batch thinking requires high initial purchase costs followed by considerable inventory, updating and sustainment costs. Best modern commercial procurement involves the frequent purchase of reliable equipment requiring less in-service support. Could this be achieved in defence? Till now no one has invested the costing resources to test this hypothesis. This paper has been written to provide a theoretical basis for doing so.

Consider the UK's purchase of Apache Longbow. If the requirement could be met by building around 70 new aircraft at the rate of 10 a year every 7 years over the proposed 30 year life of the airframe would costs rise, stay the same or fall as compared to building 70 only. The latter need to be disassembled, rebuilt and upgraded throughout their life. With the former approach one creates the essential requirement for a lean system a regular flow of demand. This would allow development, tooling and set-up costs to be spread over 210 helicopters produced in a steady flow over 30 years rather than 70 in a batch produced over two or three years.

The cost benefit analysis of such an approach is yet to be done however, a priori, savings seem possible from lower inventory, update and support infrastructure costs. To achieve this result a partnership contract would be needed over a very long period of time. The contract would not be for the manufacture of a specified number of aircraft but for a specified number of aircraft continuously updated and serviceable on the flight line throughout the proposed lifetime of the system. The shorter production cycle we have suggested would allow evolutionary fully integrated updates to be planned on a seven year cycle producing three marks of the aircraft over its lifetime.

The financial benefits of such a scheme would be enhanced if a second hand market could be created in advance for the retiring earlier marks of aircraft. The need to hold a large inventory could be eliminated perhaps. Parts would be in continuous production over the life of the system. The need for third or fourth line refurbishment could also be eliminated as new could replace old and much of the support infrastructure, of technical training staff recruitment and personnel and inventory management currently carried as an overhead by the military could be done away with.

The scenario described substitutes flow production for maintenance and sustainment stocks. This involves manufacturing at a rate that builds up a restructured inventory of equipment slowly and rotates older, or, damaged, equipment out of service to be refurbished and replaced in the line of battle with new, not refurbished equipment. Fixed price or firm downward negotiable prices on procurement need to be the norm for this to achieve the results hypothesized. Such contracts would provide incentives for generic parts to be outsourced to industry. It discourages in-house production by eliminating the gains from cost plus. This is conditional on the political realism of allowing commercial rates of return and underwriting long term contracts. One would have a core defence industry with a low internal cost base and a highly competitive infrastructure based on "dual use" activity.

The long term political benefits of a more fragmented, commercially based market extended in scope to cover activity currently carried out by staff either within defence departments or in primes could be considerable. These benefits would be in terms of enhanced industrial, and social, stability. People's jobs will depend on the functionality of the products or services they supply not the requirements of one particular customer, defence. A defence industrial infrastructure so freed from dependence on the vagaries of the political process clearly has utility. Such a system of procurement would also increase the use of what Williamson has called "high powered market incentives". Outsourcing blurs the boundary between the firm and the market. In so doing it exposes generic infrastructure support providers to the risks of wider competition in the market place while leaving the political and military risks associated with conflict and contingent preparation to handle it with the state.

IMPLICATIONS FOR COST ESTIMATING

Opportunities exist to improve the public and private parts of defence provided understandable administrative, political and military cultural blocks to change can be removed. These barriers are real. If the move to value adding flow production is to be possible these need to be removed or eased. If realistically they can only be eased rather than eliminated they will encourage rather than deliver lean production. However, the benefits to defence of the virtual organization and a costeffective global industrial infrastructure should still lower defence costs without such radical innovations.

It is clear that no matter what, the future will radically differ from the past. New cost estimating techniques will be needed to cope with the resulting devaluation of historical databases. If flow production is the end state then cost estimating becomes easier. In the limit all the resources to produce an item are brought together in one continuous flow production cell. This ensures that many costs are prices on inbound outsourced supplies priced by market competition. The rest are direct and observable as incurred. Cost measurement is then easier.

However cost forecasting becomes more difficult. New materials and production methods imply new cost structures. The change described intend to impact costs and performance. Given the lack of existing benchmarks new estimating techniques are needed. Among these could be synthetic manufacturing environments. Work on this, in the cost estimating sphere, has begun. NASA with GE is funding an engine costing initiative to transfer an existing piece of software, the Integrated Supportability Analysis and Cost System developed under UNIX, to a Windows NT/95 public domain environment. ISACS allows what if modeling of the impact of engine design changes on lifecycle costs.

One can therefore use it to trade-off the engines rated power output against in service support costs. In the UK the lean manufacturing initiative is funding Cranfield University to develop life cycle cost estimating techniques producing composite aerostructures. The initiatives are all aimed at getting over the problems for estimating costs where new processes are used. Lean production is not new. It has been successful in the private sector. Pratt and Witney have already publicly reported the effects of its use. Lean production, ironically based on old-fashioned batch thinking, is already in place in military aircraft production.

But until defence gets away from the defence financed anti-lean batch mentality there is little hope of achieving the savings already achieved in civil aerospace. These changes will not occur as long as defence departments are willing to fund the cost base underpinning the old approach. The existing mentality is underpinned in aerospace by civil aerospace's losses and until recently military aerospace's profitability.

At what speed can all this be achieved? The evidence is on short time scales Womack and Jones report 30% savings inside 6 months of starting, followed by a further 35% savings inside 2 years, followed on by continuous further proportionate cost savings and productivity and quality improvements over succeeding years. Such publicly reported results have been supported by experience at, at least, one US defence manufacturer, Pratt and Whitney. So it is reasonable to presume that there is no reason why they cannot be accessed generally. Clearly this will not be possible without a radical re-think of the defence enterprise seen holistically from factory to foxhole. To get demand pulling flow requires defence procurement to be spread out over time.

This requires the relation between military doctrine and industrial production to be thought through very carefully indeed. The military are uncomfortable with JITs. However, it was the basis for both US and British airforce operations in World War II, *i.e.* to work twenty-four hours a day every day and drop ordinance on Germany at its rate of production.

A key failure of much recent defence support thinking is that it has not dealt well with sustainability. In the Cold War we operated on the basis of a short conventional war with high rates of material consumption. When stocks were exhausted we would simply use nuclear weapons. This is not realistic for the wars contemplated now. Defence departments now seem intent on having smaller stocks of smarter more expensive weapons. With current batch thinking these can not be re-ordered when used in less than five years. This does not compute militarily. What happens when your stock of smart weapons is exhausted and the enemy is not defeated? For this reason alone defence needs flow thinking with shorter production, development and in service life cycles.

Only then can low cost, investment and production rates be in tune with the possible rate of use of technologically advanced weapons. This requires PDS and configuration management to be more technically sophisticated than it is at the moment. With proper JITs support this is possible. This is a challenge to the cost estimator and forecaster who will then have to extrapolate from commercial experience.

The raises a second order problem for the estimator. The defence market can never replicate the competitive environment commercial companies operate in. One will have to assess the impact of a monopolistic defence industrial structure on the realizable cost savings from lean manufacturing. It is clear the future provides a real challenge for the cost estimator. Synthetic environments will need to be part of the tool kit as will an understanding of the process of industrial change both from a production engineering and economic perspective.

11

Control and Profitability

All executives and managers account for cost. In various ways, all business professionals manage cost, and most managers engage in capital investment decisions, forecasting, pricing, and product or service management. All these business activities are deeply embedded in the work of cost accounting. Cost-related tasks consume a significant amount of management time at all levels of the organization. A business professional must understand the organization's cost accounting practices to competently manage a specified area and understand how personal accountabilities are calculated and tracked.

An accounting instructor with considerable experience in the field always gave her MBA students the same advice, "Learn the language of accounting. It's the language of business, and if you don't learn it, some little bean counter wearing a green eyeshade will blow your grand marketing or operations idea right out of the water!" Bellwether organizations that employ advanced management systems still run their accounting systems—"keep their books"—just as to basic cost accounting principles. Importantly, conventional practices shape advanced techniques; therefore, more mature methods cannot be fully understood without reference to their predecessors. As a baseline, an organization's executives must establish management/cost accounting practice foundations that serve decision making and operations, first, and financial accounting, second, before moving to advanced systems. To accomplish this, executives need the ability to distinguish system alternatives.

THE PROFIT IMPERATIVE: DEFINING THE OBJECTIVES OF COST MANAGEMENT

Profitability, variously interpreted as net income, equity value, and return on investment is a results-focused indicator watched more carefully than any other performance measurement category. But if these measurements depict results, what measurements show the dimensions of performance for the processes that lead to those results? At the core, profit has only two components: revenue and cost. To understand how a cost management system works.

COST

An outflow of a resource, whether in cash, as a payable, a rendered service, or as a trade or barter, that is consciously made with expectation of benefit to the organization: goods, property, or services acquired.

COST ACCOUNTING

The accounting profession is divided into two major branches:

1. Financial and
2. Management accounting.

The later is synonymous with cost accounting. The term "management" refers to the comparatively internal focus of the cost accounting field as compared with the external focus of financial accounting. The word "traditional," when used to describe cost accounting methods, refers to the standard practices that are taught in basic management accounting courses and practiced in most North American firms. The standard practices include cost systems and procedures, methods of determining costs, points of cost accountability, forecasts, cost comparisons, and budgets. The purpose of cost accounting is to assist in the wise and prudent stewardship of overall organizational resources.

COST AND EXPENSE DISTINCTIONS

Both costs and expenses are expenditures. The word "expenditures" will be used to identify an organization's total outflow of assets in all forms. In the standard income statement of a for-profit firm, costs typically refer to the categories of material, labour, and overhead appearing above the income statement's gross margin line. An example of the income statement components for a manufacturing firm. Expenditures typically called operating expenses are displayed below the gross margin line. On the income statement, the material, labour, and overhead items are called cost of goods sold. Operating expenses consist of monetary or asset outlays for general, administrative, selling, marketing, and other functions deemed to be indirectly related to production. Operating expenses are commonly abbreviated as SG&A for sales, general and administrative.

COST MANAGEMENT

The use of cost accounting systems and methods to guide current and future operations towards specified objectives; the analysis and interpretation of cost data is critical to the decision-making process.

COST MANAGEMENT SYSTEM

An expenditure information architecture that tracks, monitors, reports, and provides decisionquality information and insights. A CMS is less constrained by exacting professional standards and reporting formats than financial accounting; therefore, a CMS can and should be customised to match an organization's internal environment and specific cost structures. A CMS sets direction for resource consumption priorities and makes course corrections by emphasizing operations first and accounting practices second. A CMS specifically answers the demands of the profit imperative when it aligns employee spending behaviours with the organizational strategy. The purpose of the CMS is to understand the nature and behaviour of cost, and thereby manage valuable assets wisely through optimizing limited resources. The chief CMS responsibility is to promote improvement in cost structure.

The CMS should:

- Support understanding of the nature and behaviour of cost (and the humans doing the spending).
- Promote, track, and give feedback on value creation and continuous improvement.
- Assist management in wise use of resources.

COST TYPES

Management accountants created cost types in an attempt to understand the nature and behaviour of different resources. Cost types are designations given to categories of resource expenditures. They are based on assumptions about the ways that resources are consumed in relation to the activities to which they are applied. They are also based on the purposes for which the resources are used.

Some traditional cost types include:

- *Fixed*: Costs assumed not to vary with production/ service unit volume
- *Variable*: Costs assumed to vary with production/ service unit volume
- *Semi-fixed/variable, also called step-fixed/variable*: Costs that vary at incremental volume levels
- *Direct*: Costs that can be clearly linked, and therefore assigned to, specific product/service units
- *Indirect*: Costs that cannot easily be linked to specific product/service units, and therefore, must be allocated to production/services based on a selected cost driver

FINANCIAL ACCOUNTING

Financial accounting is the branch of the accounting field concerned with formal, aggregate reporting of transactions related to the income statement (revenue minus expense equals profit/loss), the balance sheet (assets, liabilities, and owners' equity) and other related statements (*e.g.*, working capital, cash flow). Standard report forms used across companies and an external, shareholder focus, characterize financial accounting. The primary statement in financial accounting is the balance sheet.

VALUE

When accountants talk about value they refer to "any preferred object or interest therein"; and accounting valuation is "a judgment expressing or implying preference, or relative approval or disapproval." Organizations exist to become the provider of preference by conveying value to customers, clients, and constituents. This is as true of a spiritual organization with a humanitarian mission as it is of a large corporation focused chiefly on shareholder wealth.

The path to value is different for each organization, and value has many definitions beyond those of the accountant. In the last half of the twentieth century, the focus on value became rooted in the idea of creating shareholder value.What do customers, shareholders and employees value? What do they really want? How can we differentiate ourselves from the competitor in terms of value? Should we be as concerned about internal constituents (*i.e.*, employees) as we are about customers and shareholders? How do all the converging interests of those with a stake in the organization's success or failure work together to create a mutually satisfying sense of value?

None of these questions has an easy answer, but one fact is certain:

- The first and most common cause of enterprise failure is, simply, overspending— a basic failure to manage expenditures flowing out and revenues flowing in. The solution to overspending behaviours involves little more than the skill set required to balance a checkbook. Creating value for the complex organization requires clear cost management objectives embedded in a cost management system.

OBJECTIVES

Nearly all business professionals know the major components of a general ledger (G/L) system, or at least two of the important reports generated by it: the income statement and the balance sheet. Far fewer managers can describe a cost management system—and with good reason. An effective CMS is customised to match an organization's internal environment and specific cost structures. While an experienced financial professional, and many managers, can move from company to company and quickly understand the financial statements of each, even practiced accountants need considerably more time to understand the intricacies of different cost management systems from company to company. A CMS is less constrained by exacting professional standards and reporting formats than are financial systems, with a few exceptions like the regulated cost guidelines of government contractors. Importantly, the CMS sets direction for resource consumption priorities and makes course corrections by emphasizing operations first and accounting practices second. A CMS specifically answers the demands of the profit imperative by aligning employee spending behaviours with the organizational strategy.

FOUR-STAGE MODEL

A good context for understanding the CMS is to ask not what it is, but rather how it functions. This book acknowledges and borrows from the approach used by Robert S. Kaplan and Robin Cooper, in 1998, Cost and Effect. Their "four-stage model of cost system evolution" describes how a CMS typically evolves over the life cycle of a maturing organization.

Table. Four Stage Model of Cost System Development

Stage One	Stage Two
• Broken • Many error with large variences • Inadiquate external reporting • Inediquate product, service, and cunsumer cost information • Inadiquate Operational and strategic control	• Driven by financial reporting • Meet audit standareds • External reports tailored to financial reporting needs • Inaccurate and hidden product, service, and consumer costs • Strategic feedback limited and delayed
Stage Three	**Stage Four**
• Specialized • Shared databasesbut stand alone systems with informal linkages • Same as Stage Two • Product, service, nad customer costs costs in seperate ABM systems • Strategic/operational control with several seperate performance mesurement systems	• Integrated • Fully linked databases • Financial reporting systems create external reports • Product, service, and customer integrated in ABM systems • Strategic/operational control within an integrated performence measurement system

Stage III systems are specialized, in that the cost and financial accounting systems use the same databases; however, the two systems remain isolated and specialized in application. In this stage, activitybased costing (ABC) and performance measurement systems often emerge. Stage IV systems are integrated, and present a unified reporting format supportive of operational strategy. Financial and operations data, as well as budget and actual information, are all linked. Organizations today remain spread across the Four-Stage spectrum. A healthy number of companies have moved to Stage III; but, it remains rare to find a true Stage IV company, although many claim to be.

An enterprise resource planning (ERP) implementation does not guarantee a Stage IV environment. Every executive and manager first needs to determine which stage current accounting systems are in, and then progressively move through each stage to the integrated level, whether by using the Kaplan/Cooper model or some other proven, logical method. Kaplan and Cooper caution against the high failure rate of organizations that try to jump stages. Operations Focus Is Primary The primary focuses of an effective

CMS are operations and the support of management decision making. In addition to routine bookkeeping, the CMS objectives include, but are not limited, to ten characteristics.

A CMS that supports decision making must:

- Display past, present, and future expenditures.
- Mirror the organization's cost structure and behaviours to support ongoing improvement and control.
- Support realistic, reliable strategic planning and explicit management intention.
- Influence individual and team behaviours towards goal accomplishment.
- Monitor and control resource use against mission and strategic intentions.
- Provide warning when unhealthy financial thresholds are imminent.
- Facilitate the repositioning of resources.
- Hold specific individuals and groups accountable for standards of performance.
- Assist in analyzing key discrete points of profitability: customer, process, product, and region.
- Display a 360-degree unbiased view of the organization's cost structure, one that is understood and actually used in decisionmaking by all executives and managers.

DISPLAY PAST, PRESENT, AND FUTURE EXPENDITURES

This characteristic means that historical, current, and prospective (*i.e.*, forecast, simulation) expenditure data are accessible, timely, and accurate. Accessibility is primarily judged on ease of use. In other words, can nonfinancial managers make use of the system's data and information? Accuracy is based on compliance with cost system design and with data-gathering integrity. Timeliness is based on proximity to real-time information. In the Kaplan/Cooper four-stage model, Stage I systems frequently fail all these criteria and almost never address future expenditures except in budgetary terms. Stage II systems are more reliable for past and present data but often fall short in accessibility and timeliness. Only in Stage III do CMS designs begin to fulfill all criteria. Obviously, if executives work with less than the full timeline (*i.e.*, past, present, and future), their focus will most often be on historical data, while current and future cost conditions elude them.

MIRROR THE ORGANIZATION'S COST STRUCTURE AND BEHAVIOURS TO SUPPORT ONGOING IMPROVEMENT AND CONTROL

This characteristic means that historical, current, and prospective (*i.e.*, forecast, simulation) expenditure data are accessible, timely, and accurate. Accessibility is primarily judged on ease of use. In other words, can nonfinancial managers make use of the system's data and information? Accuracy is based on compliance with cost system design and with data-gathering integrity. Timeliness is based on proximity to real-time information.

In the Kaplan/Cooper four-stage model, Stage I systems frequently fail all these criteria and almost never address future expenditures except in budgetary terms. Stage II systems are more reliable for past and present data but often fall short in accessibility and timeliness. Only in Stage III do CMS designs begin to fulfill all criteria. Obviously, if executives work with less than the full timeline (*i.e.*, past, present, and future), their focus will most often be on historical data, while current and future cost conditions elude them. In practice, profit generation has only two components: revenue/sales and expenditures (*i.e.*, costs, expenses). Therefore, when planning for profitability (or breakeven) CMS information that fairly and accurately represents expenditure information promotes realistic planning and achievement targets. Again, only Stage III and IV cost management systems possess these attributes.

Influence Individual and Team Behaviours Towards Goal Accomplishment

This attribute is among the most important for a CMS. If people do not find the cost system relevant to their daily activities and long-term responsibilities, they will not use it. Relevance includes accountability for predetermined performance standards, the prudent management of resources, and visibility of companywide cost structures and behaviours. A Stage III CMS provides opportunity for achieving this desired criterion; however, only Stage IV provides the level of integration needed to maximize this goal.

Monitor and Control Resource Use Against Mission and Strategic Intentions

This means that the cost management system assists in aligning and allocating resources where they will best serve management's strategic intentions. The managers of organizations in Stages I and II of the Kaplan/Cooper model overlook this characteristic when designing the CMS, if they give any thought to system design at all. When different managers perform budgeting and strategic planning processes at different times, the compartmentalization undermines strategic achievements that depend on appropriate resource alignment. Imagine an executive team energized from a strategic planning retreat returning to day-to-day operations, issuing mandates, directives, and a trainload of new projects, all without addressing resource allocation, budgets, or realignment of people, time, and facilities. This is a strategic plan scenario doomed to frustration and failure.

Provide Warning When Unhealthy Financial Thresholds Are Imminent

A thoughtfully designed CMS provides an early-warning system that identifies and averts overspending. It may also signal the need for additional resources due to volume and/or environmental changes. Often, CMS Stages I and II provide reactive reporting long after a decision opportunity for changing an operational process issue has passed.

Imagine the frustration of a manufacturing manager who is held accountable for subpar performance in material and labour efficiencies, but who receives efficiency reports two to four weeks after the "damage" is done. Only Stage III and IV organizations rectify these demoralizing dynamics.

FACILITATE THE REPOSITIONING OF RESOURCES

This CMS characteristic partners with number 6 by overseeing the movement and realignment of resources to adapt to strategic changes. In many companies, once an annual budget is set, woe to the manager who overspends it. If the strategic plan and the budget live separate lives, how can managers be expected to satisfy both?

Hold Specific Individuals and Groups Accountable for Standards Of Performance

A recurring error in strategic planning is the failure to assign responsibility for action plans and performance targets.When set up properly, the CMS signals expectations for cost targets and identifies the individuals/ groups responsible for meeting those targets. The CMS links cost targets with appropriate nonfinancial measures that discourage managers from working on cost and financial performance in isolation from other important indicators.

Assist In Analyzing Discrete Points Of Profitability: Custmor, Process, Product, And Region

A financial accounting system provides an aggregate consolidated view of profitability. An effective CMS provides an analytical extension that searches for suspected areas of underperformance related to specific customers, product lines, market sectors, and other identifiable objects of analysis. Although a Stage II CMS may provide rudimentary historical data on these targets of analysis, only Stage III and IV systems provide decision-quality reporting through use of such techniques as activity-based costing.

Display A 360-Degree Unbiased View of the Organisation's Cost Structure

Display a 360-Degree Unbiased View of the Organization's Cost Structure that is understood and actually used in decision-making by all executives and managers. A CMS that provides open-book views of companywide cost structures used concurrently by all managers to advance the organizational community's well-being as a whole encourages management creativity in resource use, as well as optimal use of available capacity.

In most cases, only a Stage IV CMS can satisfy this attribute requirement. To be an effective management decision-making guide, the cost management system has to be much more than a set of bookkeeping procedures, and it must not be the sole source of information for decision making. Never use a cost management system in isolation for operational decision making. Just as financial accounting delivers an important but narrow stream of results information, cost accounting also displays a critical but incomplete viewpoint.

Nonfinancial, noncost information is part of any mature cost analysis. This is particularly true for making business development decisions. For example, a research and development (R&D) function usually shows continuous losses when subjected to a profit-and-loss, P&L (*i.e.*, income statement), approach. However, the R&D function value remains invisible until seen in the context of potential future revenue and cost streams.

CONTROL AND PROFITABILITY

Every business professional wants to manage well by making the right decisions. Good decisions lead to profit. Effective management and profitability rely mutually on systems that control employee behaviour. This is the time to distinguish cost accounting and cost management. Cost accounting can be thought of in terms of structured data elements; cost management can be thought of in terms of the information yielded by analyzing cost accounting data elements.

As defined earlier, cost accounting includes cost systems and procedures, methods of determining costs, points of cost accountability, forecasts, cost comparisons (*e.g.*, standard cost systems), and budgets (operational, project, and capital).

Interestingly, in many companies, these and other functionalities exist but are not actively managed. Unless cost managers create meaning out of the cost accounting data and reports, a good portion of cost accounting effort is wasted, and critical information for decision making remains hidden. Significant resources can be applied to cost accounting work, but if executives view cost accounting simply as part of financial accounting, meaning and insight remain hidden within transaction data. Only cost management can extract and create insight and meaning from raw cost data.

The cost accounting obligation is simple in concept: Provide accurate cost information. Implementing a cost accounting system that is accessible, aimed at the right targets of analysis, and supportive of management decision making is a more sophisticated task. The cost management responsibility is equally clear: Promote improvement in cost structure. Making good on this prospect is even more challenging. Make no mistake, accounting is part of the organizational control system.

The primary purpose of the control system is to protect the organization's assets. The important place that the accounting system occupies in the overall control system becomes more intriguing upon consideration of some basic accounting terminology. One common accounting definition of assets is "costs that have not yet been used." The accounting term for this is unexpired costs. These unexpired costs represent current or future value to the organization. Controller is the title of the head accountant in many organizations.

Finally, consider that the two conventional financial statements that reflect this control and safeguarding of assets are:

1. The balance sheet, and
2. The statement of cash flows.

All this clearly speaks to the control focus in accounting activities. The next most important function of the accounting system is to monitor profitability as recorded on the periodic income statement. Profitability results from effective control. All managers follow profit across the shortest available reporting interval; however, responsibility for calculating profitability lies with financial accountants, who in turn rely heavily on cost accountants.

THE SHIFTING FOCUS OF CONTROL IN ACCOUNTING SYSTEMS

Traditionally, those charged with the maintenance of financial and cost accounting systems do not care what is happening in an organization as long as it is accurately recorded as a transaction and made available for reporting on the income statement and balance sheet. The focus of the mechanics of financial and cost accounting systems is distinctly different from the perspectives and priorities of internal control and audit systems, not to mention the concerns of executives and managers. While all accounting systems have two primary concerns—control and profitability—managers and executives must be able to distinguish the specific aspects that financial and cost accounting systems each contribute to the understanding of control and profitability.

Financial and management/cost accounting systems see business control and profitability from significantly different perspectives. Historically, the financial accounting focus has determined the organization's overriding control and profitability perspective: return on investment, which inherently includes profitability. The investor and the market in general focus on short-term financial results. Stock price performance reinforces the primacy of the financial accounting perspective. In contrast, cost accounting systems historically see business control and profitability from the operational perspective.

Financial accounting sees the organization from an external perspective; managerial accounting sees the organization from an internal perspective. Managers and executives who hope to steer their organizations towards continuous improvement have learned not to wait for the financials.They control and manage organizational performance based on continuous improvement and sustainable profit goals.

This proactive approach is supported by cost and performance management methodology and technology innovations over the last 20 years that have helped elevate the status of internal operational information. More recently, theoretical research and actual practice have shown that operational and nonfinancial elements are equally important in creating success and strategic achievement. The financial accounting system provides the motivation; the managerial cost accounting system information provides the means to improve processes and achieve profitability.

WHERE FINANCIAL AND COST ACCOUNTING SYSTEMS CONNECT

A return to the Kaplan/Cooper four-stage model helps to narrow the range of the many possible permutations of cost accounting system design. Using the context of the developmental stage of the organization's current cost accounting system, executives and managers can deliberately shepherd their cost accounting systems towards more integrated levels. Importantly, all cost accounting systems must first meet the Stage II baseline before aspiring to more advanced levels.

When business processes and accounting methods are in harmony, the aligned flow of a traditional, Stage II system would look like this:

- Plan strategic objectives → then determine budget allocations → that create expenditures → that are assigned just as to plan and budget. → Later, actual expenditures are compared to budget targets to show deviations → that lead to management intervention, as appropriate.

The accounting system tracks this overall process from financial and cost perspectives. Now consider three primary connection points that tie the cost and financial systems together as they each monitor the flow of value through business processes: inventories, capital spending, and period expenses (*i.e.*, SG&A).

Consider how an accounting system might:

- Support understanding of the nature and behaviour of cost— cost accounting.
- Promote, track, and give feedback on value creation—financial accounting.
- Assist management in wise use of resources—both.

INVENTORIES

The first connection point, inventories valuation, flows as follows:

- Material+ labour + overhead → becomes inventory recorded on the balance sheet → becomes product cost → becomes cost of goods sold (COGS) reported on the income statement.

Material, labour, and overhead are cost information items that flow through the accounting system from the inventory assets on the balance sheet to COGS on the income statement—from the cost accounting system to the financial accounting system.

CAPITAL BUDGETS

The second connection point, capital spending, has a flow that looks like this:

- Capital budget process selects investments. → Purchase is made and recorded as an asset, usually long-term. → Depreciation expense is recognized over the estimated useful life of the asset (tax methods aside). → Depreciation expense is recognized on the income statement.

In theory, traditional capital budgeting processes attempt to select long-term investments that will support strategic achievement over time. In practice, the process is often a cold-war battle between divisions, departments, or functions, wherein each attempts to garner as much investment money as possible for a parochial area. Once a capital investment is made—whether wisely or not—the expense of that investment is conventionally recognized over time by accounting formulas that most often do not reflect the actual use of the investment (*e.g.*, machine, computer system).

PERIOD EXPENSES

The third connection point, period expenses (i.e., SG&A), has a flow that looks like this:

- Administrative and selling costs are budgeted and then incurred → then assigned to the current time period → classified as SG&A → and reported on the income statement.

Many companies run into financial difficulties because they fail to manage expenditures "below the line," the SG&A expenses below the gross margin line on the income statement.

COST ACCOUNTING AND OPERATIONS

Now it is time to give due attention to support of operations as the primary responsibility of a cost accounting system. Consider the following questions, this time in light of cost accounting responsibilities to operations, compared to its obligations to financial reporting requirements.

How might the accounting system:

- Support understanding of the nature and behaviour of cost?
- Promote, track, and give feedback on value creation?
- Assist management in wise use of resources?

The answers lie in the design of the cost management system. Deliberate and careful design of a cost management system promotes organizational control, as well as workforce focus. The managerial cost accounting system mandates specific control processes by means of the design of its cost management system. More and more organizations look to their CFOs, controllers, and accountants for vital decision-making information and participation in strategic and long-term planning. In contrast, operations-oriented firms often see accounting systems as a necessary evil, required by government and creditor agencies, but for the most part simply a nuisance to internal managers. The difference in viewpoint largely depends on the accounting system design. CMS designs that remain in Stage I and II may quickly become irrelevant to management's decision-making responsibilities. The importance of CMS design extends throughout the entire organization. Dr. CJ McNair summarizes the situation eloquently. "What cost management chooses to make visible—the focus of its work—will inform and constrain the organizations of the future.

In choosing a future for cost management, the future of business will be shaped." Cost management system design is a conscientious and deliberate process that avoids irrelevant detail and integrates seamlessly with the financial system. CMS design requires rigorous, periodic review to ascertain its continuing relevance.

To reiterate:

- *Cost accounting exists for a conceptually simple purpose*: Provide accurate cost information.
- The purpose of cost management is equally clear: Promote improvement in cost structure.

This part will address the essential steps that executives and managers can take to achieve these elusive goals and thereby develop a CMS that is easy to use, aimed at the most important targets of analysis, and supportive of management decision making. In Cost and Effect, Kaplan and Cooper conclude their introductory chapter by describing the vision for such cost systems where,"cost and performance measurement systems are explicitly designed to produce the right information at the right time for essential managerial learning, decisions, and control."

HISTORICAL OBSTACLES

Any executive with even a few years of experience knows the sharp difference between an accounting function that is pro-operations and one that is pro-finance. Likewise, any experienced accountant can tell when other functions (*e.g.*, operations, marketing) see the finance function as a necessary burden and when the function is appreciated for the value it adds to the organization. As in most complex situations, the ideal practice is a blend of both perspectives. Until this becomes true in their own organizations, managers must come to understand and acknowledge the historical animosity and inherent conflicts between operations and accounting.

Passions would not run so high if the relationship between operations and accounting were not essential to business health. At the root of this friction is that, financial staff and operations people see their work from culturally different perspectives and business worldviews. These unspoken viewpoints generate misunderstandings and outright conflict. The different perspectives must be discovered, exposed, and reconciled before they can be blended. All too often, nothing happens. Both sides fear the loss of control, and each is reluctant to take on new roles.

Not long ago, a financial accounting professional might spend an entire career never setting foot on the factory floor or talking with a customer face-to-face. Huddled in back rooms with whirring pencils scratching numbers on green ledgers (and erasing them, too), accountants literally had no time for any activities other than tallying, ticking, and tying the numbers. Today, although computerized accounting systems have replaced the demanding drudgery of manual ledgers, some accountants still seldom set foot in the land of operations. Cost accountants who match this profile—then or now—cannot serve their organizations to the best of their abilities.

The connections and the conflicts within the accounting/operations dynamic are easiest to conceptualize in the manufacturing sector where the tangible nature of production makes conflict stand out.

Making the Numbers Count, Brian Maskell cites five key shortcomings with management accounting:

1. Lack of relevance,
2. Cost distortion,
3. Inflexibility,
4. Incompatibility with world-class approaches, and
5. Inappropriate links to financial accounts.

By inversely examining each of these shortcomings as attributes, the inherent connections between cost accounting and operations, whereby a CMS brings value to management, can be explored in terms of:

- Relevance,
- Cost visibility,
- Flexibility,
- Support for advanced approaches, and
- Appropriate links to financial accounts.

APPROPRIATE LINKS TO FINANCIAL ACCOUNTS

Financial statements address the information needs of a range of constituents and government regulators. Since financial statements target external users and are governed by external standards and formats, at best they provide internal managers with a highly aggregated and shallow "report card" of business performance. Consequently, while the CMS should provide external managers the necessary and sufficient information to meet financial reporting requirements, the system should do so with all due dispatch in terms of the needs of internal managers for information focus and efficiency. Inventory valuation, COGS, expense classification, and absorption are among the few important connection points at issue between the financial accounting system and the CMS.

SUPPORT FOR ADVANCED APPROACHES

Because traditional accounting systems position cost accounting in the status of servant to the general ledger/financial statement system, the poorly designed CMS may consequently attempt to make vassals out of the other business functions. Practice the reverse. The most mature cost accountants have been given permission to support their executives to design a budgeting and cost reporting system that rapidly supports decision making, encourages efficiency throughout the organization, and requires value-added information from functional managers. In this context, all standard financial accounting-related routines should be automated and transparent to nonfinancial staff.

Capital spending is another connection point between accounting and operations functions for CMS value creation. Typically, North American companies use discounted cash flow (DCF) or return-oninvestment (ROI) measurements to choose between capital spending alternatives. These financially focused frameworks are based on tenuous estimates and forecasts that frequently prove grossly inaccurate. Additionally, these traditional, exclusively financial analysis tools look for rapid returns on invested capital. This is not always congruent with operations management or long-term strategic plans.

FLEXIBILITY

Protocols often become highly standardized when financial accounting perspectives control the cost accounting system. In contrast, when the CMS serves operations first and financial accounting second, its system and report designs adapt to changing operational environments.

COST VISIBILITY

As service organizations become a larger business sector and the business landscape loses its stability in terms of organizational structure (due to mergers, acquisitions, and virtual offices), traditional cost types become increasingly irrelevant. Cost types do not facilitate cost visibility—a transparency of the nature and behaviour of costs and resource spending that sustains informed decision making. More advanced cost management systems such as activity-based costing and resource consumption accounting, clarify cost dynamics and enable wise choices grounded on business interrelationships that more closely reflect business performance.

RELEVANCE

Closing the circle, a CMS that serves operations, supports advanced cost management approaches, adapts flexibly, and clearly displays the nature and behaviour of cost, de facto, becomes relevant. In a relevant CMS, cost work investments are generally viewed as valueadded activities, and organizational management relies on them for essential decision-making information.

When a CMS exhibits these five attributes it becomes a valuable organizational asset. Inversely, for organizations missing some of these attributes, the executives and managers see one more reason for nonfinancial functions to pay less attention to CMS information.

CONTROL AND PERFORMANCE MANAGEMENT SYSTEMS

At this point, it is worth making a final connection point. Since cost is such an integral element of the "profit imperative" and profit performance is a universal organizational requirement, it is natural and inevitable that cost and performance systems become intimately associated. Organizations with CMS designs in Stages I and II use financialonly accounting systems. If it exists at all, nonfinancial performance measurement is typically fragmented and isolated within the functional domains of an organization. Everyone wants to "keep score," and without a formal measurement system, good managers will create their own scoreboard. For example, a competent production manager always has a control system in place based on the principles of quality, theory of constraints, or some homegrown paradigm.

Companies developing into a Stage III CMS almost always navigate the same important barrier: exclusive reliance on financial measures for management and accountability purposes. An intense struggle ensues between the financially based management system and the more mature emerging system that values nonfinancial measures as equally important. Consequently, this can result in two performance management systems within the same company—the original financial-based accountability framework and the more balanced performance information paradigm. The subsequent conflicts are all too familiar; but, eventually, they must be resolved so that the entire organization embraces a single performance measurement standard of accountability.

Once again, the primary responsibility of cost accounting activities is conceptually simple: Provide accurate cost information. The cost management responsibility is equally clear: Promote improvement in cost structure.

NO SEPARATION

Cost and organizational performance are inseparable. The link between cost and performance may seem obvious today, but not long ago financial results were the organizational report card of choice. From a capital market perspective, the financials still reign supreme.

That said, studies reveal the same market analysts paying more and more attention to nonfinancial measurements and intangible asset valuation, as well as to shortterm quarterly financial measures like earnings per share and price/earnings ratio. Other operational frameworks, like the Quality Movement, helped shift the emphasis to some degree. However, when, in the early 1990s, performance measurement and management systems began developing independently from financial systems, performance managers found a structured way to move beyond the information constraints of general ledger financial systems. Increasingly, powerful performance management methods and software applications support the development and reporting of nonfinancial information.

CONCLUSION

Cost management systems can be powerful allies in organizational success, but only when deliberately designed and consistently utilized.

Here are some key points in accomplishing this:

- A CMS should focus primarily on internal operations management.
- A cost management system serves its organization when it is relevant, makes costs visible, is flexible, is supportive of advanced approaches, and has appropriate links to financial accounts.
- An accounting system that meets financial reporting requirements is not necessarily adequate for management decision making.
- Cost accounting/management's first responsibility is to internal operations, and only secondarily to financial accounting.
- Finance and operations professionals must be vigilant in maintaining healthy relationships, where the contributions of each are recognized and appreciated.
- Strategy, accountability, and performance concerns are central ingredients for CMS design to drive performance that is aligned with strategic intention.
- The behavioral implications of a CMS design have to be carefully anticipated and managed.
- Traditional cost accounting systems do not always make good management systems. When a cost accounting system is constructed with a primary goal of servicing financial accounting systems, management decision-support information suffers.
- Unlike general ledger systems, a CMS is more flexible and must be customised for each organization.

12

Short-Run Planning and Control

Short-run management decisions differ in a number of respects from long-run decisions. Long-run decisions generally involve selection of courses of action that extend over perhaps many years, such as introducing a new product line. Those courses of action, once selected, require controlled implementa-tion. The latter constitutes management's concern in the short run. Short-run management objectives are therefore typically derived from the implementation requirements of long-run programmes, projects, and product lines that management has selected. Short-run management decisions are constrained by all of the factors that limit long-run courses of action.

In addition, further limitations are imposed on short-run decisions by the specific long-run courses of action that have been selected. For instance, current production volume is limited not only by the available supply of labour (a largely externally imposed constraint) but also by factory capacity, the result of past capital-budgeting decisions.

THE SHORT-RUN MANAGEMENT DECISION CYCLE

Short-run management decisions have two important distinguishing features:

1. They are usually oriented towards a period of activity, and
2. A distinct pattern of decisions is usually repeated each period (along with decisions necessitated by previously unanticipated developments).

PERIODICITY OF SHORT-RUN DECISIONS

The periodicity of short-run decisions is a result of their relationship to long-run courses of action that have been decided upon. Since the long-run programmes and product lines of an enterprise may be quite divergent in nature, time of origination, and life expectancy, there is a need for some unifying scheme to coordinate their implementation and execution. One way of achieving this is to manage all projects and programmes on a one-period-at-a-time basis repetitively over the same calendar interval, such as a month, a quarter, or a year. Another reason for periodicity in short-run implementation and execution of long-run courses of action is the need for continuous evaluation and adaptation.

Long-run courses of action are adopted in a state of uncertainty based on expectations of achievable results. As long-run programmes are implemented and executed, periodic surveillance is necessary to detect results that are significantly different from the expectations on which initial adoption of the programmes was based. Furthermore, if needed alterations in a programme are to be made on a timely basis, experience indicates that the surveillance activity should not be left to chance. Therefore surveillance and evaluation of programmes is generally formalized as part of a periodic cycle of short-run management decisions.

THE SHORT-RUN CYCLE

The preceding paragraph not only explains the periodicity of short-run management decisions, it also implies that there usually is a pattern of short-run decisions that is repeated with each new period. The pattern may be thought of as a cycle composed of two major phases-an *operations planning* phase and a *control* phase.

CONTROL

Control consists of those activities engaged in by management to ensure that:

- The programme of activities for a period is accomplished to the fullest, and
- Performance deficiencies are detected, their causes are determined, and remedial action is taken.

The cyclical aspect of short-run decisions results from the interrelationship of planning and control activities. Performance evaluation implied in the control phase of the short-run decision cycle is dependent on having a recognized plan with which to compare the results of actual activities. On the other hand, as one period's actual results are materializing and being evaluated, plans are made for the coming period's operations.

To be as realistic as possible, all new plans must incorporate the experience gained from current control activities. Thus there is a sequencing of activities with one period's control efforts based on the prior planning phase and leading into the next planning phase. Similarly, every period's plan is based on prior control experience and provides the basis of evaluation in the coming control phase.

OPERATIONS PLANNING AIDED BY ACCOUNTING INFORMATION

Many kinds of activities are involved in both the operations planning and the control phases of the overall short-run management decision cycle. Both of these phases, however, can best be described as sequences of steps necessary to accomplish the purpose of each phase. Accounting makes significant contributions to both phases. We first describe the planning phase step by step, including descriptions and illustrations of accounting's contributions.

The major steps in the planning phase of the short-run decision cycle that receive detailed attention are the following:

- Goals are assigned to responsibility centers.
- Plans are developed for responsibility centre operations.
- Production plans of responsibility centers are translated into budgets.
- Responsibility centre budgets are combined and coordinated: the master budget.
- Review of the master budget and replanning are undertaken.

GOALS ARE ASSIGNED TO RESPONSIBILITY CENTERS

Within the planning phase all requirements of long-run programmes, projects, and product lines are first interpreted and then broken down into specific descriptions of output goals or activity requirements corresponding to responsibility centers within the enterprise.

RESPONSIBILITY CENTRE

A responsibility centre is any identified organizational unit, within the enterprise, that:

- Consists of one or more individuals,
- Is given responsibility for accomplishing a specific enterprise objective, and
- Is given authority (within limits) to accomplish that objective.

As overall output goals for the whole organization are decomposed into contributing goals to be assigned to various major responsibility centers, care is taken to allow for interactions between such centers. For instance, in a typical manufacturing situation, a realistic sales objective must usually be worked out with the sales staff first. This is followed by an evaluation of inventory requirements to determine whether finished goods on hand should be increased or decreased over the period to correspond to expected increases or decreases in sales.

Only after inventory requirements are known can demands be worked out which must be made on the production department. Production schedules, in turn, are used to derive demands for labour to be scheduled by the personnel department, along with demands for materials and supplies required for production (or for various inventory stocks) to be acquired by the purchasing department. After goals are assigned to the large responsibility centers that perform major functions in the organization, each major responsibility centre further divides and subdivides its goal. The total sales goal is divided by territories and then again by salesmen within territories.

Similarly, the production goal is divided by factories, and then again by departments within the various factories. To illustrate this and other steps in the planning phase of the short-run decision cycle, we introduce a simple but comprehensive example. All Block sales over the foreseeable future are expected to be at $10 per set. Last year's sales were only 50,000 units. But production was greater than sales by 10,000 units, building inventory up to 20,000-in partial anticipation of the coming year's increase in sales. The company has followed a policy of ending each year with an inventory of finished goods equal to 20 per cent of the next year's sales estimate. Based on this policy and the sales forecasts of the coming year and the following year, the production schedule for the coming year can be worked out. The production of every Block game requires the fabrication of sets of wooden pieces.

They are the responsibility of the fabrication department. Each game also requires assembly of a play board and the wooden pieces, along with a set of instructions, into colourful boxes that the company uses to package the game. This is the responsibility of the assembly department. Since the company's operations are not too complicated, it is a simple matter to pass along the same production schedule of 104,000 units to both the fabrication and the assembly department. Both departments consist of only one foreman and a crew of hourly laborers. Hence there is no further subdivision of the production goal. Assuming that production methods, level of labour skill, and quality of materials are all predetermined, the assignment of production goals will determine the materials and labour acquisition requirements placed on the purchasing and personnel departments, respectively.

PLANS DEVELOPED FOR RESPONSIBILITY CENTRE OPERATIONS

When goals have been divided and subdivided until the smallest responsibility centers (sometimes individual employees) have been assigned their goals for the coming period, the "top-to-bottom" direction of the planning process stops. The first step in working back towards a total plan for the organization is devising the "best" (least cost) plan of operations for accomplishing the goals assigned to each of the smallest individual responsibility centers. At the lowest responsibility centre levels within an organization, where a goal may be to perform just one or two operations on each product produced, success usually hinges on minimization of costs. Thus the accountant's skill in bringing together cost data and engineering or production data often facilitates the selection of the "best" plan of operations at that level.

Example: Suppose that the management of NMC has not been entirely satisfied with the level of costs incurred in the fabricating department. The primary problem is in the production of the wooden pieces. The fabricating department uses direct material in the form of soft white pine, which machine operators cut into sets of pieces. Besides direct materials and labour, whose use varies proportionately with the number of sets of pieces produced, the process requires certain indirect inputs called overhead items, such as machine time, lubricants, gloves for the workers, heat, light, and power.

Some of these items vary proportionately with the numbers of labour hours of activity, averaging $1.50 per hour worked (under good conditions). Other overhead inputs are fixed, amounting to approximately $20,000 *per year* (under good conditions) for the whole fabricating operation, regardless of activity. Presently, the production of one set of pieces requires two feet of 1" by 10" pine board and 35 hours of labour.

The engineers feel that there are two basic ways of altering the process for better or worse:

- Change the quality of wood used, or
- Increase or decrease the level of skill of the machine operators (presently all are about medium in skill). Management has rejected lower-quality wood because it might affect sales of the game. But it wishes to consider various combinations of labour skill and either pine (now in use) or birch (a better-quality wood).

But management cannot choose on the basis of physical production estimates alone. Here the accountant serves in a coordinating role by integrating production data with price data to arrive at relevant financial or money flows. In this case, the accountant has sought out the prices of the various quality inputs with the cooperation of purchasing and personnel managers. One foot of 1" by 10" pine of proper quality can be purchased for $.30, whereas a one-foot length of birch costs $.50. *Including variable overhead* of $1.50 per hour, one hour of low-, medium-, and high-skilled labour costs $4.00, $5.00, and $6.00, respectively.

Combining this cost data with the last two columns of the production data from, the accountant arrives at per-unit costs for each production combination. The best (lowest-cost) combination is combination 3, which requires the use of the same pine wood but higher-skill labour. The engineers had already indicated that a switch in labour force could be made almost immediately by rescheduling employees around the factory plus a small amount of on-the-job training, causing a minimum of layoffs and rehiring. Management adopts the new production plan.

PRODUCTION PLANS ARE TRANSLATED INTO BUDGETS

After the best feasible production plan is determined for each responsibility centre, a financial representation of that plan, called a *budget,* is formulated. Accountants assist operating personnel at all levels in formulating budgets.

The process consists of combining:

- Individual unit resource requirements, based on a selected plan, with
- The assigned production activity goal. The budget process relies heavily on prediction of cost behaviour patterns.

Example: Based on the "least-cost" production combination selected for the fabrication department the budget for production of 104,000 sets of pieces for Block games for the coming year.

RESPONSIBILITY CENTRE BUDGETS ARE COMBINED AND COORDINATED: THE MASTER BUDGET

After a budget or financial plan has been formulated for all of the lowest-level responsibility centers, there follows a process of combining the budgets of those units into budgets for the higher-level responsibility centers of which they are a part. *Example:* At NMC, the fabricating department, along with the assembly, purchasing, and personnel departments, all come under the authority of the responsibility centre labeled "manufacturing." To get the total budget for manufacturing, we have to combine the budgets of all of the responsibility centers subordinate to it. The manufacturing budget for NMC for the coming year.

Notice that total budgeted costs for the whole manufacturing activity are greater than the sum of the budgeted costs for separate subunits of responsibility within it. This is a common phenomenon in budgeting. The reason, of course, is that some costs incurred at the higher level (like the salary, secretarial help, and supplies for the factory superintendent) are not the responsibility of lower-level managers and, therefore, are not included in their individual budgets. After the budgets of the various responsibility centers have been combined at successively higher levels, they are finally put together into a coordinated whole called the *master budget*.

MASTER BUDGET

A master budget consists of a coordinated set of financial estimates for the budget period, including a balance sheet, an income statement, and whatever other statements are considered useful. The master budget differs from the budgets of such high-level responsibility areas as sales and manufacturing in that it is not a "summing up" of lower-level budgets. Instead, it allows for the financial consequences of divergent volumes of such major activities as production and sales. *Example:* The income statement included in the master budget for NMC for the coming year might look something like the statement. Notice particularly that the statement is an income statement and therefore oriented towards sales activity rather than production activity. Thus total cost of units manufactured is adjusted to get the total *cost of units sold*.

REVIEW OF MASTER BUDGET AND REPLANNING

Since the master budget integrates the plans for all activities of the enterprise in financial terms, it provides a check on all of the individual plans. The master budget does not pinpoint potential production bottlenecks and other technical planning defects. But it is useful in other ways. For instance, if several areas of responsibility have been careless in seeking optimal plans of operation, the lack of rigor may not be discernible in their individual budgets. But when all budgets are combined in the master budget, the result will be a less-than-satisfactory estimated income figure. If the master budget produces unsatisfactory results, some form of adaptation is desirable before operations start. The exact form of the adaptation depends on the cause of the disappointing outcome. If it is felt that the cause is lack of rigorous planning on the part of the various responsibility centers or selection of overambitious goals on the part of management, the entire planning process must be reiterated. In the former case, more attention must be devoted to selecting the best (least-cost) plans for each subunit. In the latter case, more realistic goals must be assigned throughout.

On the other hand, if the cause of the disappointment is beyond the control of management in the short run, that is, if it is due to some identifiable internal or external constraint, the problem becomes a matter for the long-run consideration of management; the initial plan of operation, though disappointing, is not necessarily abandoned—unless adaptation could lead to a better plan *under the circumstances*.

CONTROL OF OPERATIONS THROUGH ACCOUNTING INFORMATION

Once management has arrived at a satisfactory set of operating plans for a period, control activity takes over. The scope of control activities encompasses virtually every effort made by management to ensure that accepted plans are executed to the fullest. Because most control activity is preventive it goes on more continuously than short-run planning, which is distinctly cyclical.

Control of operations includes all of the following types of activities to some degree:

- Organizational control
- Standard conditions and procedures for operations and related cost standards
- Selecting, training, informing, and motivating employees
- Performance measurement, evaluation, and remedial action

Although accountants become heavily involved as information specialists only in the second and the fourth activity, all of the activities tend to blend together. They interact in achieving the purpose of control. We therefore comment below on each kind of activity in turn. Special attention is given to points of substantial accounting contributions.

ORGANIZATIONAL CONTROL

The organizational aspects of control are simple in principle but often difficult to apply. Essentially, organizational control means creating recognized lines of authority and responsibility throughout the business enterprise. If plans are to be carried out properly, it is imperative that some individual within the organization be responsible for every activity included in the plans. It is equally imperative that the individual responsible for a particular activity have sufficient authority to accomplish his or her goal.

But organizational control is also a matter of balance and coordination. Obviously, no single segment of the enterprise should pursue success in its own activities in such a way as to restrict other segments from accomplishing their goals just as to plan.

Two important techniques of organizational control are:

1. Built-in redundancy, and
2. Separation of duties in certain areas susceptible to serious malfunction. Redundancy means that more than one individual is able to perform key functions. Even though only one individual may be given responsibility for a specific function at any given time, the other qualified individual is available if an emergency arises. He or she may also notice impending difficulties that escape the attention of the person with primary responsibility.

Separation of duties is another label for building in "checks and balances." In a business enterprise, separation of duties takes such forms as assigning one individual the responsibility of recording all cash receipts from customers (to reduce respective account balances), while another individual counts the customers' checks and makes the bank deposits. Neither individual is given control of both the records and the cash. This tends to ensure accuracy, and in the absence of a conspiracy of at least two employees, protects against misappropriations of enterprise resources.

STANDARD CONDITIONS AND PROCEDURES FOR OPERATIONS AND RELATED COST STANDARDS

Although the input requirements (and their costs) of any given plan of operations largely determine its desirability, many more factors determine whether a given plan can be successfully implemented and executed.

Two things that embody these "other factors" are:

1. Well-conceived sets of standard conditions and procedures for combining input resources to achieve the desired output at the lowest cost, and
2. Sets of standard input costs which characterize the level of resource sacrifice achievable through use of standard operating conditions and procedures. The former serve as guides to action for employees; the latter serve both as goals to be striven for and as a basis for evaluating actual employee performance.

To see the importance of a set of standard or recommended conditions and procedures to the success of an operation, think of the features that make up a good recipe in cooking. A list of ingredients and quantities, by itself, is usually inadequate. Without instructions on how to combine the ingredients, and in what order, the outcome of any given attempt at preparation is likely to be disastrous. The same is true of most productive activity, particularly manufacturing activity calling for specific product outputs while utilizing limited resource inputs.

To ensure success of any plan of operations, appropriate methods must be worked out in advance. As weaknesses become apparent, these methods should be corrected. Over time, the effect will be to continually move each operation in the enterprise towards its simplest, safest, lowest cost, and most easily learned form. This means that not only will the goal of low cost be achieved over the long run, but in any given period the likelihood is minimal that planned activities will go seriously awry. Earlier we noted that the selection of a best plan of operations is usually based on the *expected* costs of production, employing that plan. But the expected costs of production under a particular plan may not be the same as the *standard costs* of production under the same plan.

Standard Cost

Standard cost is the dollar amount of sacrifice associated with consumption of input resources when standard operating conditions and procedures are followed completely. Estimated costs will differ from (usually exceed) standard costs whenever management expects that standard conditions and methods will not be achieved at all times. But, although management may not expect its employees to perform consistently just as to standard procedures in a given planning period, standard cost is relevant for control purposes. If standard procedures are attainable by reasonably competent and conscientious employees, then the standard cost level of efficiency ought to be held out as a goal that employees should strive for and against which their performance may be fairly compared.

Example: The important distinction between estimated and standard costs for an operation, reconsider the National Marketing Corporation case. In planning, the activity of the fabricating department for the coming budget period, one of six possible combinations of material and labour skill was chosen on the grounds that it had the lowest expected cost. The combination selected was *expected* to consume two feet of pine board at $.30 per foot and.25 hours of highly skilled labour at $6.00 per hour ($4.50 labour; $1.50 variable overhead) for a variable cost per unit of output of $2.10.

Now, it is likely that if all the standard procedures in the fabrication operation were followed to the letter, a lower level of cost per unit could be achieved with the combination of material and labour skill selected. We can realistically assume, for instance, that if everything goes just as to standard engineering design of the operation, only 1.9 feet of wood and.24 hours of labour would be required to complete each unit. Thus, standard cost for each unit of output is (1.9 × $.30) + (.24 × $6.00) = $2.01. Provided the standard engineering design of the operation is actually achievable by reasonably motivated and industrious employees, this standard cost, not the estimated cost of $2.10, ought to be the goal for which employees should be striving.

In addition, actual employee productivity should be measured relative to the achievable standard, not the expected, costs of production. Otherwise some real potential for improved performance may be overlooked. If standard costs are the proper target and basis for evaluation of employees performing an operation, then why bother with expected costs of production in the first place? The answer is, of course, that a realistic estimate of resource consumption for each responsibility centre is necessary to coordinate planning of the various functions within the enterprise.

Example: In order for the fabricating department of NMC to produce 104,000 sets of Block pieces in the coming period, the purchasing department must acquire the proper amount of materials. If the standard materials quantity per set were used as the basis for the purchasing plans, 197,600 board feet (104,000 × 1.9') of pine lumber would be purchased. But it is realistically expected that actual usage will be 2.0 feet per set, or 208,000 feet in total. A purchasing plan based on standard performance would, therefore, result in a shortage of materials. At expected input levels and with standard materials purchased, actual production might be restricted to 98,800 finished units (197,600 ÷ 2.0), or 5,200 units short of the output goal of the fabricating department.

Thus both estimated costs and standard costs are relevant to short-run management decisions. Estimated costs form the basis for planning. Standard costs are held out as models for employee performance and are established as a basis for performance evaluation-provided the standards are considered reasonably achievable by competent and conscientious employees. Before leaving the topic of standard procedures and standard costs, an important qualification should be made. Standardization of procedures and costs in and of itself can be harmful as well as beneficial for an organization.

If standard procedures and costs become outdated, they may no longer be useful. If standard procedures are too rigid-if they do not allow for variations among employees in physical characteristics, disposition, or tolerance of fatigue-they may not necessarily produce the desired result and may even damage employee morale. In turn this may lead to costly employee turnover. A wise management will not deny latitude or flexibility in operating procedures if the variations adopted by employees result in achievement of output goals at reachable standard costs.

SELECTING, TRAINING, INFORMING AND MOTIVATING EMPLOYEES

Selecting and training employees, and informing them about what is expected of them, are all important aspects of control of operations. Part of the standard or recommended conditions for successful performance of any task within the enterprise is possession of certain qualifications on the part of an employee. To assign a task to an unqualified employee reduces the likelihood of successful performance. It may jeopardize the morale of the employee or perhaps even his physical safety. If an employee is to be qualified to perform a given task, his selection should be based on possession of any innate qualities required for the task.

Then the person must become thoroughly acquainted with the demands of the task, and, through training, innate ability should be refined into specific competence for the job. The more successful the enterprise is with respect to selecting and preparing employees, the greater the probability that they will successfully carry out planned operations. Presumably every employee's goal in working for an enterprise is to contribute the most to the satisfaction of personal wants and needs. The purpose of the enterprise in employing a person is to use the person's resources to the fullest in satisfying enterprise goals. The best results for both parties are obtained when there is a maximum of *goal congruence* between the two.

GOAL CONGRUENCE

Goal congruence is said to exist between an employee and the enterprise (management) if by working in the manner most satisfying to himself or herself, the employee is at the same time most likely to produce desired results for the enterprise. Clearly it is essential to the success of any plan of operations that the goals of the employees who perform the operations be as congruent as possible with successful performance from the enterprise's point of view. At one time during the development of business management it was assumed that man was a purely economic being, motivated wholly by wealth.

Hence it was further assumed that an employee could be induced to perform in any manner desired by management, within his or her physical and mental capability, if a sufficiently high wage or salary was offered. Experience, however, has been largely inconsistent with that theory. It is now widely recognized that human motivation is a much more complex phenomenon. Therefore, *employee motivation* is another aspect of control activity.

Employee Motivation

Employee motivation consists of actions by management taken to provide the conditions, rewards, or other incentives necessary for employees to adopt personal goals that are congruent with enterprise goals (and to conduct themselves accordingly). To be sure, in most cases *some* employee motivations fall within the realm of economic incentives that are tied directly to a desired level of productivity. Example Job Shop Machine Company hires machinists on a purely incentive system.

The company performs several kinds of machining operations on various metal parts sent to it by its customers. Since Job Shop has a limited number of machines, its profitability depends on its full use of the capacities of the available machines. Rather than pay its machinists on an hourly basis, it pays them a fixed amount for each satisfactory piece of work completed. To maximize their own wages, therefore, the machinists simply produce as many satisfactorily completed pieces per hour as possible, thus maximizing the output (and the revenues) from the machines they operate.

Assuming that all machinists working for Job Shop are primarily interested in maximizing their wages, this sort of "piece-rate" incentive system might work quite effectively in inducing them to maximize output from the machines.

But evidently many factors other than wage incentives are also important in motivating employees. Actually, the possible factors are so numerous that space limitations do not permit exhaustive coverage.

We can only list several kinds that seem to influence employee motivation:

- Employees seem to relate to small, informal groups of fellow employees and to be influenced by the values of those groups, as well as by the policies and incentives offered by management.
- Some employees seem to thrive in very authoritarian environments, while others seem to chafe under an authoritarian management.
- Some employees are challenged to excel by very high performance standards, while others may become frustrated or despondent because of the seeming impossibility of ever succeeding when such high standards are set.
- Many employees respond more favourably to standard methods and costs if they have participated in devising the methods and therefore accept the standard cost levels as "achievable" (fair) standards for measuring their performance.

The list could go on and on. And the reader can no doubt add to the list as well by imagining what things he or she would respond to favourably or unfavourably in various types of job situations.

Not only is our list incomplete, but knowledge about human motivation is still so inadequate that it is difficult to predict how various individuals will respond to the many different incentives that management may offer. It is for this reason that both practicing and academic accountants are turning more and more to behavioural sciences for relevant insights.

PERFORMANCE MEASUREMENT, EVALUATION, AND REMEDIAL ACTION

For ensuring the success of any plan of operations, the old adage "An ounce of prevention is worth a pound of cure" is very appropriate. But management cannot anticipate every problem in advance of implementing the plans for a given budget period. Periodic surveillance and adjustment of operations are also necessary and important parts of management's control activities.

They are control activities to which accounting contributes significantly. Because control activities are costly in the sense that they consume scarce management resources and perhaps employee time that would otherwise be devoted to production, the concept of *management by exception* has evolved.

Management by Exception

Management by exception is the process of detecting and devoting remedial attention to only those facilities, employees, and operations that are not performing just as to plan. The great advantage of management by exception is that time and efforts are not wasted on operations that are performing satisfactorily. But management by exception implies that management can locate trouble spots without detailed on-the-spot review of every responsibility center's activities.

To do this, management typically relies on two sources. The first source and, indeed, the first line of defence and correction, is the employee. A well-selected, well-trained, and well-motivated employee who understands the standard conditions and procedures for his operation will detect and correct many problems directly. Furthermore, he will seek help in correcting problems that are seemingly beyond his immediate control, thus bringing them to the attention of management. Management's second source for detecting performance problems lies in performance reporting systems.

Performance Reporting Systems

Performance reporting systems are formal information systems for periodically gathering data on actual production activities, comparing actual data with standard performance, and thereby highlighting problem areas for management attention. Formal performance reporting is conducted on either a physical-data or a cost-data basis. The advantage of physical data, like quantities of material and labour consumed, is that they are stated in terms of the things that employees manipulate directly during operations. But a possibly greater comparative advantage of cost data is that they pinpoint problems in various operations in uniform (money) terms. This may have relatively greater economic significance to both management and employees.

Example: An employee working with expensive material has not been following standard procedures for his task. The result is that he has been using 5 per cent less of his time per unit of output while he has been using 5 per cent more materials than standard. The trade-off may seem reasonable to him when stated in percentages of physical inputs. But he may be shocked at the results on a cost basis if, for instance, standard material costs per unit of output are $100 while standard labour input is one hour at $5 per hour. What seems to be a one-for-one trade-off in input percentage utilization is really a twenty-to-one cost trade-off.

Formal performance reporting based on cost data usually falls within the special area of expertise of the accountant. As with other contributions of accounting for management decisions, performance reporting on a cost (or money) basis involves association of costs (and revenues) with various kinds of real economic activities, such as the consumption of resources in production. Cost behaviour patterns are therefore applicable to performance reporting, just as they are applicable to other major managerial accounting contributions. One reason that cost behaviour patterns are a valuable tool for performance reporting is that it is useful to divide performance reporting into two major measures of performance called effectiveness and efficiency.

Efficiency

Efficiency refer to the input consumed (measured in quantity or costs) for a given level of output. *Example:* Suppose that the fabricating department actually completed 100,000 sets of pieces. It would be judged efficient if it incurred costs less than or equal to the standard input costs for 100,000 units; inefficient if it incurred more than standard costs for that level of output. Whereas effectiveness is measured against a goal that is set in advance, efficiency is measured with respect to actual output, which is not known until a particular performance period is over. Thus accounting performance reporting, which is mainly oriented towards measuring efficiency, must be flexible. The source of that flexibility is the use of cost behaviour patterns. Relying on cost behaviour patterns that have been determined in advance, accountants can construct standard cost levels for actual levels of output immediately after those levels are known.

Accounting performance reporting usually follows these steps:

- As operations progress during a reporting period, quantities and costs of resources used in production are recorded for each responsibility centre.
- At the end of the reporting period, a performance report is prepared for each responsibility centre on which actual costs of production are compared with standard costs *for the achieved level of output,* and variances are noted.
- Variances are analysed to highlight the nature of inefficiencies.
- Significant variances are investigated to determine the cause and appropriate action.

Before management investigates the causes of certain of the variances that require attention, further insights can usually be gained from analysis of the nature of variable cost variances. The level of *actual variable* costs is usually a function of two influences, the *quantity* of the variable input used and the average *price* paid per unit used.

Thus, variable cost variances can be due to either:

- Differences between standard and actual prices or rates paid (called price, rate, or spending variances) or
- Differences between standard and actual quantities used to achieve the actual level of output (called usage or efficiency variances).

Example: Suppose that we have the additional information (besides total actual cost of materials used) that the fabricating department used an average of 2.0 feet of wood or 200,000 board feet in total to produce its output of 100,000 sets of pieces. Now we can separate the total unfavourable material cost variance of $5,000 into two parts. We recall that the total cost of 100,000 units at standard input quantity and standard price is $57,000. By multiplying the actual materials usage of 200,000 board feet by the standard price of $.30 per foot, we find that if all wood actually used in production were purchased at standard prices, actual cost would have been $60,000.

This means that the variance due only to excess usage of wood is $3,000(U) or ($60,000 - $57,000). Now, since the $60,000 figure represents the actual quantity of wood used, times the standard price, it differs from actual cost of wood used only insofar as actual prices paid differed from standard prices. Subtracting the $60,000 from the actual cost of $62,000 gives a price variance of $2,000(U). The same reasoning as that used in the example is applicable to other variable inputs besides material. The analysis of variable cost variances helps to focus management's attention on possible causes responsible for nonstandard performance even before costly investigations are begun. Once a significant performance variance is noted and it is determined that it should be investigated, management first consults with the individual who is responsible for the activity that is not measuring up to standard.

Frequently it will be found that the cause for the off-standard performance has already been discovered and eliminated. If it has not, the investigation will start with those most familiar with and most responsible for the troublesome activity. In any case, performance reporting's role will have ended. The solution to problems highlighted by the performance report will come from one of the other three types of control activities or from revising plans and standards for the next period. Those problems that do not have satisfactory short-run solutions become inputs to long-run decision activities of management. In this fashion, management can strive continually for an improvement of overall enterprise performance.

Index

A

B

C

D

E

F

I

L

M

O

P

Q

R

S

T

V